S0-BAC-758

7O write this book the authors sifted through hundreds of news reports, opinions, statistics, and records to cull the absurd, the amusing, the great, and the not-so-great from all walks of life. Their findings are often humorous, occasionally appalling, sometimes bizarre, but always entertaining.

"TOTALLY CAPTIVATING AND INTERESTING."
—*West Coast Review of Books*

"DON'T GIVE THIS TO A FRIEND FOR CHRISTMAS. GIVE IT TO YOURSELF FOR TODAY, TOMORROW AND ANY OTHER TIME YOU NEED A LAUGH."
—*Sacramento Bee*

ARE THERE FAWCETT PAPERBACKS
YOU WANT BUT CANNOT FIND IN YOUR LOCAL STORES?

You can get any title in print in Fawcett Crest, Fawcett
Premier, or Fawcett Gold Medal editions. Simply send title and
retail price, plus 50¢ for book postage and handling for the first
book and 25¢ for each additional book, to:

MAIL ORDER DEPARTMENT,
FAWCETT PUBLICATIONS,
P.O. Box 1014
GREENWICH, CONN. 06830

There is no charge for postage and handling on orders for
five books or more.

Books are available at discounts in quantity lots for industrial
or sales-promotional use. For details write FAWCETT WORLD
LIBRARY, CIRCULATION MANAGER, FAWCETT BLDG.,
GREENWICH, CONN. 06830

Felton & Fowler's
Best, Worst, and Most Unusual

Bruce Felton
and
Mark Fowler

A FAWCETT CREST BOOK

Fawcett Publications, Inc., Greenwich, Connecticut

*FELTON & FOWLER'S BEST, WORST, AND
MOST UNUSUAL*

THIS BOOK CONTAINS THE COMPLETE TEXT OF
THE ORIGINAL HARDCOVER EDITION.

A Fawcett Crest Book reprinted by arrangement with
Thomas Y. Crowell Company.

Copyright © 1975 by Information House Books, Inc.

All rights reserved, including the right to reproduce this book
or portions thereof in any form.

ISBN 0-449-23020-1

Printed in the United States of America .

10   9   8   7   6   5   4   3   2   1

Photo Credits

Airborne S.A., Montreuil/France: page 208.
American Battle Monuments Commission, Washington D.C.: 16.
Australian News and Information Bureau, New York: 198, 296.
Peggy Barnett: 13, 14.
Belgian Consulate General, New York: 294.
Brooklyn Public Library, Picture Collection of Art and Music Division: 20, 22, 33, 42, 60, 70, 81, 121, 126.
Consulate General of Brazil, New York: 285.
De Telegraaf, Amsterdam: 147.
Esquire Magazine 90–91, 301. Reprinted by permission of *Esquire* magazine © 1965 by Esquire, Inc.
Goodyear News Bureau, Akron, Ohio: 217.
Hinckley Reporter, Hinckley, Ohio: 86.
Library of the New York Botanical Garden: 196.
Lutèce: 231.
Marlborough-Blenheim, The White Family: 290.
New York Public Library—Branch Libraries Picture Collection: 21, 67, 113, 135, 194, 195, 213, 235, 242, 259, 261, 268, 280.
Normal Street Mechanics Institute, Belvedere, California: 223. © 1973.
Oxford University Press, New York: 19.
Pro Football Hall of Fame, Canton, Ohio: 102.
RCA Records: 70.
United Press International: 157.
U.S. Navy Photo: 193.
University of Kentucky: 101.

To Judy and to Jessica

Acknowledgments

Special thanks to Laurence Ogden Booth, Judith Felton, Jessica Kaplan, and Richard Schickel for their assistance in the writing of this book.

Information House wishes to thank the following persons for their assistance in the compilation and development of this book: Pat Fogarty, Joyce Shue, Peggy Bedoya, Sheila Arnott, Irit Spierer, Anne Columbia, Nancy Doyne, Art Springer and Buddy Skydell.

Contents

Introduction

It is a very sad thing that nowadays there is so little useless information.
—OSCAR WILDE

Critics, by definition, are not reticent. They are paid not to be squeamish about saying precisely what they feel is wrong —or right—about a string quartet, a Broadway musical, or a new film, and rarely are they reluctant to antagonize their readers if their art demands that they do so.

But it's a rare reviewer who will go so far as to categorize a work of art as the absolute best or worst in its field. That, however, is precisely what we've been presumptuous enough to do in *Felton & Fowler's Best, Worst, and Most Unusual*, a miscellany of the outrageous in which we've assembled the opinions of experts in an improbable broad range of disciplines, from Beethoven on the best composer ever (Handel) to Dwight D. Eisenhower on the best movie ever made (*Angels in the Outfield*). Moreover, we've made incursions deep into exotic and unlikely regions—such as politics, religion, and psychology—where reviewers don't normally tread. The fact is, critics in the past have generally had the good sense to restrict their opinions to the field of the arts. Indeed, there is ample artistic criticism here, including notes on the best "Eggplant-That-Ate-Cleveland" film ever made, the worst love scene in literature, and the most unusual composer of all time.

But suppose, for just one moment, that you needed some solid, no-nonsense advice on where to find the best muktuk? Or the world's worst seafood dinner? We humbly suggest that you might check with *Felton & Fowler's Best, Worst, and Most Unusual*.

Like that seafood dinner—or the world's most unusual

cheese—this book is meant to be nibbled at in moderation; not swallowed whole. And despite its chapter-by-chapter progression from one discipline to the next, feel free to flip open the book at random wherever you might happen to be —on the beach, in a stalled subway, in the bathroom—and jump haphazardly from chapter to chapter according to your mood or interest.

In the midst of this jumping, the reader will also be required to make an occasional leap of faith. While reading about the most unusual beard or the worst musical instrument, you may mumble discontentedly, "Do they really expect me to believe that?" Our answer is yes—for the most part. All the facts and anecdotes we have collected are based on published nonfiction accounts purporting to tell the unexaggerated truth. As to the veracity of our sources, *Newsweek*, Plutarch, Will Durant, and *The New York Times* aren't vouching for us, and we aren't vouching for them.

The judgments offered in this book are both subjective and objective, rational and hysterical, serious and sardonic. In assessing their validity, you should bear in mind the words of Leonardo da Vinci: "I take no more notice of the wind that comes out of the mouths of critics than of the wind expelled from their backsides."

If you find yourself standing up and cheering at things that should have been said long, long ago, fine. But if, on the other hand, the claims made here offend you or strike you as arrogant—if, in fact, you find the very idea of a book of bests, worsts, and oddests preposterous, you're in good company: Film critics Rex Reed and Robert Hatch, for example, told us that the very idea of such a book is "pretentious" (Reed) and "dumb" (Hatch).

And novelist Leon Uris was even more blunt. "It's the worst idea for a book I've ever heard," he wrote us. He's probably off. There have been other books written that are unquestionably worse than this one. You'll find them described in the literature section of *Felton & Fowler's Best, Worst, and Most Unusual*.

Fine Arts

Best Art Forger: Han van Meegeren was a good painter in his own right, but he soon discovered that painting fake Vermeers was more lucrative than painting authentic van Meegerens. Unlike hack forgers, he did not copy existing works. Instead, he painted completely new works in Vermeer's style, even inventing a nonexistent middle period. Van Meegeren's first Vermeer was *Christ at Emmaus,* which was not only accepted as an original but was even hailed as a masterpiece by the critics. It was worth $250,000 to the previously impoverished painter.

During the Nazi occupation of the Netherlands, van Meegeren painted and sold five more Vermeers of the middle period; one, *Christ and the Adulteress,* was bought by Hermann Goering. This was van Meegeren's downfall. After the war, Dutch officials began to search for the collaborators who had sold the Dutch masterpiece to the Nazis, and the trail led directly to van Meegeren. Faced with a charge of treason, van Meegeren confessed his forgery; the experts laughed. Even when he explained how he had baked the paintings in the oven to reproduce the "seventeenth-century" cracks, they doubted his claim. Finally, to convince the courts and the world that he could indeed imitate the master, he undertook to paint still another Vermeer—*Christ Amongst the Doctors.*

Faced with the emergence of a new Vermeer right before their eyes, and faced with the evidence of a new X-ray technique, which proved that van Meegeren had painted all the masterpieces he claimed, the experts had to eat crow. Van Meegeren was exonerated of treason, but was sentenced to one year in jail for forging Vermeer's signature. Exhausted from the trial, the great forger died before he could be imprisoned.

11

Worst Art Collection: Are all the great religious artists of the world dead? The question is raised because, in the summer of 1974, when the Vatican decided to establish a minimuseum of twentieth-century religious art, the best they could come up with was a 542-item collection that is, in the words of *Time* magazine art critic Robert Hughes, "an aesthetic swamp." The Botticellis, the Michelangelos, the Raphaels are not among the 250 artists included in this sampling. Instead, there are endless rows of "weak, vulgar bronzes of recent pontiffs" that have all the charm of an outsized, tarnished Lincoln-head penny. And, out of an apparent dearth of genuinely religiously motivated art, there is a strange abundance of inane landscapes whose only claim to religiosity is a church steeple tucked in the corner.

None of this is terribly surprising, however, since the Vatican has let it be known that it will cut corners wherever possible in stocking and maintaining the museum and depend primarily on the gifts of artists and collectors rather than its own purchases. Says Hughes, the collection "will probably remain more of a curiosity than a museum: an embarrassing document of religion's inability in recent years to provoke aesthetic responses."

Worst Drawing: *Le Remède* by Antoine Watteau depicts a reclining Venus about to receive an enema administered by her chambermaid.

Worst Painting: There are plentiful examples of artistic incompetence melded exquisitely with thematic ignorance. An unnamed Dutch painter depicted the sacrifice of Isaac, with Abraham holding a loaded blunderbuss to his son's head. The German painter Berlin painted a Madonna and Child, with the subjects being serenaded by a violinist. In a Last Supper scene, painted by a French artist, the table has been set with cigar lighters. Another Frenchman painted Adam and Eve in Eden, fig-leafed and innocent, with a fully dressed hunter nearby pursuing ducks with a shotgun.

Worst Sculpture (European): *The Fountain of Bacchino,* found in the Boboli Garden behind the Pitti Palace, in Florence, Italy. Bacchino was the court dwarf of Cosimo I, an obscure Florentine potentate in the sixteenth century who commissioned the minor sculptor Niccolo Pericoli to design the garden and create the sculpture.

For out-and-out bad taste, the monument to Enrico Toti,

Watteau, *Le Remède*

the legless hero of the Austrian invasions into Italy in the nineteenth century, is a rival to *The Fountain of Bacchino.*

Worst Sculpture (World): A series of war dead memorials commissioned throughout the 1950s and 1960s by the American Battle Monuments Commission is, according to former *Times* art critic John Canaday, the world's worst sculpture. "If our military tactics had paralleled the absurdity with which the National Sculpture Society has memorialized our battles," he writes, "the G.I.'s would have landed on the beaches in rowboats and wearing hoop skirts. These memorials do not say 'Remember.' They do not even say 'Forget.'"

Most Unusual Art Critic: Paul Cezanne acquired a bright green parrot of excellent voice, which he taught to repeat one phrase over and over again: "Cezanne is a great painter!"

The Fountain of Bacchino

Most Unusual Conceptual Art: We could single out *one* work of conceptual art as the most unusual ever created, but as Richard Nixon might have said, it would be wrong. We'll offer several, then, and let you judge for yourself:

Californian Chris Burden had himself crucified on the roof of a Volkswagen; real nails were used and they were driven through his palms. He's also had himself filmed crawling on his naked stomach across a Los Angeles parking lot littered with broken glass.

Austrian artist Rudolf Schwarzkogler began cutting away at his penis with a knife, piece by piece, in the name of art. (He ultimately bled to death.)

Vito Acconci, who has exhibited—in more than one sense —at the Sonnabend Gallery, in New York, masturbated under a ramp over which the visitors walked. He has also dressed his penis in doll's clothing and, in yet another opus, bit himself all over his body.

Most Unusual Display of a Painting: *Le Bateau,* painted by Henri Matisse, was exhibited upside down in the Museum of Modern Art, New York City, for forty-seven days in 1961. Over 100,000 people had seen the painting before anybody noticed.

Most Unusual Painting: After touring the Mississippi River for years and making thousands of sketches, John Banvard began work on the most colossal landscape ever painted. He covered nearly three miles of canvas with a panorama of some 1,200 miles of the Mississippi shoreline.

First displayed in Louisville, Kentucky, in 1845, Banvard's panorama was exhibited like a giant scroll rolled from one huge spindle to another. Soon it was drawing hundreds of spectators each day, and Banvard, who made a pretty penny on admissions, took his work on tour throughout the United States and England. From all accounts, it was not a particularly good painting, but people enjoyed watching the countryside wind by, anticipating such highlights as Cairo, Illinois, and Memphis, Tennessee.

Detractors disputed that Banvard's panorama was a full three miles long, though no one doubted that it was at least a mile in length. Upon his death, the work was cut into sections, and, for many years, parts of it were used as backdrops in South Dakota theaters.

Most Unusual Painting Technique: The ancient Egyptians embalmed their dead in asphaltum, a preservative which makes an excellent base for paint, especially when aged. In recent centuries, Egyptians have taken to exhuming mummies and grinding them to dust to produce the paint which is so greatly prized among discriminating artists.

Most Unusual Photograph: Chris Burden arranged to have himself shot by a friend with a Winchester .22 while a third participant recorded the experience in a sequence of photographs. Burden's intention had been only to be grazed but the marksman had an off-day and Burden wound up in the hospital with a nasty gunshot wound in his left arm. In any event, he sold the pictures, along with several others, to a New York art dealer for $1,750.

Most Unusual Sculpture: *Mierda d'Artista,* consisting, as one would suspect, of several cans of the artist's feces. The artist in this case is Piero Mangoni, of Milan.

War Dead Memorials
  (Top left) Airman, Cambridge, England
  (Top right) Normandy WW II cemetery and memorial, Cal-
vados, France
  (Bottom left) Honolulu WW II and Korea memorial, Honolulu,
Hawaii
  (Bottom right) East Coast WW II memorial, Battery Park, New
York City

If we stretch the word "sculpture" just a bit beyond its conventional definition, we might also include, as runner-up, the work of Swiss artist Michael Heizer. The main event of an exhibition of his works consisted of the artist using a house-wrecking machine to demolish the asphalt in front of the Berne, Switzerland, museum where the show was held.

Incidentally, ice cream magnate Louis Sherry commissioned sculptor John Bertolini to do a bust of then President Richard Nixon in ice cream in 1970. Sherry had difficulty marketing the work and it was ultimately relegated to storage in a freezer vault in Brooklyn. And Nixon's wife Pat had her likeness done in macaroni in 1971 when she was voted Macaroni Woman of the Year by the American Macaroni Institute.

Literature and Language

Best Dictionary: The Compact Edition of the *Oxford English Dictionary,* published in 1972. Through a miracle of modern-day printing technology, the thirteen volumes of the OED have been condensed into two. (The miracle part is that four pages of the original edition are reproduced on each page of the condensed version. This could make for a lot of squinting, but a high-quality reading magnifier is included with each set.) For under $100 you can purchase a dictionary that is vastly cheaper than the original, normally priced over $300, and actually easier to use. The OED's monumental ninety-one-page bibliography, citing the works of Shakespeare, Hilaire Belloc, and Sir Thomas Bastard (author of a 1598 anthology of epigrams), is reproduced in full. The real value of the OED is in the elaborate etymologies provided for each word.

Best Library in the World: The best library in the world, from the scholarly researcher's point of view, is the British Museum. (See also *Best Museum in the World.*) There are over six million printed volumes in the British Museum's collection and an additional sixty thousand unpublished manuscripts, including the Codex Alexandrinus and the Codex Sinaiticus, and the world's most extensive collection of Greek papyri from Egypt.

The Bibliotheque Nationale, in Paris, also stocked with six million volumes, is a similarly great library, although its holdings are not quite so varied as those of the British Museum.

Best Mystery Writer: Ross Macdonald. The highest praise one can bestow upon a writer of mystery novels is to call him an artist rather than a hack, and, as former *Newsweek* critic R. A. Sokolov has noted, Macdonald "has reached a break-through into the charmed circle of detective novelists who

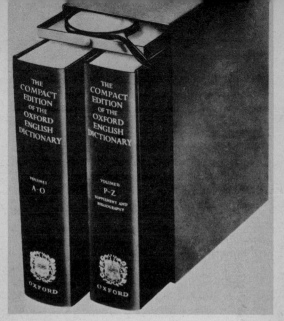

The Compact Edition of
the *Oxford English Dictionary*

have been accepted as literary artists." The best of his Lew
Archer novels—which *The New York Times* calls "the finest
series of detective novels ever written by an American"—is
probably *The Underground Man* (1971). A murder and kidnapping set against a devastating brush fire in southern
California are the key elements in what may well be one of
the best mystery novels ever written.

Best Novel of All Time: *War and Peace.* It took Leo Tolstoy
six years to write *War and Peace,* less time, perhaps, than
most people need to read this monolithic novel peopled with
over 500 characters. It is the story of the intertwining fates
of several Russian families set against the background of
Napoleon's invasion of Russia from 1805–1820.

Tolstoy led a troubled life almost from birth (his family
and friends nicknamed him Crybaby Leo) and he fought
continually with his wife, finally leaving her at the age of
eighty-two when they argued bitterly over his intention of
dividing up all their property among their servants. In 1910,

19

Count Leo Tolstoy

accompanied by his daughter, he left home, caught pneumonia, and died in a railway station.

Best Novel (American): *Moby Dick.* Herman Melville was an unknown when he wrote *Moby Dick* in 1851, and he died an unknown in 1891. Those who had heard of him knew him only as the man who had lived among cannibals in the South Seas (which he had, in his earlier years, collecting material for the books that made him famous after his death. He learned a lot about whales then, enough to note in an introduction to his great novel that "the breath of the whale is frequently attended with such an insupportable smell as to bring on a disorder of the brain").

In the 1920s, Melville's ghost was reawakened and he was recognized, at long last, for the genius he was. Since then, his sprawling novel of Captain Ahab's obsessive pursuit of the great white whale "has come to be regarded as the most eminent American novel," according to Max J. Herzberg. William Rose Benét called it "one of the greatest novels . . . in the literature of the world."

Herman Melville

Best Novel (English): *Great Expectations*. Dickens was the favorite of many of the world's greatest writers, including Tolstoy and Dostoevsky, and Pip's story, told with peerless grace and poignancy, is easily the best of his work, free of the improbable coincidences and awkward plot contrivances that marred much of his earlier work. In 1955, sixteen of France's most noted intellectuals, including François Mauriac and André Maurois, were asked to select the twelve greatest non-French works of fiction for a special series to be published by the French state press. As the greatest novels of all time they chose *War and Peace*—and *Great Expectations*.

Best Novel (French): Some say Flaubert's *Madame Bovary*, others favor *The Red and the Black* by Stendhal, but it would be unfair to rate either of them higher than *Remembrance of Things Past*, the sixteen-volume novel that was the life's work of Marcel Proust and which Somerset Maugham has called "the greatest novel of the 20th century." Says Clifton Fadiman, "For some this is the greatest novel in the world. For others it is unreadable."

In any event, Proust's fame rests almost entirely on this epic of introspection, and its sixteen volumes—the most famous of which is *Swann's Way*—were brought out between 1913 and 1928. Collectively, they describe through the eyes of Marcel, the first-person narrator, the lives of three families—the aristocratic Guermantes, the middle-class Swanns, and the vulgar nouveau riche Verdurins. Their fortunes are

21

Charles Dickens

played out against a background of salons, cafes, soirees, and indiscretions, and always there is Proust's obsessive attention to detail and introspection. He spends pages on the manifold ramifications of a cup of tea.

Proust was sickly, asthmatic, and neurotic, and spent most of his waking hours in bed, swaddled in scarves, gloves, and blankets, writing frenetically, his room lined with cork to keep out noise. His windows were always tightly shut, even during the most sweltering Parisian summer days. Visitors to his room were choked with the smell of inhalants.

Best Novel (German): *The Magic Mountain.* Thomas Mann's masterpiece, along with those of Proust, Joyce, Tolstoy, and Melville, seems to bear out the connection between high quality and literary indigestibility. Frank Donald Hirschback wrote of it that "it bids fair to join the list of immortal works of world literature which people bring back from their summer vacations—unread." But it's worth the effort.

Written in 1927, it is the story of Hans Castorp, a young German engineer who visits a cousin recovering from tuberculosis in a sanitarium in the Swiss Alps and is himself infected and forced to take up lodging there. He remains in the diseased atmosphere of Haus Berghof for seven years, and his experience there is a comment on the root of evil in western civilization. Mann won a Nobel Prize in 1929, and later took up residence and citizenship in the United States. He died in 1955.

Best Novel About Baseball: *The Universal Baseball Association, J. Henry Waugh, Proprietor* by Robert Coover. We might also have chosen *The Natural,* by Bernard Malamud, or Ring Lardner's *You Know Me, Al.* In both, as in Coover's 1968 masterpiece, the game itself is of secondary importance. But we'll go with Coover, whose novel, for its originality and depth, is really without peer. J. Henry Waugh is a bank teller whose one consuming passion in life is playing—by himself—a tabletop baseball game he's invented. The meticulous record books he's kept compulsively over the years are peopled with ballplayers of his own invention, and to Waugh, they mean more than life itself. Says critic Wilfrid Sheed, *The UBA* "is the finest book to date about baseball in an admittedly thin field. But not to read it because you don't like baseball is like not reading Balzac because you don't like boarding houses."

Best Novel About World War II: *The Naked and the Dead.* Norman Mailer fans are split into two camps: Those who favor his later work and those who think he never did better than *The Naked and the Dead.* But few feel there has ever been a better novel of World War II. David Dempsey of *The New York Times* wrote that *The Naked and the Dead* "is undoubtedly the most ambitious novel to be written about the recent conflict," when it came out in 1948, and that "in scope and integrity it compares favorably with the best that followed World War I." C. J. Rolo of *The Atlantic* called it "by far the most impressive piece of fiction to date about Americans in the Second World War." Other novels with a World War II setting that are rated highly are *The Young Lions,* by Irwin Shaw, and James Jones's *From Here to Eternity.*

Best Novel of Postwar America: *Invisible Man.* Ralph Ellison's magnum opus (not to be confused with H. G. Wells's novel of the same name, which science fiction pundit John Baxter calls "the best novel ever written about invisibility"), written in 1952, was voted best novel of the postwar era in a poll of 200 noted American writers, editors, and literary critics conducted by *Book Week* magazine in 1965. It's a novel, says critic Alfred Kazin, "that has proved the most believable of the many current novels of the embattled self's journey through an American reality defined as inherently absurd." And, we think, Ellison ranks as the best of the black

23

American novelists, outclassing James Baldwin and Richard Wright.

Best Novel (American) of the 1970s: *Gravity's Rainbow*. Thomas Pynchon's massive (760 pages) third novel touched off something akin to a vast, sustained universal orgasm of praise among the nation's literary critics. "If I were banished to the moon tomorrow and could take only five books along," Christopher Lehmann-Haupt of *The New York Times* rhapsodized, "this book would have to be one of them." And Bruce Allen of *The Library Journal* noted that *Rainbow* was his choice for "the most important work of fiction produced by any living writer." At the kernel of the book's labyrinthine —and at times almost impossibly intricate—plot is the development of the V-2 rocket during, and just after, World War II. But the story line takes off into distant realms far removed from, but somehow ultimately connected to, rocketry: sex, wartime London, parapsychology, obscene limericks, psychohistory, and eastern religions.

Best Novel (American) of the Twentieth Century: *The Sun Also Rises*. This is the novel Ernest Hemingway himself was most pleased with, the one many critics today regard even more highly than *The Great Gatsby* and *Light in August*. Written in 1926, *The Sun Also Rises* is the novel that captured better than any other work of the period the spirit of the Lost Generation, as it focuses on a group of American expatriates living in Paris. The persona is Jake Barnes, an impotent journalist hopelessly in love with Lady Brett Ashley, who eventually falls in love with a young Spanish bullfighter. The prose is spare and lean and almost parodies itself at certain points.

Best Novel (English) of the Twentieth Century: *Ulysses*. "With *The Magic Mountain* and *Remembrance of Things Past*, *Ulysses* is ranked as one of the greatest novels of the 20th century and also one of the greatest novels of all time," notes William Rose Benét, whose prose is incomparably more explicit than Joyce's: "Avowal, *Sonnez*. I could. Rebound of garter. Not leave thee. Smack. *La cloche!* Thigh smack. Avowal Warm. Sweetheart, goodbye!

"Jingle. Bloo."

Ulysses is the greatest of the stream-of-consciousness novels, an epic description of a single day—June 16, 1904— in the life of three Dubliners, Leopold and Molly Bloom and

Stephen Dedalus. Joyce establishes a parallel between the events in Dublin and those in Homer's *Odyssey*, with Molly the counterpart of Penelope, Bloom the counterpart of Ulysses, and Stephen the counterpart of Telemachus. He uses a variety of techniques, including newspaper headline montage, questions and answers, play dialogue, puns, parodies of literary styles, and free association. All of it is sprinkled throughout with a sufficiently heady dose of explicit language to have kept the book banned from the United States for fourteen years until 1934.

Best Novel of the West: *The Ox-Bow Incident,* by Walter van Tilburg Clark. A good novel if not a great one, *Ox-Bow* is the story of a lynching, and it's done with compassion and insight—qualities you rarely see in the westerns. (The movie, starring Henry Fonda and Dana Andrews, does justice to the book.) The same praise can be accorded Bret Harte's classic short story of enforced exile, *The Outcasts of Poker Flat,* which is better than any full-length western novel ever written, with the possible exception of *Ox-Bow.* Dissenting opinion: Robert Benton and David Newman call Zane Grey's *Riders of the Purple Sage* "the best of the West." Perhaps. In any event, it's certainly the best novel of *any* genre ever penned by a minor league center fielder (which Grey was. Yes, he was.).

Best Novelist (American) of the Twentieth Century: William Faulkner. *The Saturday Review* was "astonished," by its own admission, at the unanimity with which America's major literary spokesmen selected Faulkner as the best novelist of the century. Typical of their comments was this statement by novelist Bernard Malamud: *"The Sound and the Fury, As I Lay Dying, Light in August,* and *Absalom, Absalom!*—these four novels, written in less than ten years, are the work of a great writer, no matter how frail or frenetic the 'vessel.' "

Best Novella: *Metamorphosis.* If we accept E. M. Forster's dictum that anything over 50,000 words is a novel and anything shorter—but longer than a short story—is a novella, then Franz Kafka's *Metamorphosis,* written in 1916, is the best yet written, according to the sixteen-member panel who voted in France in 1955 to select the cream of non-French writing. Kafka's story tells of Gregor Samsa, the man who awoke one morning to find that he had turned into a monstrous vermin.

We might also consider *The Old Man and the Sea* which, if it is a novella and not a full-blown novel, is on a par with Kafka. Largely on the basis of this book, Hemingway won the Nobel Prize for Literature in 1954.

Best Poet (American) of the Twentieth Century: Robert Frost. For Alfred Kazin, it's actually a toss-up between Frost and Wallace Stevens (who sometimes jotted poetic notes to himself on his shirt cuffs while commuting to work at the Hartford Accident and Indemnity Company). While we'll stick with Frost, you might also consider stuffy old T. S. Eliot, of whom Leon Edel says, "He was the supreme case of 'a man of letters.'" There is also Ezra Pound, crazy as a hoot but brilliant beyond description. Indeed, the *best single poem of the twentieth century*—in any language—is either the collected *Cantos* of Pound, or Eliot's *The Waste Land*.

Worst Book: Ordinarily a book would have to endure the test of time and be subjected to decades of critical scorn in order to earn the epithet *the worst*. But in preparing this manuscript we have received some advance assessments suggesting that the appearance of *Felton & Fowler's Best, Worst, and Most Unusual* marks the darkest day in publishing history. For example, we contacted novelist Leon Uris as part of our research to solicit his opinions on the superior, inferior, and bizarre in literature. In his reply, Mr. Uris states emphatically, "I think your idea is disgusting. . . . This is the worst idea for a book I've ever heard."

In all modesty we suggest that you may now be reading *the* worst book, but for the final judgment we will have to await the opinions of those who, in contrast to the above-mentioned reviewers, have actually read the work.

Worst Children's Book: In colonial times, children were treated to a rich panoply of books, stories, and poems about the death of infants. The message was always the same: In the eyes of God, the death of a sinless child is as blessed an event as his birth. This tradition in children's literature continued to bear fruit well into the nineteenth century, and is highlighted by such titles as *A Legacy for Children; Being Some of the Last Expressions and Dying Sayings of Hannah Hill . . . Aged Eleven and Near Three Months; Christian*

26

Character Exemplified in the Life of Adeline Marble, Corresponding Secretary of the Female Juvenile Mite Society of New Haven, who Died May the 3d, 1882; and George Headley's *A Memorial for Children, Being an Authentic Account of the Conversion, Experience and Happy Deaths of Eighteen Children.* The worst, in terms of the horror which is struck into the hearts of the young—a gauge, in those days, of its value—was *A Token for Children, being an Exact Account of the Conversion, Holy and Exemplary Lives and Joyous Deaths of Several Young Children.* Typical of its hellfire-and-brimstone admonitions were these lines: "My days will quickly end, and I must lie/Broyling in flames to All Eternity."

The American poet Julia A. Moore (see *Worst Poet [Female]*) was concerned with the moral upbringing of children. In an 1878 collection of her verse entitled *A Few Choice Words to the Public and New and Original Poems* she waxes lugubrious over the fate of Little Libbie: "While eating dinner, this dear little child/Choked on a piece of beef." Unspeakable.

As for something a bit more of this world, an early geography text, written in 1784 by Jedidiah Morse, was as stuffy and pedantic when the first of its nineteen editions was published as it would be if it were in use today. It's called *Geography Made Easy,* but the goal implied in the title is thwarted by the presence of only one map of the United States in the entire text—and that one is just a few inches square. The book is peppered with pious homilies on the virtues of learning and model dialogues for student and master (mostly student): "I am very thankful, sir, for your entertaining instruction, and I shall never forget what you have been telling me. I long, sir, for tomorrow to come that I may hear more of your information."

Worst History Book: *History of America in Rhyme,* written in 1882 by Major Frederick Howe. Historic events and the concept of history taken more broadly have inspired some of the world's greatest poetry (including much of Shakespeare's work). But there is a school of poets—happily limited—who have tried to bring off a systematic history of the world in verse. It doesn't work, and Major Howe's opus is about the worst. As Walter Hart Blumenthal writes, "The Major may have been a good soldier, but as a versifier his spurs were on his tongue."

Another favorite is Adrian Hill's 381-page epic, *The Grant Poem, Containing Grant's Public Career and Private Life from the Cradle to the Grave,* published in 1886.

A third choice might be *The Tempter of Eve,* by Charles Carroll, a history of mankind from antediluvian times to 1902, the year the book was published in Saint Louis. *The Tempter of Eve* is pious, hysterical, and badly written. Carroll's main contention is that the black races, having descended from the apes (as the white races have not), are most decidedly inferior and ought to be carefully suppressed—religiously, socially, and politically.

Worst Literary Critic: Delia Bacon, author of *The Philosophy of the Plays of Shakespeare Unfolded.* A frustrated New England spinster, Miss Bacon became possessed by the notion that Shakespeare was a clod, and an illiterate clod at that, and that he could not possibly have written a laundry list, much less the thirty-seven plays commonly attributed to him. She thus made it her life's work to expose him and prove her thesis that the Bard's works were actually written by Sir Francis Bacon (no relation), assisted by Sir Walter Raleigh, Sir Philip Sidney, Lord Buckhurst, Lord Paget, and the Earl of Oxford.

In 1857 she published her book, which stated in 700 pages of garbled prose that the thirty-seven plays had been written over a relatively short period of time and that it had been the purpose of those involved in their writing to educate the masses. When the plays were ready to be performed, she claimed, Ben Jonson acted as public relations man, introducing them to a gullible public. Beyond the lunacy with which her views are saturated, her prose is all but indecipherable, and reading it is very much like slogging waist-deep through a sea of sludge. Says Irving Wallace in his book, *The Square Pegs,* "To be trapped in mid-page was like being caught in an armed riot."

Miss Bacon was attacked as a lunatic by her contemporaries, and to some extent they were borne out: The year after her book was published, she died in an insane asylum.

Worst Love Scene in Literature: In *Justine,* by the Marquis de Sade, a passionate kiss between two lovers with a penchant for the bizarre makes for what may well be the most tasteless and repulsive love scene in all literature. Before they embrace, our hero thrusts his finger down his throat as far as it will go, touching off the antiperistaltic muscles that cause him to vomit. He immediately covers his lover's mouth with his own, upchucking the semi-digested contents of his stomach into *her* mouth. Our heroine, it goes without saying, immediately responds in kind, whereupon he bounces it all back at her again. Their mouths never come unglued and this alimentary tennis volley continues for a few minutes until our lover and his lass collapse exhausted in the muck.

Worst Memoir: *Sordid Amok!* is a 1901 work by the French madwoman Clarin de Breujere, whose prose is as incoherent as the title. In it she chronicles six months spent in a Paris insane asylum. She writes, "Human beings, looking out over the entire expanse encompassing all the marvels of the science and the Genius of Civilizations, Ancient and Modern, are still unable even to make an 'Eyelash,' which carries in itself its own inherent mystery of extension." Her motto, emblazoned on a coat-of-arms which she designed for herself, was "My Rights or I Bite."

Worst Nonfiction Book: *Euthanasia: The Aesthetics of Suicide* by Baron Harden-Hickey, the self-styled American founder of Trinidad. Harden-Hickey's treatise on the noble art of ending it all was published in 1894 by the Truth Seeker Company, an antireligious society and publishing house that has also offered such works as *What Would Christ Do about Syphilis?* In presenting his book to a world-weary public, the baron assembled some 400 quotations from the world's greatest thinkers, claiming only to have written the preface. (He lied: Most of the quotes were spurious.) The Baron offers some splendid methods of dispatching oneself in style—he is partial to drugs, poison, and scissors—and his book is illustrated with pen-and-ink drawings. One shows a well-dressed dandy in his throes, a drained tumbler of poison beside him. Another shows a fully dressed man sitting contemplatively on the edge of his bed, holding a pistol to his head. "May this little work contribute to the overthrow of the reign of fear!" Harden-Hickey writes. "May it nerve the faltering arm of the poor wretch to whom life is loathsome. . . . Let him calmly, without anger or joy, but with the utmost indifference, cast off the burden of existence. . . . The only radical remedy for a life of misery is death; if you are tired and weary, if you are the victim of disease or misfortune, drop the burden of life, fly away!" The baron dropped his own burden in 1898 with the aid of an overdose of morphine.

Worst Novel of Postwar America: *Peyton Place*. Grace Metalious's tale of love among the patios was called by Stanley Kauffmann the work of a fifth-rate talent working at peak capacity. *Esquire* called it "a novel so rotten and yet so horny that every reader stayed until the finish." Worst line: " 'Hurry,' she moaned. 'Hurry, hurry.' "

Worst Novelist (English) of the Twentieth Century: Eden Phillpotts. "Eden Phillpotts," wrote H. L. Mencken in a 1923 article in *Vanity Fair,* "seems to me to be the worst novelist now in practice in England." Phillpotts's interminable tales of life in Dartmoor have been compared to the Wessex novels of Thomas Hardy, but that seems altogether blasphemous and not at all fair to Hardy. Phillpotts wrote plays as well as novels and several mysteries under the pseudonym of Harrington Hext. His was a singularly versatile dullness, and he could bore you to death a dozen different ways. *The Treasures of Typhon,* a 1924 work, prompted these remarks from a New York *Tribune* reviewer: "Under the guise of conjuring up the flavor of antiquity, Mr. Phillpotts talks very much like our old friend Polonius. He not only talks very much like our old friend Polonius, but he talks very much."

Worst Poem Ever Written: There is an embarrassment of riches to be found in *The Stuffed Owl,* a 1930 anthology of bad verse edited by Wyndham Lewis, but the worst, the absolute schlock bottom, may well be "Catastrophe," by the nineteenth-century English poet Cornelius Whur. Whur's inspiration for these deathless lines was a young artist born without arms who supported his parents and himself through his painting:

> "Alas! Alas!" the father said,
>   "O what a dispensation!
> How can we be by mercy led,
>   In such a situation?
> Be not surprised at my alarms,
>   The dearest boy is without arms.
>
> "I have no hope, no confidence,
>   The scene around is dreary.
> How can I meet such vast expense?
>   I am by trying weary.
> You must, my dearest, plainly see
>   This armless boy will ruin me."

30

The works of two other nineteenth-century woodsmiths rate an honorable mention at the very least. Conceivably, you may regard them as vastly inferior to "Catastrophe" and thus more worthy of the "worst" designation. First, there is Erasmus Darwin, grandfather of Charles, and poetically obsessed with the wonders of nature as evidenced by such titles as "The Loves of the Plants" and "The Birth of KNO_3." Two of his individual poems bear special mention:

"Ae Fond Kiss, and Then—"

So still the Tadpole cleaves the watery vale,
With balanc'd fins and undulating tail;
New lungs and limbs proclaim his second birth,
Breathe the dry air, and bound upon the earth.
Allied to fish, the Lizard cleaves the flood,
With one-cell'd heart, and dark frigescent blood;
Half-reasoning Beavers long-unbreathing dart,
Through Eirie's waves with perforated heart;
With gills and lungs respiring lampreys steer,
Kiss the rude rocks and suck till they adhere;
With gills pulmonic breathes th' enormous Whale,
And sprouts aquatic columns to the Gale.

"The Maiden Truffle"

So the lone Truffle, lodged beneath the earth,
Shoots from paternal roots the tuberous birth.
No stamen-males ascend, and breathe above,
No seed-born offspring lives by female love.
. . . Unknown to sex the pregnant oyster swells,
And coral-insects build their radiate shells.

Robert Southey, a favorite target of Lewis Carroll and Alexander Pope, was the progenitor of some exquisitely wretched verse, of which "The Early Call" is a simply magnificent example:

By that lake whose gloomy shore
Skylark never warbles o'er,
Where the cliff hangs high and steep,
Young St. Kevin stole to sleep.
"Here at Last," he calmly said,
"Woman ne'er shall find my bed."
Oh! the good saint little knew
What the wily sex can do.

Even now while calm he sleeps
Kathleen o'er him leans and weeps.
Fearless she had tracked his feet
To this rocky wild retreat;
And when morning met his view,
Her mild glances met it too.
Ah! your Saints have cruel hearts!
Sternly from his bed he starts,
And with crude, repulsive shock,
Hurls her from the beetling rock.

Worst Poet (American) of the Twentieth Century: Edgar A. Guest, the most telling criticism of whom is this anonymously penned rhymed couplet:

I'd rather fail my Wassermann Test
Than read the poems of Edgar Guest.

His work is consistently mawkish and treacly, his insights bland and repetitious. Guest's worst poem may well be "Home":

It takes a heap o' living in a house t'make it home,
A heap o' sun an' shadder, an' ye sometimes have t'roam
Afore ye really 'preciate the things ye lef' behind,
An hunger fer 'em somehow, with 'em allus on yer mind.
It don't make any difference how rich ye get t'be,
How much yer chairs an' tables cost, how great yer luxury;
It ain't home t'ye, though it be the palace of a king,
Until somehow yer soul is sort o' wrapped round everything. . . .

Worst Poet (Female): Mrs. Julia A. Moore—"the Sweet Singer of Michigan" to her admirers—was partial to war and patriotism, but utterly enchanted by death and disease. In these stanzas from "The Brave Page Boys," she fused them all:

Enos Page the youngest brother—
    His age was fourteen years—
Made five sons in one family
    Went from Grand Rapids here.
In Eight Michigan Cavalry
    This boy he did enlist.
His life was almost despaired of
    On account of numerous fits.

32

Walt Whitman

The unutterable mediocrity of Mrs. Moore's work was equaled only by Nancy Luce, who raised chickens on her Martha's Vineyard farm and wrote poems about them—bad poems full of poor grammar, forced rhymes, and mawkish conceits. And on every egg that she sold, she inscribed in an elegantly cursive hand the name of the bird that produced it.

Worst Poetry by a Great Poet: Regardless of Walt Whitman's greater capabilities, he wrote some of the most overblown, extravagantly incoherent poetry ever to see print. Writes Walter Mermon, "That graceless, banal English of his . . . indicates a man without feeling for words, who would not shrink today from the horrible jargon of the follow-up letter of the in-reply-to-your-favor-would-say school of English composition." Contemporary critics of *Leaves of Grass*, Whitman's magnum opus, characterized it as "hexameters bubbling through sewage," and *Song of Myself*, his most famous poem, contains these lines, certainly among the worst American poetry ever published: ". . . a gigantic uvula with imperceptible gesticulations threatens the tubular downward blackness occasionally from which detaching itself bumps clumsily into the throat a meticulous vulgarity. . . ."

Worst Review: It was the age of discovery when Sir Thomas More's *Utopia* first appeared, and many critics were duped into believing the well-imagined communist community was a real island. One poor reviewer, a gentleman named Budaeus, went so far as to recommend that missionaries be sent to the newly discovered isle to convert the wise citizenry to Christianity.

Worst Rhymster: Neither Julia Moore nor Nancy Luce had a patent on bad grammar and ersatz rhymes—or if they did it was patently ignored by Rev. William Cook of Salem, Massachusetts, who wrote during the mid-1800s. "Indian Corn," which is found in a booklet of poems entitled *Talk about Indians*, which he published in 1873, has a charm all its own:

> Corn, corn, sweet Indian corn,
>   Greenly you grew long ago.
> Indian fields well to adorn,
>   And to parch or grind hah-ho!
> Where shines the summer sun,
> And plied his hoe or plough
>   Blessings to men have you not gone
> Making food of your dough?
>
> In England, in France and Germany
>   At morn, at eve, at noon
> Johnnie-cake and harmony
>   Increase the family boon.

Worst Slip of the Tongue: The slipperiest tongue on record belonged to the Reverend William A. Spooner (1844–1930), who was for many years dean of New College, Oxford. Reverend Spooner committed so many verbal blunders that the word "spoonerism" entered the language, meaning the unintentional interchange of the initial sounds of two or more words. For example, Spooner once explained that "It is kisstomary to cuss the bride." On another occasion he remarked that "Work is the curse of the drinking class." Spooner was capable of charging headlong into a sentence and making a half-dozen errors before it was all over. He rebuked one of his students with these immortal words: "You have hissed all my mystery lectures; I saw you fight a liar in the back quad; in fact you have tasted the whole worm." But Spooner's admirers generally agree that his finest error occurred when he referred to the good and elderly Queen Victoria as "the queer old dean."

Worst Title: A farce published in the seventeenth century was titled *Chrononhotonthologos, the Most Tragical Tragedy*

That Ever Was Tragedized by Any Company of Tragedians.
The first two lines read:

> Aldeborontiphoscophosnio!
> Where left you Chrononhotonthologos?

Most Unusual Alphabet: Dr. Alimamed Kurdistani of Azerbaijan, U.S.S.R., has invented a universal alphabet, combining the characters of all the world's major languages (excluding Chinese). Dr. Kurdistani's ABC's are now being studied by the United Nations and other world organizations.

Most Unusual Bibliography: A ninety-four-page treatise on the extermination of fleas, published in 1739 by F. E. Bruckmann, contains the most extensive bibliography ever prepared on flea-related literature. Bruckmann's book also features a detailed description of a newly invented "curious flea-trap for the complete extinction of fleas," which is worn around the neck and captures its quarry live. The author notes that the captive insects may then be "dispatched in some way, by murder, drowning, beheading, hanging or some similar end."

Most Unusual Dictionary: Lexicographers in Wales have been working on a dictionary of the Welsh tongue for over fifty years. As of 1970 they were up to the letter H.

Most Unusual Epigram: Sir William Collingborne was executed for writing this punful little poem: "The Rat, the Cat, and Lovel the dog,/Rule all England under the Hog." Of course, he was not executed merely for bad puns; there was politics involved. In 1484, *Cat*esby, *Rat*cliff, and Lovel were the prime henchmen for Richard III. Lovel was a popular name for dogs, like Spot or Fido. And a white boar appeared on Richard's coat of arms. In a number of productions of Shakespeare's *Richard III*, these words have been appended and given to a character about to be executed. (See also *Most Unusual Shakespearean Lines.*)

Most Unusual Hack Writer: The hack writer is a Faustian hero, a character of great psychological complexity, a person who will do anything for a buck. Prominent in the hack writer hall of fame (there is no such institution, but there should be) is John Mitford. Mitford lived in the most trying period for hack writers (1782–1831) when, no matter how versatile you were or how low you stooped, it was difficult to make ends meet and at the same time satisfy your alcoholic habit.

Between binges, John Mitford wrote for religious and pornographic publishers, as well as editing *Scourge,* the *Quizzical Gazette,* and penny-pulp journals in the poorest of taste. While composing his eminently forgettable novel, *Johnny Newcome in the Navy,* Mitford received what was probably the highest salary of his life—a shilling a day. To put his earnings to the best possible use, he slept out-of-doors for the forty-three days he was working on *Johnny Newcome,* eating only two pennies' worth of bread, an onion, and a slice of cheese each day; he spent the rest of his money on gin.

Most Unusual Letters: The Simon and Schuster publishing house owns the unusually brief correspondence between Victor Hugo and his publisher. To inquire how the editors liked the manuscript for *Les Miserables,* Hugo composed the following letter, quoted here in its entirety: "?". The publisher responded: "!". Such brevity is all the more remarkable when one considers that *Les Miserables* contains one of the longest sentences in the French language—823 words without a period.

Most Unusual Library: In the sixteenth century, a library near Cassel, Westphalia, housed "books" which had no pages and were made of wood. Each "book" was actually a book-sized box, the spine made of the bark of a specific tree and the sides made of slats of polished lumber taken from the tree. Inside the box were samples of leaves, berries, insects, moss, and fruit peculiar to that tree. All the "books" were labeled, naturally, and proportionate in size to the size of the tree which they represented.

Most Unusual Library Collection: The British author Delpierre noted in 1860 that there existed at the University of Cambridge library a separate shelf for books written by deranged persons and morons.

Most Unusual Novel: The avant-garde writer Juan Luis Castillejo, in an attack against "the tyranny of words we call literature," published a book in 1969 consisting of "several hundred pages printed randomly with the letter 'i'," according to the London *Times*. Sales were not terribly encouraging and Castillejo did not follow through on his plans to commission several translations.

Also, in 1969, Georges Perec published his novel *La Disparition (The Disappearance)* in which the letter *e* does not appear at all. The letter *e* is the most commonly used letter in French, as it is in English.

An earlier attempt at an *e*-less novel was Ernest Vincent Wright's *Gadsby*, published in Great Britain in 1939. This literary curiosity runs some 50,000 words in length and Wright's prose is surprisingly smooth and straightforward. In fact, the e's are never missed, as one may gather from the following passage:

"Gadsby was walking back from a visit down in Branton Hills' manufacturing district on a Saturday night. A busy day's traffic had had its noisy run; and with not many folks in sight, His Honor got along without having to stop to grasp a hand, or talk; for a Mayor out of City Hall is a shining mark for any politician. And so, coming to Broadway, a booming bass drum and sounds of singing told of a small Salvation Army unit carrying on amidst Broadway's night shopping crowds. Gadsby, walking toward that group, saw a young girl, back towards him, just finishing a long, soulful oration, saying: '. . . and I can say this to you, for I know what I am talking about; for I was brought up *in a pool of liquor!*' "

Most Unusual Novelist (English): William Dampier, whose most famous work is *A Memoir of John Carter,* written in 1850. Dampier was a quadriplegic who not only wrote by holding a pen in his mouth but illustrated his books with pen-and-ink drawings in the same way.

Most Unusual Poem: "Dentologia: A Poem on the Diseases of the Teeth," written in 1840 by Solyman Brown, a New York dentist. The poem is amply footnoted with advice that is "Practical, Historical, Illustrative and Explanatory," and followed by a list of three hundred qualified dentists throughout the United States.

On a par with "Dentologia" is "Syphilis Sive Morbus Gallicus," or "Syphilis, the French Disease," a book-length poem written in Latin hexameters by the Italian Renaissance poet Girolamo Fracastoro.

Less arcane, but unique in its own right is "The Dream of a Spelling Bee," by Charles C. Bombaugh:

Menageries where sleuth-hounds caracole,
　Where jaguar phalanx and phlegmatic gnu
Fright ptarmigan and kestrels cheek by jowl,
　With peewit and precocious cockatoo.

Gaunt seneschals, in crotchety cockades,
　With seine net trawl for porpoise in lagoons;
While scullions gauge erratic escapades
　Of madrepores in water-logged galloons.

Flamboyant triptychs groined with gherkins green,
　In reckless fracas with coquettish bream,
Ecstatic gargoyles, with grotesque chagrin,
　Garnish the gruesome nightmare of my dream!

Most Unusual Pornography: On September 30, 1970, the Presidential Commission on Obscenity and Pornography issued its 646-page official report. The twelve-member panel, handpicked by President Nixon, concluded with a recommendation that all sexually explicit films, books, and magazines intended for adults be legalized (a conclusion that the president immediately condemned as morally "bankrupt").

William L. Hamling, a West Coast publisher, abridged the commission's report, added 546 immodest photographs, and distributed it for $12.50, over twice the price of the Government Printing Office's official, unillustrated edition. Within three months Hamling had sold over 100,000 copies; then the law moved in. Hamling was arrested and charged with eleven counts of "pandering to pruriency" for mailing out brochures advertising his version of the commission's finding. He was found guilty, fined $87,000, and sentenced to four years in prison.

Most Unusual Spoken Sound: Several tribes of South Africa, among them the Xhosa, speak languages featuring a tongue click. The word Xhosa begins with this sound *(click)ho-tza*, which occurs nowhere else in the world. In Arabic the *l* sound occurs only in the word Allah (God).

Most Unusual Text: A book entitled *Liber Passionis Domini Nostri Jesu Christi cum Characteribus Nulla Materia Compositis,* which once belonged to Rudolphus II of Germany, is unique. Each letter was painstakingly and beautifully scissored out of fine vellum and attached to a blue paper backing.

Another rare book, now in the Gutenberg Museum, Mainz, Germany, measures only about an eighth of an inch square. Believed to be the smallest book ever printed with movable type, it contains the Lord's Prayer in seven languages.

Finally, a library in Uppsala, Sweden, holds a translation of the Gospels printed with metal type on purple vellum. The main body of the text is in "ink" of pure silver, and the initial capitals are in gold.

Most Unusual Translation: In "The Jabberwock Traced to Its True Source," a paper that appeared in the February 1872 issue of *Macmillan's Magazine,* the Greek scholar Robert Scott claimed, with his tongue fixed immovably in his cheek, that Lewis Carroll's famed masterpiece of nonsense verse is no more than a competent translation of a medieval German ballad called "Der Jammerwoch." To allay suspicions that he was staging a hoax, Scott offered the complete text of the German poem.

Scott's German rendering of "Jabberwocky" is but one of several "translations" that have appeared since the 1855 publication of Carroll's poem in *Through the Looking Glass.*

Most Unusual Word Origin: A Mr. Daly, manager of the Dublin Theater, bet a pub pal of his that he could introduce a new word into the language within twenty-four hours. Overnight, Daly hustled around the town chalking the letters Q-U-I-Z in bathrooms and other public places. The next morning, the Dublin citizenry were all asking one another, "What does 'quiz' mean?" Daly won his bet. The probable explanation for the durability of the term is its similarity in sound and meaning to "inquisition."

Drama

Best Broadway Musical: *My Fair Lady* beats out such other topdrawer musicals as *South Pacific* and *Showboat* because, apart from the music and lyrics—which are the wittiest and most tuneful we've ever heard—the book can stand on its own for dramatic value and dialogue. (After all, take away the sound of music from *The Sound of Music* and you're left with a weekday afternoon soap opera. Take away the songs from *My Fair Lady* and you still have *Pygmalion*.) *My Fair Lady*, with music by Alan Jay Lerner and lyrics by Frederick Loewe, opened in New Haven in February 1956 (where it most decidedly did not bomb) and then went on to a run of 2,717 consecutive performances in New York.

Best Child Actor (Current): It has been said that the only thing more insufferable than a precocious child is the mother of a precocious child. The fact is, it's a rare child who actually makes a polished or even believable actor, regardless of how talented he may be. One notable exception is Tatum O'Neal, whose single film credit to date—her performance in *Paper Moon*—qualified her as the best child actor in the business today.

The late Brandon de Wilde was, perhaps, even a better actor, and he was never better than in the 1950 cinematization of Carson McCullers's *Member of the Wedding*, made when he was seven years old. O'Neal and de Wilde seem to be comfortable as children, and therein lies their success. They try neither to imitate adults nor to be overly precious.

For the *best child actor of all time*, it's necessary to turn back to the early years of the nineteenth century. W. H. W. Betty ("Master Betty" as he was known as a child) was born in London in 1791 and made his stage debut in Dublin in 1803. The London aristocracy fought among themselves for tickets to his S.R.O. performances and the lower classes lived for a glimpse of him as he left his dressing room to board his carriage after a matinee. The enthusiasm over his performances—he was said by many to be a better actor than Garrick himself, even in the roles that Garrick had made famous—was widespread and all but hysterical. Within three or four years of his debut, however, the cheering died away and as an adult actor, Betty had a mediocre reputation at best. He retired from the theater at the age of thirty, and died fifty-three years later, on August 24, 1874.

Best Comedy: *The Prisoner of Second Avenue* doesn't even come close. You'll be closer—right on target, in fact—if you choose *The Misanthrope*, by Molière. George Brandes called it "the unapproachable masterpiece of the foremost of comic dramatists." Alceste is the hero of the play, a humorless but relentlessly sincere young man desperately in love with the flighty Celimene. Molière played opposite his wife in early performances of the comedy, and there is no question that he injected much of his own passion and anger into the writing and acting of the more heated arguments between the two leads. In real life he suspected, with good cause, that Mme. Molière was unfaithful.

Best Elizabethan (non-Shakespearean) play: Figure it this way: Whatever it is, it's got to be something by either Ben Jonson or Christopher Marlowe. If you opt for Jonson—as we do—then it's *The Alchemist*, commonly hailed as his best play and considered by Samuel Taylor Coleridge as one of the three best plays ever written. The action takes place during the London plague of 1610, and the names of the characters —Face, Doll Common, Sir Epicure Mammon, Tribulation Wholesome, and our personal favorite, Dame Pliant—are alone worth the price of admission.

If you favor Marlowe, the choice is likely to be *Edward II*, written in 1590. According to critic Joseph Shipley, Marlowe's characterization of the young Edward III makes for "the best drawn child in the Elizabethan drama." The play was a great favorite of Havelock Ellis.

Best Play (American) of the Nineteenth Century: The American dramatic imagination in the nineteenth century could hardly be described as fertile, but one possibility for best play of the century is Frank Murdock's *Davy Crockett*, of which stage historian Lawrence Hutton wrote in 1891, "It is almost the best American play ever written." *Davy Crockett* is in four acts of unrhymed verse and depicts a Crockett in-

George Bernard Shaw

nocent, free and unspoiled by the trappings of civilization. He is illiterate, naive, a physical superman, totally honest, and in all ways the personification of Rousseau's noble savage. The play was enthusiastically received and reviewed when it opened in 1873, although there have been no major productions of it in recent memory.

Best Playwright of the Twentieth Century: George Bernard Shaw. Backing us up is former New York *Times* drama critic Brooks Atkinson, who rates Shaw the best if only because Shaw's "intellectually brilliant" plays—and the best of them is probably *Candida*—were the major force in world theater throughout much of the century. For *Newsday* drama critic George Oppenheimer, the choice is the Irish dramatist Sean O'Casey, whose *The Plough and the Stars* and *Juno and the Paycock* "are two of the great plays of our time." The *best American dramatist since 1900*—and perhaps the best in the world—was Eugene O'Neill. In this category the *Saturday*

Review noted that *all* of the writers and critics it polled agreed that O'Neill was the best.

Best Shakespearean Play: *Hamlet* or *Othello*. Opinion is divided among literary critics as to which of these two was the best of Shakespeare's efforts, although one thing is certain: Of the thirty-seven plays Shakespeare wrote, there was none better than his "great tragedies": *Othello, King Lear, Macbeth,* and *Hamlet.* Many critics, Leo Tolstoy among them, have found *Lear*'s greatness diminished somewhat by a lack of psychological credibility, and virtually *nobody*—with the notable exception of Abraham Lincoln—ever claimed publicly that *Macbeth* was the best single play Shakespeare ever wrote. *Hamlet* is the choice of Oscar James Campbell, who notes that the drama "possessed an inexhaustible and infinite variety." Dr. Ernest Jones, the eminent psychoanalyst and biographer of Freud, has called *Hamlet* Shakespeare's "greatest work." In an essay entitled *Hamlet and Oedipus,* he expressed great fascination with the young prince's childhood and suggested that Hamlet was motivated in thought and deed by repressed hostility towards his late father.

As for *Othello,* critic A. C. Bradley calls it "the most perfect of the tragedies in point of construction," and Samuel Taylor Coleridge wrote this of the drama: "The beauties of this play impress themselves so strongly upon the attention of the reader that they can draw no aid from critical illustration."

Worst Actor: The nineteenth-century British eccentric Ronald Coates, says Irving Wallace in his book, *The Square Pegs,* "was probably the worst actor in the history of the legitimate theatre." A Shakespearean by preference, Coates saw no objection to rewriting the Bard's great tragedies to suit his own tastes; in one memorable production of *Romeo and Juliet* in which he played the male lead, he tried to jimmy open his lover's casket with a crowbar. Costumed in a feathered hat, spangled cloak, and billowing pantaloons—an outfit he wore in public as well—he looked singularly absurd.

Coates, who proclaimed himself a second Garrick, was frequently hooted and jeered offstage for his inept, overblown performances. Quite often he had to bribe theater managers for a role in their productions and his fellow thespians, fearing violence from the audience, demanded that he provide police protection before they would consent to go on stage with him. He was slandered and laughed at throughout the British Isles and often threatened with lynchings, but he persisted in his efforts to act. At one performance, several members of the audience were violently convulsed by laughter and had to be treated by a physician. Coates was struck and killed by a carriage in 1848 at the age of seventy-four.

Worst American Actor: The worst actor in the history of the American stage was actually a British import—George Jones, who came to the United States from England in 1828. Known familiarly as Count Johannes, Jones became psychotically obsessed with the role of Hamlet, and played it to the exclusion of virtually everything else. As his career progressed he grew increasingly more insane, and his performances were always laughed at. Eventually, he became too mad to act any longer—too mad, in fact, to play the role of the Mad Prince, as one contemporary critic said.

Jones was also a writer of sorts. *The Original History of Ancient America, Anterior to Columbus,* which he published in 1843, claims that Tyrians and Israelites were among the first people to inhabit the Americas.

Worst Comedy (American): *Pleasure Man.* Mae West—yes, Mae West—was the author of this sordid little horror which opened at New York's Biltmore Theatre on October 1, 1928, and was closed by the police after two performances. Rodney Terrill, an actor, is careless with his women until the angered brother of one of his recent discards attempts to set him straight by castrating him. The brother overshoots his mark, however, and Rodney dies. It all takes place at a Broadway party attended largely by female impersonators.

While *Pleasure Man* may have been the unfunniest comedy of all, the dreariest comedy ever written came from the pen of the nineteenth-century dramatist-housewife Mrs. H. L. Bateman, and was called *Self.* Mrs. Bateman touted her work as "an original New York comedy in three acts." In Act I, a young girl, with a pile of money stashed in the mattress, dutifully hands it over to her drooling father. Mom, in the meantime, puts the son up to writing a bad check on the cash. In Act II the crime is attempted, botched, and discovered, but our heroine covers for her undeserving mother and

44

brother by saying that *she* did it. She is thus turned out of the house in disgrace. This leaves it all up to a *deus ex machina*, in the form of a doting uncle, to set everything aright in Act III, and the play ends happily if drearily. It opened in 1856.

Worst Play: In 1941 an all-star cast including Jean-Paul Sartre and Simone de Beauvoir, under the direction of Albert Camus, introduced Pablo Picasso's *Désir Attrapé par la Queue* (Desire Caught by the Tail) to a Paris audience. Since that time, thankfully, it has been performed only three times, most recently in 1967 at the Festival of Free Expression in St. Tropez. With characters named Big Foot, Fat Anxiety, and Thin Anguish, *Désir* combines features of medieval morality plays with twentieth-century smut. The St. Tropez production featured a bleached blonde stripper in the role of Tart, who disrobed to the throbbing rhythms of a rock band while a chorus of go-go dancers boogalooed and slides of Picasso paintings flashed on the backdrop.

Picasso's only theatrical effort deals with elemental themes —food, money, and sex—although from the dialogue it might be difficult to figure that out: "We sprinkle the rice powder of angels on the soiled bed sheets and turn the mattresses through blackberry bushes!" Big Foot shouts at the end of the play. "And with all power the pigeon flocks dash into the rifle bullets! And in all bombed houses, the keys turn twice around in the locks!" he states categorically.

The highlight of *Désir* comes when Tart urinates on stage as a variety of disgusting sound effects play over the loudspeakers. When the mayor of St. Tropez objected to this scene, the director, Jean-Jacques Lebel, moved the play outside of the city limits. "We're not at liberty to emasculate a work of art in order to pander to bourgeois sentiment," *Time* quoted Lebel as saying.

Worst Shakespearean Play: *Titus Andronicus.* This was the first of Shakespeare's tragedies and, many critics feel, his worst. Set in Rome during the time of the Gothic invasions, the drama runs heavily to savagery and gore with several beheadings, dismemberments, and a rape. Possibly the most tasteless scene in the Shakespearean repertoire occurs towards the end of Act IV, when two brothers who have raped and dismembered Lavinia, daughter of Titus, are methodically mutilated by her father. After severing their heads, Titus grinds their bones to powder, which he mixes with their blood. The viscous mixture is then rolled into a thin doughy paste which is wrapped, in pie-crust fashion, around the severed heads. The dish is served to their unsuspecting mother. Marchette Chute wrote that the play "wallowed in the kind of atrocities that are still the mainstay of cheap journalism and cheap fiction." Critic J. C. Maxwell said of *Titus* that it is "the only play of Shakespeare which could have left an intelligent contemporary in some doubt whether the author's truest bent was for the stage."

Another Shakespearean lemon is *Timon of Athens,* set in ancient Greece. Says English literary critic Barrett Wendell, "In *Timon* there is such weakness of creative imagination that we can hardly realize how what goes on might really occur anywhere." And the late Mark van Doren called the play "plotless."

Worst Theatrical Act: When impresario Oscar Hammerstein found himself in a financial hole, he decided on a new approach. "I've been putting on the best talent and it hasn't gone over," he told reporters. "I'm going to try the worst." On November 16, 1896, he introduced Elizabeth, Effie, Jessie, and Addie Cherry to New York audiences at his Olympia Theatre. A sister act that had been treading the vaudeville boards in the Midwest for a few years, they strutted out onto the Olympia's stage garbed in red dresses, hats, and woolen mittens. Jessie kept time on a bass drum while her three partners did their opening number:

> Cherries ripe Boom-de-ay!
> Cherries red Boom-de-ay!
> The Cherry sisters
> Have come to stay!

New York audiences proved more merciful, at first, than those in the Midwest. They held off pelting the girls with garbage and overripe tomatoes at first, staring goggle-eyed in disbelief. Said the New York *World* of their premiere, "It was awful." Said *The New York Times,* "It is sincerely hoped that nothing like them will ever be seen again." One critic wrote, "A locksmith with a strong, rasping file could earn ready wages taking the kinks out of Lizzie's voice." Eventually, the Cherry sisters put up a wire screen to protect themselves from the inevitable hail of missiles showered on them by the audience, although in later years they denied that anything had ever been thrown at them. Despite their reputation as "the world's worst act," they played consistently to standing-room-only crowds, wowing their fans with such numbers as "The Modern Young Man" (a recitation), "I'm Out Upon the Mash, Boys," "Curfew Must Not Ring To-night," and "Don't You Remember Sweet Alice Ben Bolt?"

Most Unusual Play: *Breath,* by Samuel Beckett, was first performed in April 1970. The play lasts thirty seconds, has no actors, and no dialogue.

Most Unusual Shakespearean Lines: Two popular and often-quoted lines from *Richard III* were not written by Shakespeare at all. "Off with his head; so much for Buckingham" and "Conscience avaunt, Richard's himself again!" were actually composed by Colley Cibber, an actor and frequent butt of Henry Fielding's jokes.

Most Unusual Shakespearean Production: Patients at the Orthodox Jewish Menorah Home and Hospital for the Aged and Infirm in New York produced and staged *Macbeth,* or a reasonable facsimile thereof, in 1964. Sample dialogue: LADY MACBETH: Did I do bad? I wanted my husband to be a somebody. MACBETH: A king I hed to be? A fifteen-room kessel vasn't good enough for you?

As alternates, you might like to consider these productions:

British playwright, Donald Howarth, journeyed to Cape Town, South Africa, to put on Shakespeare's *Othello.* He immediately ran into casting difficulties. Employing a black man to play the part of Othello in an otherwise all-white cast was ruled a violation of South Africa's apartheid laws. As the San Francisco *Chronicle* (6/19/72) reported, Howarth went ahead and produced *Othello* without Othello, writing in three new parts for white characters to replace the Moorish protagonist.

In a January 1956 production of *King Lear* at New York's City Center, Orson Welles, who had fractured his ankle in a fall, played the title role from a wheelchair.

47

The Movies

Best Adaptation of a Novel: *Gone with the Wind* (as if there were any question). Margaret Mitchell, who was killed when struck by an automobile in Atlanta in 1949, admitted that she wrote *GWTW* with an eye cocked to movie rights, and had thought of Clark Gable as she created the character of Rhett Butler. Gable's use of an undeleted expletive when he leaves Scarlett ("Frankly, my dear, I don't give a damn") was unprecedented and hailed as an omen of the coming corruption of the cinema, but no matter—the film to date has grossed millions. In 1950, a poll of 200 Hollywood bigwigs voted *GWTW* the greatest movie ever.

Best Antiwar Film: *All Quiet on the Western Front*. And perhaps the most widely viewed film as well, just as the Erich Maria Remarque novel on which it is based is one of the best sellers of the twentieth century. The first of the antiwar movies—all war films prior to *All Quiet* glorified war and the gore of battle—it is considered by *The New York Times* to be the best ever made. Lew Ayres starred in *All Quiet,* a film in which 2,000 ex-G.I.'s were hired as extras for the battle scenes. When the movie opened in 1930, the New York *American* could not contain its enthusiasm, calling it "the mightiest war drama ever screened in the ages of history." It has also been one of the most savagely censored movies. When it played in Germany in the early 1930s—to enthusiastic audiences, incidentally—Nazi saboteurs released snakes and rats in the theaters where it was shown. During the Korean War, only heavily cut versions of the film were allowed to be shown in the United States.

Best Children's Film: *The Wizard of Oz*. Bosley Crowther found a place for *The Wizard of Oz* (a 1939 Victor Fleming production) on his 100-best list—the only children's film in the lot. With a cast headed by Judy Garland, Bert Lahr,

Jack Haley, Ray Bolger, and Billie Burke, *Oz* counts not only as the all-time best of the children's movies but one of the greatest musicals ever made, says Pauline Kael. By the way, leave your color-adjusting dial alone when you watch *Oz* on TV—the first 18 minutes are in black and white.

Best Comedy: *A Night at the Opera.* The Marx Brothers were never better than in this 1935 classic, and the rudeness of Groucho, as the fly-by-night showman Otis B. Driftwood, is positively exquisite: "Waiter, the bill. . . . *Nine dollars and forty cents*—that's an outrage!" Looking up at straight woman Margaret Dumont: "If I were you I wouldn't pay it." Granted, there wasn't much to laugh at in 1935, but the controlled lunacy of Groucho, Harpo, and Chico, aided by Allan Jones, Kitty Carlisle, and Miss Dumont, had depressed (and Depressed) Americans laughing themselves silly. The stateroom scene alone is worth the price of a ticket.

Best Documentary: A dead heat—more or less—among these four: Marcel Ophuls's *The Sorrow and the Pity,* Antonioni's *Point of Order,* and two by Robert Flaherty, *Louisiana Story* and *Nanook of the North.* The Ophuls opus, the longest of the lot and certainly the most ambitious, is also the most recent, and *Esquire*'s Thomas Berger has written that it is "the finest documentary ever made."

Louisiana Story, however, with its splendid background score by Virgil Thomson, placed fifth on the all-time movie greats list in the 1952 British Film Institute poll.

And then there are those exquisitely delicious few moments in *Point of Order* in which Joseph Welch puts the screws to Joseph McCarthy for slandering Welch's legal assistant ("At long last, sir, have you no sense of decency? Have you no shame?")

Which brings us to *Nanook,* which scratchy, silent, and fifty-two years old, still has the edge over the others. The film is neither fiction nor fantasy, but a hard, truthful look at life in the arctic as it really was—without tears (but with tons of ice and whale blubber). The stars of this film are the Eskimo hunter-frontiersman Nanook and his family, seen struggling for survival in surroundings both beautiful and hostile. In one memorable sequence, Nanook single-handedly constructs an igloo for his family when they are caught in a storm during a hunting expedition. Working with unbelievable speed and dexterity, he cuts out bricks of ice with his whaling knife and fits them together with a watchmaker's attention to precision. Two years after this remarkable movie was made, Nanook died of starvation.

Best of the "Eggplant-That-Ate-Cleveland" Films: *King Kong*. We're speaking, of course, about films in which a prehistoric monster, mean, angry, and skyscraper-tall, runs amok in a large city, derailing subways, gnawing away at building foundations, chewing up little girls, and the like. The fifties were rife with such epics: *The Beast from 20,000 Fathoms, It Came from Beneath the Sea, Rodan, Godzilla,* etc. All the same, the best of them is still that 1933 masterpiece, *King Kong,* at least as far as special effects and photography are concerned. *Kong,* in recent years, has come to mean many things to many people—the Black Man enslaved, sexual frustration, the danger inherent in man's attempt to control nature. The phallic imagery of the finale, in which Kong scales the Empire State Building, is unmistakable, if unintended. David O. Selznick produced this classic and Faye Wray screamed a lot. Rod Steiger says he's seen the film twenty-three times.

Best Film: *Citizen Kane* (1941), produced and directed by Orson Welles. "Boy Genius" Orson Welles was twenty-four years old when he made *Citizen Kane,* a cynical cinematization of the life of newspaper magnate William Randolph Hearst. Critics raved about the movie when it opened—"It comes close to being the most sensational film ever made in Hollywood," wrote Bosley Crowther of *The New York Times* on May 2, 1941—and their enthusiasm has grown over the years. In a 1962 British Film Institute survey, seventy critics from eleven nations voted *Kane* the best film in motion-picture history, and *Kane* was the only American movie—and one of only three "talkies"—on a list of twelve all-time movie greats selected by 117 international film historians in a poll at the 1958 Brussels World's Fair. Pauline Kael of *The New Yorker* has written that *Citizen Kane* "is more fun than any great movie I can think of. . . . It is also a rare example of a movie that seems better today than when it first came out." The same might be said of *Angels in the Outfield,* Dwight D. Eisenhower's unabashed favorite. Late in his second term he confided to a *Newsweek* reporter that he had seen *Angels* fifteen times since its 1948 premiere.

Other films that rate high are Michelangelo Antonioni's early sixties' drama *L'Avventura,* Renoir's 1939 satire of prewar France *The Rules of the Game,* and Sergei Eisenstein's silent masterpiece *Potemkin* (1925) (see *Best Historical Drama*).

Best Film Biography: *Ivan the Terrible*. A hazily defined category, if only because so many great films, such as *Citizen Kane* and *All the King's Men* straddle a thin line between biography and fiction. Sergei Eisenstein's two-part dramatization of the life of the Russian czar was released in 1945, the first two-thirds of a never-to-be-completed trilogy. Balked in his efforts by Soviet strictures against using montage sequences and offending Stalin, the picture seems extremely formalized today. Bosley Crowther calls *Ivan* the greatest of Eisenstein's films and the British Film Institute named it the sixth greatest movie of all time in 1952.

Best Film in Which an Artist of Great Promise is Stricken with a Fatal Disease: We use the term "artist" broadly, and in this case it boils down to musicians and athletes. The pickings here are slim: *Love Story, Rhapsody in Blue, The Eddy Duchin Story, Rockne of Notre Dame* (Ronald Reagan, playing George Gipp, is the hero in question), etc. The best of the genre, undoubtedly, is *Pride of the Yankees,* the 1942 biography of New York Yankee star Lou Gehrig, starring Gary Cooper and Teresa Wright. Leonard Maltin calls it a "superb baseball biography," a movie which is "beautifully photographed and directed, tastefully written." Watch for cameo appearances by Babe Ruth, Bill Dickey, and other Yankee greats.

Best Full-Length Cartoon: *Pinnochio* or *Yellow Submarine*. The former is a classic of visual art and widely accepted as the best that Walt Disney ever did. The latter integrates music that has been compared favorably with the *lieder* of Schubert and a strikingly imaginative screenplay. ("Do you ever get the feeling that things are not as rosy as they appear underneath the surface?") Says Vincent Canby of *Pinnochio*, it's the film in which Disney "reached his pinnacle of creativity and technical mastery."

Best Historical Drama: *The Battleship Potemkin*. And, until *Citizen Kane* came along, this 1925 Sergei Eisenstein opus was widely hailed as the greatest motion picture ever made. *Potemkin* is the story of a naval uprising in Odessa harbor in 1905, and of the czarist quashing of it. One scene stands out as perhaps "the outstanding single sequence of all time," according to Bosley Crowther and a host of other critics—the massacre of the peasants by Cossack guards on the great steps of Odessa harbor. Said James Agee, it was a scene "as brilliantly organized as a movement in a Beethoven symphony." Early in the movie, a bystander is shot full in the face by a stray bullet; this scene, otherwise unremembered, was the model for a similar sequence in Arthur Penn's 1967 *Bonnie and Clyde,* in which a bank guard, likewise uninvolved, is shot during a bungled getaway attempt by the two outlaws.

Best Horror Film: For sheer blood-curdling repulsiveness, *The Night of the Living Dead* wins in this category. But for a more profound sort of horror spiced with greater cinematic creativity, we'll opt for *The Cabinet of Dr. Caligari.* This silent relic released in 1921 will still frighten the socks off the most hardened of filmgoers. A product of the cinematic renaissance in post-World War I Germany, it is the story of Dr. Sonnow, the maniacal proprietor of a lunatic asylum who, under the name of Dr. Caligari, performs a unique hypnotic act at a local fair with an inmate known only as Cesare.

Cesare is stored in a cabinet—*the* cabinet, naturally—and at night, when the crowds have left, Caligari commands him to murder and multilate enemies of the good doctor. *Caligari* is just about the only horror film that ever makes it to anyone's list of all-time favories—including those of Dwight MacDonald and the novelist Henry Miller—as well as the list of all-time bests chosen by the Brussels symposium in 1958. Robert Wiene was the producer.

Best Monster Film: *Frankenstein.* Boris Karloff was never better than in this 1931 John Whale classic, but the real star of the show was make-up man Jack Pierce, who labored over Karloff for nearly five hours every day during the filming: "There are six ways a surgeon can cut the skull and I figured Dr. Frankenstein, who was not a practicing surgeon, would take the easiest," he told a New York *Times* reporter in 1939. "That is, he would cut the top of the skull straight across like a pot lid, hinge it, pop the brain in, and clamp it tight. That's the reason I decided to make the monster's head square and flat like a box and dig that big scar across his forehead and have two metal clamps hold it together. . . . The lizard eyes were made of rubber, as was his false head.

I made his arms look longer by shortening the sleeves of his coat. His legs were stiffened by steel struts and two pairs of pants. . . . His fingernails were blackened with shoe polish. His face was coated with blue-green grease paint. . . ." David Zinman says that "Karloff set the standard for Hollywood horror films to come." As for Karloff—the make-up ordeal alone cost him a twenty-pound weight loss.

Best Musical: *Singin' in the Rain*. Gene Kelly and Stanley Donen co-directed this 1952 classic that Pauline Kael calls "just about the best Hollywood musical of all time." Set in Hollywood in the late 1920s, *Singin'* takes a wry, mirthful look at the dilemma faced by squeaky-voice matinee idols like John Gilbert as the movie industry moved from silents to talkies. Starring Kelly, Donald O'Connor, and Debbie Reynolds, *Singin'* has attracted a broad-based following in the twenty-odd years since its release, including such critics as Jay Cocks of *Time* magazine and Rex Reed, who counts himself as one of the "devoted, dyed-in-the-wool *Singin' in the Rain* fans," and John Russell Taylor, who notes that *Singin'* seems always to be first among the films "that one would take to the moon or choose to see immediately before going into solitary confinement."

Best Mystery: *The Maltese Falcon*. "I think *The Maltese Falcon* is the best crime picture ever made in Hollywood," says Dwight MacDonald of the 1941 thriller, and Leonard Maltin concurs: "John Huston's first fling at directing, from Dashiell Hammett's story, adds up to the greatest detective film of all time. Everyone (Humphrey Bogart, Peter Lorre, Sidney Greenstreet, Elisha Cook, Jr., Mary Astor, et al.) is great, but when Lorre calls Greenstreet a 'blundering fathead' it's sheer ecstasy." Bogart's Sam Spade is deftly faithful to Hammett's original—callous, brilliant, and wholly without fear. "But you love me!" protests Mary Astor as he prepares to turn her over to the police at movie's end. "Sure I love you, but that's beside the point," Bogart tells her. "If they hang you, I'll always remember you."

Best Science Fiction Film: *The Incredible Shrinking Man*. Scott Carey is sunning himself aboard his cabin cruiser one fine summer day when a cloud of insecticide passes by and engulfs him and his small craft. Six weeks later he begins mysteriously to shrink in size, losing an inch or two at first, and then half his normal height. His marriage flounders (in spite of the old saw about short men being the most virile) and he seeks comfort in a quickie affair with a circus midget, which ends when he discovers he's become even smaller than she. Dejected beyond words, he returns home and moves into a dollhouse, but is chased out by his cat, now monstrously large. Taking refuge in the cellar, he struggles for survival against starvation, tarantulas, exhaustion, and isolation. As the movie ends, he slips through a ventilator to the great outdoors—his front yard—looking up at the heavens to ponder the meaning of it all.

The special effects in this 1957 Jack Arnold production are masterfully executed, even the acting is competent, and the screenplay, based on a novel by Richard Matheson, is excellent. It's a film, says sci-fi critic John Baxter, "that for intelligence and sophistication has few equals. Arguably, it is the peak of sf film in its long history."

Best Silent Film: *The Gold Rush*. Or so said a twenty-six-nation poll of 117 film historians who met at the Brussels World's Fair in 1958 to compile a list of the greatest movies ever produced. Hard-pressed to come up with a single all-time best, the group placed Charlie Chaplin's 1925 silent comedy among the six greatest motion pictures of all time. *The Gold Rush* also rated highly in a poll of seventy international film critics conducted by the British Film Institute in 1962, and was named the third greatest movie of all time by a similar poll ten years later. Written, produced, directed, and partially financed by Chaplin, who starred in the movie as the Lone Prospector, the movie cost $2 million to make. Best scene: a starving Chaplin, desperate for food, cooks his shoe with the finesse and care of a cordon bleu chef, serving it up basted in its own juices and garnished with laces. He devours the meal with bittersweet gusto.

Best Western: *The Gunfighter* is unquestionably the greatest Hollywood western ever filmed—unless, of course, you prefer *High Noon, Shane, The Searchers,* or *The Ox-Bow Incident,* all of which rate highly and none of which has ever made it to *anyone's* ten-best-movies' list (nobody takes westerns very seriously these days, it seems). In any event, Dwight MacDonald likes *Gunfighter*—a 1950 film which Henry King directed and Gregory Peck starred in—because it shows a stock character "behave realistically instead of in the usual terms of romantic cliche."

Worst Comedy: *The Big Noise.* The bubbles had just about fizzed out of Laurel and Hardy by the mid-1940s, and this 1944 dud is as depressing as it is unfunny. The action finds Stan and Laurel as detectives, hired to guard a bomb. (The French title, significantly, was *Quel Petard*—or *What a Bomb.*) Bosley Crowther wrote in *The New York Times* that the movie "has about as much humor in it as a six-foot hole in the ground." Runner-up is *The Courtship of Andy Hardy,* which film critic Leonard Maltin calls "the most unbearable in a now-obnoxious series. If Rooney doesn't get you the Forties' slang will."

Worst Editing of a Film: A movie theater manager in Seoul, South Korea, decided that the running time of *The Sound of Music* was too long. He shortened it by cutting out all the songs.

Worst Film: An admittedly difficult choice. *New York* magazine has called Ken Russell's *The Devils* "cinematic excrement," a judgment it has yet to confer on any other film. There is also that monumental turkey of 1948, *The Babe Ruth Story,* with William Bendix. But the real winner may very well be *Myra Breckinridge.* *Time* reviewer Jay Cocks wrote of this 1970 cinematization of the Gore Vidal novel that it is "about as funny as a child molester. It is an insult to intelligence, an affront to sensibility, and an abomination to the eye." A surreal tale about a transsexual actor who undergoes sex-change surgery and emerges as a voluptuous siren bent on seducing Hollywood, the film drew universally scathing notices. *McCall's* said that "the principal horror of the film [is] its overwhelming inhumanity." And film critic Rex Reed himself, who played the presurgical Myron Breckinridge to Raquel Welch's Myra, told a nationwide audience weeks before the opening that he had seen previews of the film and that it was "terrible." If the story intrigues you, read the book. It isn't Vidal at his best, but it's vastly better than the movie. More fun, too.

Worst Film Biography: Three contenders for this one. First, *The Magnificent Rebel,* a cinematic biography of Beethoven produced in Germany in 1961 by Georg Tressler. Treacly and dull, the movie, notes film historian Lotte Eisner, features a young Beethoven "with false eyelashes, played by a mediocre actor with a broad face."

Next we have *The Babe Ruth Story,* made in 1948, starring William Bendix as the Babe and Claire Trevor as his wife, which may well have been *the* worst film bio Hollywood has ever come up with. It's a casebook of sports film clichés and Bendix, who throws like a girl, is a monumental flop. The deathbed scene is even more sickening than its counterpart in *Love Story* and is to be avoided at all costs.

Finally, the *Harlow* twins. In 1965, when Joseph E. Levine announced plans to produce a film version of the life of Jean Harlow, the Hollywood screen siren, low-budget film-maker Bill Sargeant got on his celluloid horse and decided to scoop Levine. Sargeant's cinematic mugging of Miss Harlow was filmed, spliced, edited, packaged, and in the theaters in eight days (including time out for coffee and danish and two days lost due to bad weather). Starring Carol Lynley in the title role and Ginger Rogers and Barry Sullivan as her parents, it was made of 100 percent pure plastic without a fleck of humanity or an iota of truth.

In the twilight period between the opening of Sargeant's *Harlow* and the premiere of Levine's *Harlow,* film critic Howard Thompson of *The New York Times* wrote that "Whatever the second *Harlow* picture looks and sounds like, it can't be much worse than the first." As it turned out, it was actually a little bit better.

Worst Love Story: *Love Story,* appropriately enough. Critics generally found this 1970 production of Erich Segal's best seller—which wasn't any better than the movie—a model of sheer pretentiousness and high-gloss plasticity, and Judith Crist's characterization of the film as "*Camille* with bullshit," was not untypical. One reviewer who differed with the majority of critics was Richard Nixon: He liked the film just fine, although he was appalled by its "excessive profanity."

Worst Miscasting: Connoisseurs of the incongruous recall with fondness Clark Gable's unfortunate portrayal of the title character in *Parnell,* an inept 1937 biography of the Irish revolutionary hero. Our own favorite is Charles Boyer's Napoleon in the 1938 Clarence Brown film, *Maria Valeska.* Not that Boyer is not an admirable actor, not that he doesn't put his all into the role. It's just that, as film historian Lotte Eisner has pointed out, he's too *tall* to be Napoleon and spends the entire film walking around stooped over.

Worst Western: *The Tall Men.* "In just 15 minutes watch three big stars sink slowly in the west," writes Leonard Maltin. The stars included Clark Gable, Robert Ryan, 1,500 Indians, 4,000 head of cattle, and Jane Russell, whose aching feet were the only point of interest in this titanic bore released in 1955. (Some nice scenes, though, including Miss Russell purring sexily in a Montana log cabin while Gable munches eagerly on a piece of mule meat. "After a long ride," he explains, "I get as hungry as a bear.")

Most Unusual Film: *Sleep,* the first movie ever made by America's most unusual moviemaker Andy Warhol. A 1963 opus, *Sleep* features close-ups of a naked man getting his eight hours. It is, appropriately, eight hours long.

Warhol also produced *Eat,* in which the artist Robert Indiana eats mushrooms for two hours; *Empire,* a seven and one-half hour view of the Empire State Building, shot from the top floor of the Time-Life Building, and ****, which is twenty-five hours long in the uncut version. Actually, to call it uncut is redundant, since *nothing* ever winds up on Warhol's cutting room floor. What he shoots is what you get, and that includes not just all the footage but the celluloid leaders at the ends of the film used to thread the film onto the sprockets of the spools.

Most Unusual Film Rating: Boston newspapers ran an advertisement in 1970 for Walt Disney's *Peter Pan* which carried an "R" rating (Children under eighteen not admitted without parent or guardian).

Most Unusual Pornographic Movie: At England's Chessington Zoo, officials embarked upon a revolutionary plan to perk up the chimpanzees' flagging sex life and get the apes to mate: show them skin flicks. First step in the program, before the chimps would be graduated to hard-core porn, would be a BBC documentary film showing chimpanzees cuddling. "We tried it in three cages in the ape house," said zoo spokesman Andy Bowen. "The orangutans were only interested in the projector. The gorillas became aggressive. But Cressida [an eight-year-old female chimp] was just overcome with passion."

Music

Best Ballet Dancer (Current): Rudolf Nureyev. Critical acclaim for this forty-year-old Russian-born premier danseur is unanimous—from Clive Barnes to Hubert Humphrey (who once bubbled after a Nureyev performance, "Excellent, wonderful—and I don't usually cotton to that kind of dancing"). Hubert Saal, music editor of *Newsweek,* has called Nureyev "the reigning prince of dancers," and Serge Grigoriev, the noted Soviet ballet dancer, says of Nureyev that "he is every bit as good as Nijinsky." In London, Saal reports, Nureyev has become something of a latter-day matinee idol, "transforming Victorian reserve into Elizabethan enthusiasm. Covent Garden audiences are highly spiced with bobby-soxers who shower the stage with flowers and chant, 'We want Rudi, preferably in the nudi.' "

Best Ballet Score: *Swan Lake,* by Pëtr Ilich Tchaikovsky. It's the music we're concerned with here, not the choreography or the staging, and many critics agree that in *Swan Lake,* in his last three symphonies, and in his violin concerto Tchaikovsky reached the height of his creative powers.

Composed in 1875, *Swan Lake* was not well received at first, but is today a fixture of the standard concert repertoire—with or without dancers. (You may be interested to know that *Swan Lake,* as ballets go, is especially hard on a dancer's feet; the average ballet dancer, in a typical production of *Swan Lake,* will completely wear out four pairs of ballet shoes.)

Best Chamber Work: Beethoven's String Quartet no. 14 in C# Minor (opus 131). The best Beethoven is late Beethoven, and his five last string quartets, opus nos. 127, 130, 131, 132, and 135, composed in the final years of his troubled life, are commonly regarded as the pinnacle of Beethoven's aspirations and the greatest works of chamber music ever composed (as well as among the most difficult to play and appreciate). "For variety and complexity of texture—thin, transparent passages contrasted with densely woven contrapuntal ones; bristling pizzicato phrases alternating with sweeping legato themes—these quartets had never been equalled," writes Walter E. Nallin. Of the best of them, the C# Minor, Beethoven said, "Never have I written a melody that affected me so much." Says critic Martin Bookspan, the Quartet "is perhaps the most consistently 'other-worldly' and 'sublime' of Beethoven's final quartets—and probably of all music."

Best Choral Work: Bach's *The Passion According to St. Matthew*. Not that there aren't others that might also fill this spot—two, to be exact: Brahms's *German Requiem,* which he composed in 1868, and Handel's oratorio, *Saul,* composed in 1739, four years before the completion of *Messiah.* The Brahms and the Handel are certainly more immediately accessible than the *St. Matthew Passion,* and more *fun* at first, too. The drama of the Brahms requiem is more readily apparent and *Saul* abounds in the catchy tunes and rousing choruses that *The Passion,* on first hearing, may seem to lack. But in the final analysis, Bach's *St. Matthew Passion* may well be the most moving, human choral music ever heard. It was written in 1729.

Best Composer: Ludwig van Beethoven, who straddled the classical and romantic periods of music, may well be regarded as the Big One, the composer who single-handedly turned the symphony from a pleasant enough parlor diversion into a medium of artistic expression. The only other two possible choices, it would seem, would be Mozart and Johann Sebastian Bach—except that Beethoven himself once wrote that George Frederick Handel "was the greatest composer who ever lived."

Best Composer (American): Charles Ives or George Gershwin. Both are favorites, but Ives seems to have the edge. Leonard Bernstein, who gave Ives's monumental Second Symphony its first public hearing in 1951—it had been composed in 1897—calls Ives "our first really great composer—our Washington, Lincoln, and Jefferson of music." Ives, like the poet Wallace Stevens, was a highly successful insurance executive by trade, and never tried very hard to have his music performed publicly. Of all his compositions, his best

Ludwig van Beethoven

are thought to be his four symphonies and the revolutionary *Concord* Sonata for piano. When it was first performed on January 20, 1939, at New York's Town Hall, Lawrence Gilman of the New York *Herald Tribune* had this to say: "The sonata is exceptionally great music—it is, indeed, the greatest music composed by an American and the most deeply and essentially American in impulses and implication. It has passion, tenderness, humor, simplicity and homeliness. It has imaginative and spiritual vastness. It has wisdom and beauty. . . ." And so on. Some of the piano chords in the *Concord* Sonata and in Ives's Fourth Symphony are so complex that they can be struck correctly only with a specially sized block of wood.

Gershwin, of course, is better known. The prevailing sentiment is that he might well have become the greatest American composer bar none, had he not been cut down at his peak: He was only thirty-nine when he died of a brain tumor. He had completed his most ambitious concert work to date, the Concerto in F for Piano and Orchestra, and was just turning his talents more fully to symphonic composition when he died.

Best Composer of the Twentieth Century: Igor Stravinsky. While Bela Bartok may have composed the *best single piece of orchestral music* of the twentieth century—the Concerto for Orchestra—Stravinsky is unchallenged as the century's best composer. While the composer was still living, Joseph

Machlis wrote of him that "for half a century [he] has given impetus to the main currents in contemporary music." Stravinsky's best-known work, the *Rite of Spring*, may also be his best, but when it premiered in Paris in 1913, praise was scant. Fistfights broke out among the audience and some of the performers were hooted off the stage. Fortunately for Stravinsky, and for us, the work and its composer's genius were ultimately vindicated.

Best Opera: Mozart's *The Magic Flute*. Mozart may well have been the greatest of the operatic composers, and *The Magic Flute*, his last opera and the next-to-last work he composed before dying a pauper's death of Bright's disease at the age of thirty-five, is the ultimate synthesis of music and poetry. "That Mozart was equal to any demands of the theater, in whatever style, is shown by his triumphant treatment of the libretto," Robert Lawrence has written. Meanwhile, Alan Rich, of *New York* magazine, finds another Mozart opera—*The Marriage of Figaro*—the best opera ever composed.

But then there are the two supreme achievements of Giuseppe Verdi, *Otello* and *Falstaff*, and there are those who feel that it was Verdi, not Mozart—and *certainly* not Wagner—who brought opera to its apotheosis. "When we examine the pages of an *Otello* or a *Falstaff*," Olin Downes says, "we come across such expressions and such admirable theater, and such a master's treatment of orchestral resources delegated to their place in relation to the stage, as neither Wagner nor any other composer of his school ever dreamed of."

Best Opera Singer: When Puccini heard Enrico Caruso perform *Manon Lescaut* with the New York Metropolitan Opera the composer whispered, "He is singing like a god." While it is, of course, nearly impossible to compare modern singers with those who performed before the invention of the Victrola, we can say with confidence that Caruso was the most popular, famous, and successful opera singer of all time. It was the exceptional power displayed throughout his magnificent range that won him his highest compliments. That range is well demonstrated in an excerpt from *La Juive*, which he considered his finest recording.

All in all, his personal appeal and his treasured recordings vastly extended the audience for opera. There was scarcely ever an empty seat at one of his performances, and when he sang in Europe, tickets were auctioned off at unheard-of prices. Edouard de Reszke, an outstanding bass with the Metropolitan, described Caruso's attraction simply: "I have never heard a more beautiful voice."

Best Performance of the 1812 Overture Ever: Performances of Tchaikovsky's 1812 Overture have traditionally been augmented by the sounds of cannon and gunfire. In a recent working of the overture in Atlanta, conductor Robert Shaw added real explosives to the score. When he pressed the button smoke filled the concert hall and a loud blast shook the audience. The smoke set off a supersensitive fire alarm that alerted the local fire department who arrived, axes and hoses in hand. The concert ended early.

Best Pianist (Contemporary): Vladimir Horowitz. The lines began to form at the box office of New York's Carnegie Hall twelve hours before tickets went on sale in 1965 for Vladimir Horowitz's first piano recital in twelve years. Horowitz played to a packed house and rave reviews on that now-historic night, and Harold C. Schonberg, music critic of *The New York Times,* noted the following morning, "He still has a staggering technique—all the color and resonance in the world and a sonority that is unparalleled in the history of piano playing." A specialist in the works of the early romantics, Horowitz's *piece de resistance,* surprisingly, is a piano transcription of John Philip Sousa's *Stars and Stripes Forever,* which he introduced at a 1953 recital marking the twenty-fifth anniversary of his American debut. The performance was a tour de force, in which Horowitz's keyboard was magically transformed into a full-scale march band, complete with piccolo and sousaphone. One reviewer described Horowitz's performance as "possibly the most phenomenal pyrotechnical exhibition in the entire annals of piano playing."

Best Piano Concerto: Beethoven's Fourth. Beethoven wrote five concerti for piano in all, and the most famous, certainly, is his Fifth, the *Emperor,* although there are some who call it that more for its pomposity than for its grandeur. The real plum among Beethoven's piano concerti, his Fourth in G Minor, fell into obscurity during his lifetime, but was restored to popularity by Felix Mendelssohn, who played it publicly in Leipzig in 1836. "Although it does not offer virtuosos such an excellent chance to show off as the Fifth," write Wallace Brockway and Herbert Weinstock, "it is flaw-lessly constructed, original in detail, and inspired in melody." Beethoven accomplishes a bit of musical tradition-snubbing by opening the concerto with a statement by the unaccom-panied piano and not by the orchestra.

Other possibilities are two concerti of Mozart's—his A Major (K. 414) and his C Minor (K. 491)—and Brahms's Piano Concerto no. 1 in D Minor. Don't look for the same jewellike craftsmanship in the Brahms as you'll find in the Mozart. Brahms was a troubled, brooding man writing in the turbulent idiom of romanticism, and this concerto—which he originally intended as a full-blown symphony—is over-powering in its intensity and lyrical beauty. It was used effectively as background music for the Leslie Caron film, *The L-Shaped Room,* in the early sixties.

Best Piano Sonata: Again, Beethoven. This time, it's his Piano Sonata no. 32 in C Minor, opus 111. Beethoven's earlier keyboard classics—the *Moonlight Sonata,* the *Appassionata,* the *Pathetique*—are all beautiful, but they've been done to death. (You'll notice, once again, that we've excluded non-Beethovian candidates. The piano sonatas of Brahms and Mozart are great music, but they lack the depth and inven-tiveness of Beethoven's.) Musicologists Wallace Brockway and Herbert Weinstock write that "in the realm of musical history, it is not easy to be dogmatic, but it may be affirmed positively that Beethoven here set the limits of the piano so-nata. No other composer has even remotely approached it in amplitude of conception, perfection of design, vigor of movement or rightness of detail."

Best Rock Group: The Beatles did for rock music what Henry Ford did for the automobile and Babe Ruth did for baseball—infused it with new life and made it respectable. Their first album-long departure from rock orthodoxy—*Sergeant Pepper's Lonely Hearts Club Band,* released in 1966—maintains an almost impossibly high level of quality in every song. One critic likened the songs on that album to the art song cycles of Schubert and Mahler. Some say the Rolling Stones did as much for rock as the Beatles did, but remember, the Beatles did it first. And, we think, better.

Best Rock Song: *Sergeant Pepper's Lonely Hearts Club Band* is still the best rock album ever released. Appropriately, side two closes with the best song in rock history—"A Day in the

Life." It's a drug-induced vision of timelessness and despair, with a final chord that takes *forever* to disappear.

Best Symphony: Beethoven's Ninth Symphony. Of all the symphonies ever composed—and there've been thousands—the possible choices for "all-time best," it seems, boil down to just six: Beethoven's Third (the *Eroica*), his Fifth, and his Ninth (the *Choral*); and Mozart's last three—nos. 39, 40, and 41. Many critics have singled out the Mozart 40th in G Minor as being the most flawlessly constructed, the most melodic, and the most substantial of the six. But musicologist David Ewen feels that the mighty Ninth Symphony is Beethoven's "highest flight of fancy in the symphonic form—one of the most indestructible masterpieces in the entire realm of art." And T. S. Eliot wrote that Beethoven, in the last movement of the Ninth, was somehow aspiring to transcend music and reach for something almost divine.

Best Symphony Orchestra: The Chicago Symphony, with Georg Solti conducting. If the Philadelphia is the Cadillac of orchestras, the Chicago is a Maserati at the very least. *Esquire* calls the Chicago the best in the world, which it's clearly become since the Hungarian-born Solti took over the reins in 1969. The Chicagoans have a well-rounded repertoire, but do best with the Romantics. Their Mahler symphonies are superb.

Best Violin Concerto: Tchaikovsky's Violin Concerto in D Major. As fashionable as it has become to deplore the emotional excesses of romanticism, Pëtr Ilich Tchaikovsky managed to get it all together in his violin concerto—a magnificent synthesis of sensuality and substance. A virtuoso piece in the extreme, enormously difficult to play, its melodies are more engaging than those in the Beethoven violin concerto in D Major, and more stirring and substantial than those in the Mendelssohn E Minor concerto. Tchaikovsky, who was to die of cholera in 1893, was long troubled by feelings of artistic and creative inadequacy and freely admitted that he was "no Beethoven." But Rosa Newmarch has said that the "brightness and infectious gaiety" of the concerto's fourth movement "would probably have delighted Beethoven."

Worst Avant-Garde Concert: At the Third Annual New York Avant-Garde Music Festival in 1965, Korean composer Nam June Paik presented his lengthy *Prelude in D Minor*. Space prevents us from reviewing the performance in full, but we do feel that the highlights should be recorded for posterity. Perhaps future generations can learn from this mistake.

The composition opened with an action painting by Mr. Paik entitled "Homage to John Cage" (see also *Most Unusual Composer*); the composer applied black paint to the canvas with his hands and hair. This was followed by the demolition of an upright piano, the cracking of several eggs (amplified for the audience's benefit), and the production of various ear-splitting feedback shrieks.

The concert then moved into its second phase as nails were driven into another amplified piano. Showing intelligence that few gave him credit for, Paik proceeded to cut off his paint-soaked hair. In the *Prelude,* as in many avant-garde works, audience participation figured importantly in the performance. The composer ran out into the rather sparse crowd and squirted shaving cream on a number of appreciative music lovers. One man allowed Mr. Paik to scissor off his tie and shirt.

In the *Prelude*'s final movement, cellist Charlotte Moorman entered clad only in a *cello*phane sheath. A man dressed in black, poised motionlessly on all fours, served as her bench. For a while Miss Moorman played variations on a theme from Saint-Saens' *Le Cygne*. Then, midway through the piece, she put down her bow, ascended a six-foot ladder (assisted by Mr. Paik), and executed a "swan" dive into an oil drum filled with water. Emerging from the drum with the cellophane adhering tightly to her body, Miss Moorman finished off *Le Cygne*.

Howard Klein, a critic for *The New York Times,* termed the *Prelude in D Minor* "a study in instant ennui. Fraught with pretensions of profundity," Klein continued, "Mr. Paik's efforts lacked any spark of originality, sensitivity, or talent." Still, the *Prelude* was only the opening event of the week-long series, and Klein expressed some optimism about upcoming performances: "Maybe the festival will improve. It couldn't get worse."

Worst Ballet Score: *Ballet Mecanique,* by George Antheil. The French composer George Antheil—who was born in Trenton, New Jersey—conceived his *Ballet Mecanique* as a musical evocation of America, Africa, and steel. Scored for two airplane motors, eight xylophones, two octaves of musical bells, sixteen mechanical pianos, an automobile horn, a siren, two large sheets of tin and two of steel, and assorted humming and buzzing devices, alarm clocks, torpedoes, fan belts, electric screwdrivers and police whistles, the piece caused a near-riot when it premiered in 1926. Critics on both sides of the Atlantic were outraged and called Antheil's effort a monument to cacophony. And the *Times* of London had this to say about the ballet's premiere in Britain: "The concert is being organized as a benefit to Mr. Antheil and the promoters hope that the proceeds will enable the composer to remain in Europe and continue working there. In self-defense a concert should be organized on this side to enable Mr. Antheil to return to New York and pursue his studies quietly there."

Worst Baton Technique: During a 1975 concert in Mexico City, Uruguayan conductor José Serebrier accidentally stabbed himself through the hand with his baton. While musicians and chorus members gasped, blood gushed from the wound, staining his white tuxedo shirt and splattering his shoes. "The baton broke into pieces," the conductor later said. "One piece was sticking through my hand. Ironically, I never use a baton. But I decided to use one for this performance because I thought it would help achieve greater musical control. That was a mistake." Nonetheless, Serebrier continued conducting without missing a beat, deftly removing the wooden fragment from his hand and wrapping the wound tightly in a handkerchief during a lull in the music. He was treated at a nearby hospital following the concert and was back on the podium—sans baton—the following evening.

Worst Beethoven Composition: *Wellington's Victory,* or *The Battle* Symphony, opus 91. American and European music critics are all but unanimous in their choice of *Wellington's Victory* as rock-bottom in the Beethoven repertoire. Beethoven composed the work at the request of the German inventor-showman Johann Nepomuk Maelzel, the inventor of the metronome, as a demonstration piece for the "Panharmonicon." This was a Rube Goldberg-like device which Maelzel was touting as a mechanical orchestra. It consisted of an interconnected assortment of wind instruments through which a bellows blew with the notes controlled by a revolving brass cylinder with pins. Maelzel's plans foundered, but the

Max Reger

ymphony, commemorating the Duke of Wellington's 1813 ictory over Napoleon at the Battle of Vitoria, in Spain, emains. Today, it is occasionally performed by a live human rchestra, augmented with all manner of muskets, cannon, nd small-gage howitzers. Much of it is reminiscent of the oundtrack for a grade B western.

Worst Composer: "I remember meeting Max Reger in those ears," Igor Stravinsky reminisced. "He and his music reulsed me in about equal measure." On other occasions travinsky made the unflattering comparison, ". . . as dull as leger." In short, Max Reger is a prime candidate for honors s the worst composer.

No one accuses Reger of being without talent, but rarely as such technical virtuosity been put to poorer use. Working around the turn of the century, he incorporated two divervent influences into his music: the contrapuntal style of the ixteenth century and that of marching bands, of which he vas inordinately fond. His compositions are generally rearded as ponderous, overworked, and cluttered with too hany notes. Critic David Ewen puts it gently: ". . . he tilized formidably complex harmonic and contrapuntal tructures, generally too intricate for their own good."

Of course, Reger had his good qualities: He was endowed vith perfect pitch and is credited with a number of quotable, austic aphorisms. "The life of a composer is work, hope, nd bicarbonate of soda," he once said. Indeed, as a habitual drunk, Reger must have relied heavily on bicarbonate of soda. Even when he was abstaining from alcohol he still drank compulsively, downing as many as eight cups of beef bouillon at a sitting. Once he became ill from overindulging in lemonade. His physical appearance is best described as sniveling, and Paul Rosenfeld once remarked that Reger resembled "a swollen myopic beetle with thick lips and a sullen expression."

His music has been largely ignored, although he did receive some posthumous recognition when Hitler singled him out as a personal favorite. But still Max Reger is remembered as a musical reactionary who did his best to put the phony back in symphony.

Worst Composition of the Twentieth Century: Edgar Varese was the composer of *Ionization,* a musical representation of the action of ions with atoms. "It recalls schooldays in the chemical laboratory, where hydrogen sulfide was produced to the merriment of students and the horror of teachers," wrote the music reviewer of the Havana *Evening Telegram.*

Worst Concert: Tommy Dorsey brought eight members of his band to the monkey house of the Philadelphia Zoo in 1940 for a historic experiment designed to determine whether simians appreciate music. Well, you ask, did they dig it? ". . . The monkeys couldn't stand it," according to a zookeeper interviewed by the musical journal *Etude.* "The band first played some violent jazz. The chimpanzees were scared to death. They scampered all over the place, seeking the protection of their keepers and hiding under benches. . . . One chimp tried to pull the trombone away from Tommy Dorsey." The response to that number was so bad, in fact, that the band was forced to stop playing. One old chimp in particular had such a wounded and resentful look on his face that the band members couldn't bear to continue.

Then Dorsey tried a different style, launching into the mellow strains of his theme song, "I'm Getting Sentimental Over You." Almost immediately the animals began to calm down. They sat patiently on their benches, the keeper said, showing none of their previous agitation and "watching the players with interest."

Worst Musical Instrument: Louis XI of France commanded the Abbot of Baigne to invent a preposterous musical instrument to entertain His Majesty's friends. The Abbot good-naturedly agreed to undertake the assignment, and after a few hours at the drawing board, he gathered together a herd of hogs—ranging from nursing piglets to full-fledged swine. Under a velvet tent, he lined them up with the low-voiced porkers on the left, the middle-range sows in the middle, and the soprano piglets on the right. Then the Abbot modified an organ keyboard, attaching the keys to a complex apparatus terminating in a series of small spikes, one poised over the rump of each pig. The courtiers were gathered together and the Abbot played his keyboard, causing the spikes to prick the pigs, who naturally let out a piercing squeal, each in its own particular voice range. The tunes were actually recognizable, and the concert was adjudged a success by all.

There is another, similar story in French musical history about a fellow in the mid-1800s who trained cats to howl on command. He publicly performed a work called *Concert Miaulant* or Meowing Concert, which was also quite well received.

Worst Opera: *The Padlock,* a comic opera first produced at London's Drury Lane Theatre in 1768 (libretto by Isaac Bickerstaffe, music by Charles Didbin). The protagonist is Mungo, an inarticulate West Indian slave with a burning urge for self-expression, as evidenced in this aria:

> Dear heart, what a terrible life I am led!
> A dog has a better that's sheltered and fed
>   Night and day 'tis the same;
>   My pain is deir game
> Me wish to de Lord me was dead!
> Whate'er's to be done
> Poor black must run
> Mungo here, Mungo dere,
> Mungo everywhere;
> Above and below,
> Sirrah, come, sirrah, go;
> Do so, and do so.
> Oh! Oh!
> Me wish to de Lord me was dead! (and so forth)

Mungo ties one on in Act III and stays drunk until the final curtain, making himself generally obnoxious and losing whatever sympathy he may have earned for himself in Acts I and II.

Florence Foster Jenkins

Worst Opera Singer: Florence Foster Jenkins was involved in a taxi crash in 1943 and afterwards found that she could warble "a higher F than ever before." Yet even with her new and higher F, few would dispute that she was the worst opera singer of all time.

No one knows how many singers fail in the nation's showers, but Mrs. Jenkins dared greatly, failing in drawing rooms from Philadelphia to Newport, and ultimately on October 25, 1944, failing before a jammed house at Carnegie Hall. For a number of years, Mrs. Jenkins's career was an in-joke among cognoscenti and a few music critics, who wrote intentionally ambiguous reviews of her performances: "Her singing at its finest suggests the untrammeled swoop of some great bird," Robert Lawrence said in the *Saturday Review*.

A wealthy and well-padded matron (pictured here as the "Angel of Inspiration"), Mrs. Jenkins bore a resemblance to Margaret Dumont, the *grande dame* of the Marx Brothers movies. It was impossible to keep the diva's true talent a secret for long. Her Carnegie Hall appearance and her recording, "The Glory of the Human Voice," (RCA LM 2599) brought her national attention. Reviewing her record, *Newsweek* opined, "In high notes, Mrs. Jenkins sounds as if she was afflicted with low, nagging backache."

Mrs. Jenkins was aware that people were laughing at her when she sang the Bell Song from *Lakmé* or her favorite arias from *Die Fledermaus*, but they also applauded energetically. She was convinced that she brought her audiences pleasure with her singing; and surely she did.

Worst Piano Concerto: It was Max Reger who produced the world's worst piano concerto. These remarks, by former New York *Times* music critic Olin Downes, are typical: "The Reger Piano Concerto is to our mind a most inflated, pretentious bag of wind. . . . The orchestration is . . . swollen, thick and prevailingly in bad taste. Little bits of ideas are pretentiously and noisily bunched together and they get nowhere. . . . What incredibly bad taste, and poor invention!"

Worst Popular Singer: Elva Miller. Mrs. Miller, as her admirers know her, has a voice about as good as your mother-in-law's, but she wasted no time hitting the charts in 1966 with a nightmarish rendition of "Downtown." Some 250,000 fans bought the Capitol Records single and later Mrs. Miller came out with an album of old favorites.

Worst Rock Song Ever: What makes a rock song memorably bad? Is it the mind-smothering lyrics, the non-melody, the offensiveness of the performer—or of the pimply faced blind date you first heard it with? Actually, most bad rock songs are eminently forgettable. One called "Only in America," released in 1964, still clings leechlike to our unwilling memory:

> Only in America
> Land of opportunity,
> Would a classy girl like you
> Fall for a poor boy like me.

And so forth.

Worst String Quartet: Critical reaction to Max Reger's String Quartet opus 109 was similar to that which greeted virtually all of his works: scandalized, sarcastic, enraged. Irving Kolodin, writing in the New York *Sun*, observed that while the piece looks like music, sounds like music, and "might even taste like music," it remains stubbornly "not music . . . Reger might be epitomized as a composer whose name is the same either forward or backward and whose music, curiously, often displays the same characteristic."

Worst Symphony: Any one of the nine symphonies of Louis Spohr, a mid-nineteenth-century German composer, has a fair crack at the title, but our choice is his Symphony no. 2. Bland, yet pretentious; unmemorable, yet grating to the ears; altogether, a colossal bore. Although Spohr was in the vanguard of the German romantic revolt in music, he had little use for Beethoven's later works and didn't care a hoot about the music of Weber either. At the age of seventy-three he broke his left arm and was no longer able to play the violin. He died heartbroken two years later.

The fourth symphony of the Austro-American composer Ernst Krenek has also inspired some choice critical prose. Critic-composer Virgil Thomson called it "a pseudomasterpiece, with about as much savor to it as a paste-board turkey." Music critic John Briggs, of the New York *Post,* wrote after a performance of the work in 1947, that hearing it is like "suddenly being transported to Mars and not knowing whether to be amused or infuriated." In calling Krenek's output sterile and barren of passion, Olin Downes was considerably more generous than the Russian critic V. Gorodinsky, who said about *Jonny Spielt Auf,* Krenek's best known opera, "There is nothing in it but filth, dirt, cold cruelty and sticky frog-like sexuality, combined with the dry rationalism of a biped calculating machine."

Worst Tone Poem: The tone poems of Edgar Varese have inspired some of the most vitriolic criticism ever penned. New York *World* critic Samuel Chatzin wrote that *Ameriques* "seemed to depict the progress of a terrible fire in one of our larger zoos." Ernest Newman, of the New York *Evening Post* wrote that *Integrales* "Sounded like a combination of early morning in the Mott Haven freight yards, feeding time at the zoo, and a Sixth Avenue trolley rounding a curve, with an intoxicated woodpecker thrown in for good measure." And F. Brust, writing in the Berlin publication *Germania,* said that *Arcana* was reminiscent of "an insanely raging zoo . . . or a mass of men thrown into the crater of an erupting volcano in a hideous slaughter."

Most Unusual Composer: Harry Partch. It wasn't enough for Harry Partch that he toss the twelve-tone scale, good enough for the likes of Beethoven and Irving Berlin, into the dustbin and invent his own forty-three-note octave; he found it necessary to invent and build his own musical instruments as well. They included the Whang Gun, a seventy-two-stringed surrogate cithara, glass bells which he called "cloud chamber bowls," a strange, marimbalike instrument called a "boo," and his most famous creation, the bloboys, consisting of three organ pipes, a bellows, and an automobile exhaust pipe.

Partch began composing in 1923 at the age of twenty-two, but it wasn't until the late 1960s that he made his New York debut. He was best known in California, where a succession of grants from the Carnegie, Fromm, and Guggenheim foundations kept him sufficiently above water to continue composing and attacking what he called "the tyranny of the piano scale, a wholly irrational, oppressive lid on musical expression." Some of Partch's music was recorded on Columbia records, and it included such pieces as "Visions Fill the Eyes of a Defeated Basketball Team in the Shower Room," "And on the Seventh Day Petals Fell on Petaluma," "Daphne of the Dunes," "Water, Water," and "U.S. Highway," which incorporates the conversation of hoboes on a freight train.

Equally unconventional are the compositions of John Cage. His father was an inventor whose influence may go far toward explaining Cage's music. The foremost avant-garde composer for thirty years, Cage proved his durability at a recent retrospective at New York's Alice Tully Hall in honor of his sixtieth birthday; after all these years his compositions still drew enthusiastic cheers and heartfelt boos from the audience.

Cage's early work emphasized percussion. For example, his *Third Construction* (1941) was scored for rattles, drums, tin cans, claves, cowbells, a lion's roar, cymbal, ratchet, texponaxtle, quijadas, cricket caller, and conch shell. More recently, however, he has placed as much emphasis on the event as on the sounds. It is interesting to note the differences between Cage and Handel; in Cage's *Water Music* (1952), the performer repeatedly pours water from a full container into an empty one, carefully regulating the timing of the slosh with a stop watch; the composition also includes the riffling of playing cards and static produced by a radio. This is what the composer calls "everyday music," derived from a heightened awareness of the world around him. He explains it this way: "Now I go to a cocktail party. I don't hear noise. I hear music."

Cage's compositions also show the input of Eastern philosophy. Many works are scored to include the casting of Chinese dice (the fortune-telling process of the *I-Ching*) to determine the order of the sounds to be performed; this is known as "aleatory music." On other occasions Cage relates Zen parables as a part of his performance. The Zen Buddhist fascination with silence can also be detected in his music. *Four Minutes Thirty-three Seconds* (1952) is intended for one or any number of instruments; it consists of three silent movements of 30", 2'23", and 1'40", during which the performers sit poised with their instruments without playing.

One of Cage's most remarkable works is *Theater Piece* (1963), first staged in Rome. Fusing Marx Brothers' antics with neodadaist art, the pianist enters by throwing a dead fish into his instrument. One musician walks around the stage dragging a chair loudly across the floor, while another, wearing a nightgown, hands out soggy pizzas to the audience.

John Cage is now a musical director with the Merce Cunningham dance company. He spends much of his spare time collecting and writing about mushrooms.

And while we're considering unusual composing techniques, both Schubert and Beethoven are said to have composed some of their greatest works in the bathtub.

Most Unusual Mozart Composition: Franz Joseph Haydn, Mozart's mentor, challenged his young pupil to write a piece for the piano that the elder composer could not play on first sight. Mozart accepted the challenge on the condition that if Haydn failed to play the composition, he would buy the champagne that night at dinner. In five minutes, Mozart finished what appeared to be a rather simple little score. Haydn launched into it confidently.

Halfway through the piece, Haydn found his left hand down at the bottom of the keyboard, his right way up at the top; astonishingly, the score called for the performer to play a solitary note right in the middle of the keyboard at the same time. Haydn broke off in disgust. "Nobody can play such music!" he said. Mozart then took the sheet music and sat down at the piano himself. He rushed through the simple first section, arriving at the part with his hands stretched wide apart. At the appropriate instant, Mozart leaned over and struck the "unplayable" note with his unusually large nose.

Haydn bought the champagne.

Most Unusual Popular Singer: No one knows what Alan Stivell is trying to say when he sings "Ur blank, ur blank, ar chopinad/ar chistr 'zo eit bout evet," but he is, nonetheless, having great success as a top-billed musical attraction throughout France. Stivell, who hails from Brittany and sings in Breton, is intensely nationalistic about his heritage, and his music, he says, "is an expression of outrage against French colonialism and its tools of TV and radio." Stivell accompanies himself on an electric thirty-one-string Celtic harp, or on the Cornish bagpipes, and is backed up by one of the best rock bands on the European scene.

Pop Culture

Best Board Game: Monopoly, which has been around since the 1930s when $2,000 was a lot of rent to pay on a hotel on Boardwalk, still has more fantasy-based appeal than any of its imitators. There is just enough skill involved in the game to make it interesting, but not so much as to make it a tedious and taxing mental exercise. And, more than any other game, it satisfies the oral-acquisitive needs of most people.

Best Hobby: "Nearly every family has a favorite pet, such as a cat, dog, or parrot, to which they become attached and would like to have preserved when it dies," says Alfred Burkley. "By knowing taxidermy, and often from personal knowledge of the pet, you can preserve such specimens just as they were in life." Burkley knows whereof he speaks: He is president of the Northeastern School of Taxidermy in Omaha, Nebraska, a seventy-one-year-old correspondence school that has graduated some 450,000 satisfied bird-and-animal stuffers throughout the world.

The dimensions of taxidermy are varied. In addition to the stuffing and mounting of moose, horned toads, raccoons, and family pets, there is also "novelty taxidermy . . . a novel and fun-to-do sideline of regular taxidermy." Enjoying this amusing spin-off of the taxidermist's art takes only a good sense of humor and good aim with a rifle; the idea is to bag all the frogs, newts, rabbits, and squirrels you can find and dress their stuffed little corpses in anything from Prince Albert coats to Chicago White Sox uniforms—whatever tickles your funnybone—and arrange them in humorous real-life settings. Thus, in a NST brochure, we see a small group of coked-up frogs playing in a small jazz combo; a rabbit business executive having his hair cut by a rabbit barber while a rabbit manicurist does his nails; and a family of nattily dressed chipmunks out for a Sunday stroll.

The standard fee for stuffing a lion is $800; for stuffing a deer's head, $90. If you're good, you can earn $14,000 for stuffing an elephant. In fact, Sotheby's, the chic London gallery, recently auctioned off a stuffed great auk for $21,000.

Best Mystery TV Series: *Time* magazine film critic Richard Schickel chooses "Peter Gunn," which premiered back in 1958 starring Craig Stevens, Lola Albright (remember *her*?), and Herschel Bernardi. "Gunn" was infinitely more true-to-life, better written, and better acted than others of the genre.

Somehow "Alfred Hitchcock Presents" should be mentioned here, even though comparing it with "Peter Gunn" is a little like trying to add apples and oranges. Hitchcock's droll introductions and his epilogues, in which (in keeping with federal law) he punished an evildoer who may have gone scot-free during the drama itself, were sometimes as good as the rest of the show itself.

Best Parade: The Festival of Dionysus was always a time for luxury and revelling wherever there were Greeks. In honor of the god of wine, Ptolemy II (309–246 B.C.), Macedonian ruler of Egypt, orchestrated a splendid procession including all the animals of the Alexandria zoo—the finest in the ancient world.

The crowd gathered in the stadium in the early morning hours, as the parade was scheduled to begin at dawn and continue to dusk. One of the early features was a lavish float carrying a tremendous statue of Dionysus, attended by a host of admiring priests, priestesses, and dancing girls; the float was drawn by twenty-four straining men. There were countless men dressed as satyrs, frolicking lasciviously with women in Eastern dress, and all the while the wine flowed and flowed.

Then, according to the chronicler Athenaeus, the menagerie was led in. At the head was a tremendous elephant, the tallest ever seen, covered with trappings of gold and festooned with ivy leaves, and on top of his back was a satyr cavorting and directing the great beast. The lead elephant was followed by 24 elephant-drawn floats, 60 drawn by billy goats, 12 by lions, 6 by nanny goats, 4 by wild asses, 15 by buffalo, 8 by ostriches, and 7 by stags.

Next came the camels. Ptolemy II introduced camels to Egypt and he was particularly proud of his one- and two-humped stable. The camels drew a series of wagons, each carrying a romantic-looking tent "in the fashion of the bar-

barians" with an enticing woman in slave dress dancing alongside. Then came troops of Abyssinians loaded down with ivory tusks, ebony, trunks filled with jewels, and sacks of gold dust. Hunters crowded into the arena accompanied by thousands of fierce mastiffs. There were exotic birds in reed cages, flocks of sheep, a two-horned rhinoceros, more camels laden with spices and perfume, countless statues of the gods, Ptolemy, and Alexander; bevies of concubines carrying banners proclaiming the names of every Greek settlement in the world, a choir of 600 men in precious crowns, an orchestra playing richly ornamented citharas, 2,000 perfectly matched bulls, censers, potted palm trees, and, of course, vats brimming with wine. Finally, there were two colossal sculptures—one of Jupiter and one of Alexander—and a last chariot sending up clouds of incense.

Best Stand-up Comedian: Henny Youngman (see also *Most Unusual Stand-up Comedian* and *Worst Stand-up Comedian*).

Best Television Documentary: It was Edward R. Murrow of CBS who introduced the documentary to television, and by 1960 he had achieved virtual perfection in the form. "Harvest of Shame," a 1960 "CBS Reports" study of the plight of migrant farm workers in the South was as incisive as *Grapes of Wrath,* as eloquent, and in many ways more immediate.

Best TV Quiz Show: "The G. E. College Bowl." Why, *why* did they ever take America's favorite question-and-answer game off the air? Fast-moving, gripping, and *honest,* "College Bowl" became a national institution and was the one thing that made Sunday night, surely the most depressing time of the week, bearable. ("There's the whistle to start the first half—you're playing for a thirty-point bonus. In what Shakespearean play did an English king receive a gift of tennis balls from the Dauphin of France?") Sadly, Allen Ludden, the show's first "man with the questions," later sank to the plumbless depths of "Password" (a better parlor game than a TV show) and became, we think, the worst quizmaster/emcee in TV history. (His only evidence of talent, writes George Frazier, "would seem to be an inane grin.")

Best TV Quiz Show Host: Groucho Marx. That is, if you really do consider "You Bet Your Life" a quiz show—and you really do consider Groucho a host. (*Our* parents taught us that a host was always polite to his guests and Groucho was forever saying things to contestants like "You're a model? What do you model—clay?") George Fenneman was almost as good a straight man as Margaret Dumont.

Best TV/Radio Newcaster: Edward R. Murrow. For nearly thirty years the greatness and mediocrity of broadcast journalists has been measured against the achievement of Edward R. Murrow, who is generally regarded as the greatest newsman in radio and television history. Murrow's "See It Now" series in the early 1950s—and in particular, the episodes in which he publicly confronted Joseph McCarthy at a time when the rest of the broadcast profession sat tight, waiting to see what move the Wisconsin demagogue would make next—are still unmatched for eloquence and courage.

Murrow died of lung cancer at his home in Pawling, New York, in 1965. ("I doubt that I could spend even half an hour without a cigarette with any ease or comfort," he said on a documentary he did on the dangers of cigarette smoking.) At the time of his death, Eric Sevareid of CBS said, "He was a shooting star and we will live in his afterglow a very long time."

Best TV Show: Attempting to choose the best television show ever screened is, we admit it, quite a dilemma. After all, can anyone say that Ed Murrow was better than Richard Boone—or that "Playhouse 90" was a better show than "See It Now"?

All the same, we'll make a choice. The all-time best TV show was probably the old Sid Caesar Saturday night classic "Your Show of Shows," with Imogene Coca, Howard Morris, Carl Reiner, and a staff of writers that included Woody Allen and Mel Brooks.

Best TV Situation Comedy: "You'll Never Get Rich," known more widely if less accurately as "The Phil Silvers Show." Silvers starred as the ever-enterprising Sergeant Ernest G. Bilko ("Line forms to the right for tickets to the Come-as-You-Were-on-the-Day-You-Were-Drafted-Dinner-Dance,") and Nat Hiken wrote most of the scripts, which still play well as reruns. An episode starring a chimpanzee who is inducted into the army was probably the high point of the series.

Dick Van Dyke made some of his earliest TV appearances on the Bilko series, and later was the star of "The Dick Van Dyke Show," thought by many critics, including *Time* film reviewer Richard Schickel, to be the funniest, most sophisticated family sitcom in television history. Produced by Sheldon Leonard and featuring a can't-lose cast—Van Dyke, Mary Tyler Moore, Rose Marie, and Morey Amsterdam—the show, say Arthur Shulman and Roger Youmans, "differed from many of its contemporaries in the situation comedy field in that it was often genuinely funny."

Best TV Western: "Have Gun, Will Travel." Richard Boone starred as Paladin, the first of the *thinking* cowboys, and the title of this series, as everyone must know by now, was lifted from his calling card: "Have Gun, Will Travel—Wire Paladin, Hotel Carlton, San Francisco." Paladin puffed expensive cigars, quoted Byron, and, as Arthur Shulman and Roger Youmans write, "completed his rounds with a unique combination of epicurean zest, Spartan valor and existential ennui."

Many critics, nonetheless, prefer "Gunsmoke," in which James Arness, fresh from his sensitive portrayal of "the Thing," starred as the equally formidable, if somewhat more communicative, Matt Dillon, assisted by gimpy sidekick Dennis Weaver, Amanda Blake as Miss Kitty, and Milburn Stone as Doc.

Best True Confession Story: In 1791, Alexander Hamilton, first Treasury secretary of the United States and co-drafter of its Constitution, found himself in a bit of a pickle. Earlier that year, he had listened sympathetically to the plight of Maria Reynolds who had come to his office in dire need of financial help since her husband had recently deserted her. Responding as much out of ardor as out of magnanimity, Hamilton agreed to do what he could, and a few nights later appeared at her home with the needed cash. Mrs. Reynolds was grateful, to say the least—so grateful, in fact, that she melted in Hamilton's arms, whereupon the great statesman, who was married and the father of five children, had his way with her.

And continued to have his way with her whenever the duties of state and family allowed him to get away. It all went quite smoothly until Mrs. Reynolds's AWOL husband reappeared on the scene and handed Hamilton an ultimatum: Pay or be exposed as an adulterer. Hamilton, of course, had no choice but to pay off Reynolds. Having satisfied his blackmailer, he continued his liaison with Mrs. Reynolds without interruption.

A year later Reynolds was convicted of shady dealings with

Alexander Hamilton

the government and went to jail and soon after that Hamilton and Mrs. Reynolds ended their affair. But five years later, some political foes of Hamilton's falsely accused him in public of having been an intimate of Reynolds and conspiring with him to defraud the government. Hamilton's reputation was at stake and rather than be marked forever as a crook, which he was not, he told the entire story of the Maria Reynolds affair and all its sordid details in a pamphlet that had as big an audience in its day as *Forever Amber* and *Peyton Place* had in theirs. Alternately spicy and bathetic, it was the first of the great true confession stories, and it cleared Hamilton's name as a public statesman. And, happily, Mrs. Hamilton forgave him as well.

Worst Board Game: Something called Group Therapy, which came out a few years ago and is packed in a black box that's just full of mischief. The game equipment includes a stack of cards that contain such no-nonsense instructions as "Tell the person on your right a secret you've never told anyone before," and "Hold each player in a way that shows how you feel about him." If played right, the game stirs up a lot of anxieties without actually allowing the players to resolve them comfortably. A must for the masochistic.

Worst Commercial: Oxydol detergent ran an ad campaign in 1965 that included a TV commercial showing black women discussing their wash. This early attempt at representing the black buying public in advertising was marred by an announcer saying "When it's whiteness you're after . . ." and at the end, "Colored things come out nice, too."

Worst Fad: In the early 1960s, the specter of nuclear war frightened some 200,000 families throughout the United States into taking their government's advice and building concrete-reinforced fallout shelters beneath their homes. Fallout shelters, as you may recall, were drab, windowless affairs at best, stocked with drinking water, medicine supplies, food, clothing, blankets, playing cards, and anything else needed to survive a two- or three-week enforced confinement physically and psychologically intact. Many shelter-builders also kept a handgun or high-powered rifle handy against the possibility of an invasion by an unsheltered neighbor who demanded to be taken in and given protection. In fact, debating the merits of shooting your best friend between the eyes rather than letting him elbow his way into your shelter and drain off your family's oxygen supply was a favorite dinner-table/cocktail party diversion throughout the nation.

Worst Hobby: Annetta Del Mar of Chicago had a hobby that made members of Polar Bear clubs (who go swimming in the winter) seem like pikers. She used to freeze her entire body, except for her head, in ice. Turning professional for the New York World's Fair in 1939–1940, she had herself frozen as often as thirty or forty times a day. She attributed her remarkable ability to withstand cold temperatures to "willpower."

Worst Record (Spoken Word): A long-playing record of George McGovern reading from the great inaugural addresses of Washington, Lincoln, Jefferson, and Theodore Roosevelt is available from Spoken Arts, Inc.

Worst Stand-up Comedian: Henny Youngman (see also *Best Stand-up Comedian* and *Most Unusual Stand-up Comedian*).

Worst TV Broadcasting Gaffe: The Oakland Raiders were down by nine points in a crucial game against the New York Jets, broadcast live over NBC on a Sunday evening in 1968. As the Raiders made a concerted dash towards paydirt, millions of screens across the nation went blank as NBC prematurely cut short its coverage of the game and put on a regularly scheduled production of "Heidi" in its place. While the NBC switchboards were swamped with phone calls from apoplectic fans—so swamped, in fact, that the incessant ringing drained the power from the switchboard and the entire system broke down—the Raiders miraculously scored two quick touchdowns in the final seconds of play and won the game.

Worst TV Mystery Series: "Martin Kane, Private Eye," which premiered in 1949 and featured four different actors playing the lead in four successive seasons. (This must be a record of sorts—comparable to Joe DiMaggio's fifty-six-game hitting streak.) "Kane" was the first in the TV detective-mystery genre and in its shoot-em-up primitivism was probably the worst.

Worst TV Quiz Show: Maud Walker, a fifty-four-year-old Australian housewife, was a big winner on the daytime television game show "Temptation." The excitement was too much for her, and she suffered a fatal heart attack on camera. As sort of a consolation prize, a station executive offered a videotape recording of the show to the Walker family: "I'm sure they would like to see how happy she was," he explained.

To lay to rest an old rumor, Pinky Lee did not have a heart attack on his television show. Actually, it was his sinuses: His acute sinus infection brought on a convulsion.

Worst TV Show: Considering the hypnotic appeal they had to a large segment of the television-viewing public, "Strike It Rich," the Lever Brothers-sponsored tearjerker/giveaway show of the early 1950s, and the similarly based "Queen for a Day" probably represent television programming at its nadir. Both shows limited their contestants to those with sob stories to tell ("Mrs. Eustace's husband was fatally injured on the job last summer when he fell into a steaming vat of airplane mucilage, leaving her with nine children and a brain-damaged Lhasa apso to look after."). On one memorable "Strike It Rich" episode, a pregnant young woman, recently deserted by her husband, threatened to give up her child for adoption unless someone could come up with some cash for her—fast. Jack Gould, TV-radio reporter for *The New York*

Times, called it "an example of television programming gone berserk."

Worst TV Situation Comedy: Lots of contenders here, but top honors, we feel, go to "I Dream of Jeannie," which came along in 1965 and still haunts the airwaves with incessant reruns. At one point in the history of this unnecessary series, NBC was badgered with letters and phone calls from irate viewers who objected to what seemed a rather tasteless episode-by-episode shrinking of Jeannie's already abbreviated attire. As it turned out, Jeannie, played by Barbara Eden, was pregnant, and grew more pregnant with each episode while the costume remained the same.

We have other favorites in this category, and had you caught us on another day, we might just as well have chosen any one of them as absolute worst: "Ozzie and Harriet," "Gidget," "Gomer Pyle," "The Beverly Hillbillies," and perhaps the most tasteless ongoing series in broadcasting history, "Hogan's Heroes."

Worst TV Western: "Bonanza." It was just about everyone's Sunday night favorite in the early and mid-1960s, but that doesn't make it *good.* This simpleminded series about the Cartwrights was all tears and flapdoodle with frequent doses of low comedy that were more inane than genuinely funny. Richard Schickel calls it the worst western ever.

Most Unusual Circus Act: In the summer of 1859, French acrobat Charles Blondin crossed a 1,300-foot rope strung across Niagara Falls. To stave off boredom, he walked some of the way with his hands and feet tied, some of the way on stilts, and some of the way with his feet in a gunnysack. Finally, he took a small stove out on the rope and fried up an omelet.

Most Unusual Commercial: The London *Daily Mail* noted in 1971 that a Protestant clergyman, Rev. Ronald Stephens, had been signed to endorse Blue Brand margarine in a television commercial. "I believe it is my duty to spread the Gospel at every opportunity," he told reporters, some of whom assumed that "the Gospel" was the brand of margarine he would be plugging. Sample line: "Margarine has goodness in it and the body needs the fats in margarine as the soul needs God."

Most Unusual Dance: In their annual snake dances, the Moqui Indians of Arizona hold rattlesnakes in their hands and mouths as they whirl around ecstatically. The rattlers are neither drugged nor defanged, yet only rarely is a dancer bitten, and even then the results are scarcely ever serious. Perhaps the dancers gradually immunize themselves with injections of venoms, or perhaps they have a secret antitoxin; it is a mystery known only to the initiates of the cult.

The ceremony in some ways resembles the services of certain Christian fundamentalist sects who test their faith by treading on serpents or holding them between their teeth. They find the justification for this unusual worship service in Mark 16: 18, in which Jesus describes the signs distinguishing true believers: "They shall take up serpents; and if they drink any deadly thing, it shall not hurt them." A Tennessee judge ordered an end to such rites after rattlers bit several worshippers, killing one, at a revival meeting in 1973.

A more lighthearted dance is the Rhathapygizein in which young Balkan misses kick their bare feet back up against their own buttocks, turning both buttocks and feet quite pink.

Most Unusual Festival: With the regularity of the swallows returning to San Juan Capistrano—and on the same day—hundreds of buzzards flap back from their winter homes to the dead, twisted trees of Hinckley, Ohio. Now, the citizens of Hinckley are no fools. They recognize a great and salable natural wonder when it hovers ominously over their heads, and they have honored the buzzards accordingly. Policemen in Hinckley wear a shoulder patch featuring three hungry buzzards against the background of the golden sun. And every March 15, the merchants of Hinckley sponsor a buzzard festival that attracts upwards of 20,000 tourists to welcome the migrating scavengers to their summer nesting grounds.

Most Unusual Juggler: Quadriplegic Matthew Buckinger (1674–1722) of Nuremburg, Germany, overcame his handicap and became a proficient musician, entertaining on the flute, bagpipes, dulcimer, and trumpet. Married four times, he supported his wives and eleven children with the money he earned as an artist and writer. But what startled Buck-

Buzzard Day Festival, Hinckley, Ohio

inger's contemporaries most of all was his considerable skill as a juggler.

Most Unusual Parade: In Sparta, celibacy was a crime, and the state designated the appropriate age for marriage—thirty for men and twenty for women. Men who remained bachelors beyond that time lost their right to vote, and, worse still, they were forbidden to attend the processions in which the young men and women danced and revelled in the nude. Not that the unmarried did not have their chance to march through the streets without any clothes on. According to Plutarch, the holdouts were frequently ordered to parade naked for the amusement of their fellow citizens—even in the February snows—while singing a song in which they proclaimed themselves justly punished for having flouted the marriage laws. And Plutarch records that chronic misogamists ran the risk of being attacked, scratched, kicked, and beaten by bands of furious women.

Most Unusual Record (LP): Staten Island, New York, speech pathologist Jerry Cammarata says his latest brainchild, a fifty-two-minute-long LP record labeled "Auditory Memory," "makes a great gift," and indeed, it does make a great gift for the man who has everything, except, perhaps, for his hearing. Both sides of the record are completely silent.

Cammarata, who occupies an unchallenged double berth in *The Guinness Book of World Records*—for sitting in a bathtub seventy-five hours straight and for singing for ninety-six hours nonstop in the New York City subway system—says that "being forced to sit and listen to nothing gives you a chance to conjure up previously learned musical experiences," which all people have, he notes, "except for imbeciles." Moreover, it provides a welcome relief from noise pollution, the tensions of everyday life, and the relentless din of rock 'n' roll which, he suggests, "is damaging to your ears."

Most Unusual Stand-up Comedian: Henny Youngman. "Man walks into a psychiatrist's office, says, 'Doc, nobody listens to me.' Psychiatrist says, 'Next.' "

Youngman is no skinflint when it comes to dispensing punch lines, dealing out two-liners at five a minute with brief pauses to drag his bow across his violin strings. Percentage-wise, relatively few of his jokes would make it on their own, but he hits his audience with such a carpet-bombing barrage that the sheer speed of his delivery is hilarious. In 1972

87

Youngman taped 230 of his best (or worst) jokes to be dispensed with candy bars from a chain of vending machines in Dallas.

Most Unusual TV Documentary: In 1966 the British Broadcasting Company offered on their nightly news program a five-minute docu-feature on the complexities of spaghetti-growing in Italy. "Throughout Italy millions of pasta farmers are working harder than ever before to harvest their crop before it falls prey to the pests that ravaged much of the crop last season," an even-voiced announcer told his audience. His narration was the voice-over to BBC footage of farmers in broad-brimmed hats working their way up neatly trimmed aisles of spaghetti plants in the Italian farmlands, plucking sun-ripened strands of spaghetti from the branches and storing them in wicker baskets. "Special efforts have been taken this year to ward off the spaghetti weevil, which has been especially destructive in recent years," he said. Not a word was mentioned about levity or satire; no smiles were cracked, no giggles escaped, and millions of British viewers accepted, if with some surprise, the fact that spaghetti grew on trees.

Most Unusual TV Show: In 1970, thousands of viewers took seriously "The Million Mark Game," a game-show parody broadcast over West German TV. The emcee designated several "victims" who were assigned to proceed toward a specific destination and were promised a million marks if they reached it safely. In the meantime, a search party of "killers" was similarly assigned to hunt down the "victims." In a modern-day replay of Orson Welles's classic 1938 radio dramatization of "The War of the Worlds," several thousand people panicked. At the same time, several "victims" phoned in to say that for a million marks, they'd be willing to take their chances. One man, evidently fascinated by the whole thing, telephoned the TV station after the hoax was made public, and asked if he could be considered as a future victim in case the producers decided to bring the show back on a serious basis.

Journalism

Best American Daily Newspaper: *The New York Times.* The Great Gray Lady of American newspapers has come in for a lot of criticism in recent years as being too indiscriminating in its presentation of the news, too selective in weeding out material that might embarrass the Establishment, too stodgy —and even too inaccurate. All the same, it still heads just about every list of best American newspapers, including one by *Time* magazine in 1964 and another by *The Saturday Review. Esquire* magazine says, "Let's face it. *This* is the national newspaper; all the rest are regional collections of press releases. If you still care about living in America and the world, you need it *bad.*"

There is one other candidate for all-around top-drawer professionalism and it also comes out of New York—*The Wall Street Journal.* Its thrust is largely financial, true, but you're making a mistake if you think that the only people who read it are investment bankers and drab-looking men in white shirts and wing tips. Says British journalist Henry Fairlie, it's the only American paper to have mastered "the technique of the background news story."

Best Circulations: The most widely read newspaper in the United States is the New York *Daily News,* with a daily circulation of 3,108,832. *Asahi Shimbun,* a Japanese daily, is the best-circulated paper in the world, with a circulation of 9,257,000. As for magazines, *Reader's Digest* leads the list with a monthly circulation of 17,586,000.

Best Comic Strips: The Washington *Post.* That is, if you mean the newspaper with the biggest—and presumably best—selection of comic strips of any daily in the United States, according to a survey by *Time* magazine.

As for the *best single strip,* front runner is "Peanuts," by cartoonist Charles Schulz. Rarely inane, often insightful, and

II.
THE WORLD'S HARDEST CROSSWORD PUZZLE

A two-letter word for the Egyptian sun-god. Not on your seven-letter word meaning obsolete means of photographic representation. (The answer will appear in our issue of October, 1965.)

ACROSS

1 Symbol (s) representing an initial central vowel sound
6 Hero of "Lalla Rookh" tale
11 Pretty: Colloq.
16 Shrill trilled sounds
17 Part of a name in Robin Hood tales
18 Character in "A Masked Ball"
20 Fawn-colored
21 One type of alcohol
22 With: Dial.
24 Its symbol is X
25 Where the Byelikha is
27 Gem of changeable color
29 Testimonial: Abbr.
31 Drumlin
33 Hero of Thackeray burlesque
35 Star in the news, June, 1958
36 Author of "Louisiana Hayride"
37 Common noun suffix
39 Es — de (as regards): Fr.
40 Cloth of undyed wool
42 Type of church proclamation
43 Heads of vegetables, as cabbages, in Britain
45 Basically
48 Ornamental plasterwork
49 Joins together, as if by dovetails
51 Item used in drafting
52 Wind of flower or moss
53 Till
55 Wave Trim is
56 Indian girl's short-sleeved bodice with very low neckline
57 Squirrel's nest
60 Cape of Smith Island, off N.C.
62 Riffian's neighbor
63 Yesterday: Lat.
64 Musical direction
67 A number: Abbr.
68 Coffee plantation in Brazil
70 Prismatic crystal
72 Paper screen serving as wall or sliding door
74 Ahead of the game
76 A hater of tobacco smoke
78 Profits for distribution; Slang
79 Part of the Empire State
80 Sea eagle
81 Famous citizen of Toledo
83 Whidah
84 Passai's waterfront
5 — right, legal term
85 Twenty, in combinations
87 Wildcat akin to the jaguarundi
89 Powder used as a photographic developer

90 Roger's relatives
91 Make a gesture of respect
92 Cimo's neighbor
93 Europeans
95 Name in the news, 1922
99 Via haywire, in way
103 Vin, perennials do
105 Love song, old style
106 Aqueous solutions of gum
108 Chorus, in a way
109 Native of region S of the Hindu Kush
110 Certain prices in Wall Street
111 Oversupply
113 Skate, French style
114 Early version of the adding machine
115 Opera from voice
116 Gallic tongue
118 Verthndh, for example
120 — heredes
121 Uralic people living in Siberia
124 Combining form in many medical terms
126 One of the ologies
127 Formidable feature of the Bernese Oberland
130 Radio and signaling expression
131 Vertical grooves on the median lines of upper lips
133 Of improvidently generous size
134 Getting on
135 Nymph in Greek myth
136 Small Persian rug
137 One of a trio in baseball broadcasting
138 Greats and others

DOWN

1 Wild sheep of Asia
2 Top, in Italy
3 Viking who ruled over what is now Normandy
4 First —
5 Vest, for one
66 Results of serendipity
69 Variety of apple
71 Pour — (for fun): Fr.
73 Dweller on the shore of Mindanao
75 Large villages
77 Variety of green quartz
82 Buoyancy
86 Exclamation of impatience
88 Showy tanagers of South America
8 Tall and thin
91 Language of the Vogul
9 Common French phrase
94 Slangy term from 1959
10 Blend by imperceptible degrees
95 Birds of the genus Nestor
12 Amount by which a container of liquor falls short of being full
96 Greet, in archaic refrain
13 Dissimulation
97 Burden of a "wobblies" song
14 Slight modifying quality
98 Have — in
15 Abbreviation in medical parlance
99 Severe or harsh: Dial.
16 A thousand years
99 Not downas
19 Mount Cook, in New Zealand
100 Famous name in turf lore
20 Doric garment
102 Relative of Vendettine
23 African fox with outsize ears
104 Gaiety great
24 Moderate reddish-orange color
107 Phenomenon possibly connected with increased rainfall
26 Sentence in controversy
110 Part of O'Henry's last words
28 In the bag
112 Start of many an
30 Shakespearean role
Alma Mater song
32 Part of a proverb dining back to 1150
115 God represented as half man and half fish
34 Entries on a free chart: Abbr.
116 Wine town of S. Italy
36 Bombay site of ancient rock-cut temple
117 Sponge, in zoology
38 One of Hawaii's symbols
118 Relatives of 116 Across
40 Rossetti's — Beatrix
121 Be the author of
41 Part of a coronation ceremony
122 Berlin's "always"
42 Idolatry
123 Mightly, in combinations
44 Musical term
125 Mongol of Chinese Turkestan
46 Third group of a certain series
128 Endings for town, train, etc.
47 Very high up
130 One type of chemistry: Abbr.
50 Bearing: Comb. form
132 Places to live: Abbr.
52 One of the Yampa River
54 Describing many a notion in schools
56 Works with a bricklayer's tool
57 Loincloth worn by Hindus

58 Term in typesetting
59 Famous first name in music
61 Hebrew letter
64 First —
65 Vest, for one

(Answers appear on page 301.)

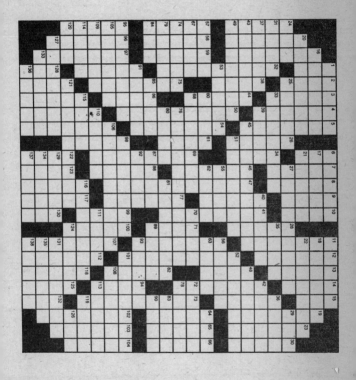

almost always funny, "Peanuts" outstrips (if you'll pardon the pun) any of the other *funny* funnies, with the possible exception of Walt Kelly's "Pogo," and is heartwarming to boot, without ever being gushy. Martin Jezer notes that "Peanuts" "probably holds the distinction of being clipped out of more newspapers and posted on more bulletin boards, lockers and walls than any other of its newsprint relatives on the comics page."

The *best single line ever uttered by a comic strip character* was uttered by Pogo: "We have met the enemy and he is us."

Best Crossword Puzzles: Again, *The New York Times*. The best crossword puzzles are in New York—and, more specifically, some feel, in *New York* magazine. But the puzzle that graces the last page of that weekly is merely an import from the *Times* of London. So it really doesn't count.

With that dismissal we turn to *The New York Times*, which, for day-to-day consistency of quality, offers the best puzzles anywhere. Will Weng took over from Margaret Farrar as puzzle editor of the *Times* in 1968, and the puzzles have since grown a bit—but *just* a bit—easier. Nobody knows how many daily readers of the paper turn to the puzzle first, even before glancing at the first page or the obits, but chances are it's a sizable percentage of the total readership. "Some people say the puzzle is a waste of time," says Weng, a one-time reporter and copy desk editor of the *Times*. "Well, it's like the movies, concerts—they're all wasting time. Which one you choose depends on how much pleasure you get out of it." The puzzles are constructed by free-lancers, but it's editor Weng who's at the receiving end of both the praise and the invective that the puzzles often prompt. One of his favorite letters was from a faithful solver who was outraged by what he considered a below-the-belt use of numerals in one Sunday puzzle. "If I ever meet you in a restaurant and you are under four feet tall, I will be very abusive," he wrote.

The best single puzzle ever to appear anywhere—if difficulty is a measure of quality—was published in the February 1965 issue of *Esquire* magazine and touted as "the world's hardest crossword puzzle."

Best Humor Columnist: Russell Baker. Art Buchwald, whose thrice-weekly column is distributed by the Los Angeles *Times* syndicate to 363 United States newspapers, is the favorite of millions, but he's completely outclassed by Russell Baker of *The New York Times*. Baker is a better writer than Buchwald, more inventive, more profound, more literate, and—most important—much funnier. Buchwald's columns, particularly in recent months, have a formularized look about them, as if they'd been stamped from a cookie cutter. Funny, yes—but they've rarely diverged from the rather outworn topic of presidential politics. Baker's subject matter is much more varied than Buchwald's and he is stylistically more versatile.

Best Magazine: *Encounter,* of which *Esquire* magazine has said, "probably not as good now as when it was backed by the CIA, but still the best general monthly magazine going." *Esquire* itself is responsible for what is certainly the biggest—542 pages—and probably the best single issue of any magazine ever published anywhere in the world: its October 1973 issue, marking the fortieth anniversary of the magazine. Most of the material in that issue had previously been published in *Esquire,* but with writers like Hemingway, Fitzgerald, Faulkner, and Baldwin filling its pages—who cares?

Best News Photography: The New York *Daily News* has been billed for umpteen years as "New York's picture newspaper," and its photography, especially in the centerfold, is probably as good as any daily photojournalism to be found anywhere in the United States, although that is a distinction of dubious worth. Better quality is found across the Atlantic. Says *Esquire* magazine, the Sunday supplement of the *Times* of London offers "the best example of photography used in support of an idea. The fusion of pictures and text is often aimed at by other magazines, but rarely accomplished."

Best Sunday Edition of a Newspaper: *The New York Times.* It used to be said of the mammoth old *Saturday Evening Post* that reading it in bed was a hazard; should you fall asleep, it would fall on you and crush you to death. Today the same *caveat* might apply to the Sunday *Times* which, at sixty cents, is still the biggest journalistic bargain in the United States. The average issue has 350 pages and weighs nearly three pounds. In addition to the same splendid news coverage as in the daily edition of the *Times,* there is also the *Times* magazine, which is still the best Sunday supplement in America despite a reputation in some circles for superficiality and blandness; the Sunday "Book Review," on a par with the *Times Literary Supplement* (of London) and alone worth the price of the paper; and the "News of the

Week in Review," which scoops *Time* and *Newsweek* by two days and has better news coverage and in-depth analysis of current issues than either of the two major news magazines.

Worst American Newspaper: The Manchester *Union Leader*. The *Union Leader*'s fair-to-middling circulation of 64,000 is a deceptively modest indication of the paper's real sway—not only in northern New England but throughout conservative America. Its closest companion, the Nashua *Telegraph*, boasts but a third of the *Union-Leader*'s circulation, and the *Union Leader* is the only daily newspaper distributed throughout the state of New Hampshire.

The editorial alter ego of right-wing blatherer William Loeb, the paper's news columns and editorials betray a narrow isolationism tinged with bigotry and ignorance that places the paper among the ten worst newspapers in the United States according to the journalistic review [*More*]. Loeb once ran a lead editorial in his paper scoring the formation of a gay students' organization at the University of New Hampshire. The headline: BOOT THE PANSIES OUT OF UNH. On another occasion, he printed a scathing indictment of Henry Kissinger under the heading: KISSINGER THE KIKE?

Another favorite of [*More*] is the New Orleans *Times-Picayune*, which, after 138 years of daily mediocrity, still boasts a circulation of well over 200,000. "This bloated, sluggish, myopic giant of the Delta morn," says [*More*], is still peppered with some eminently forgettable features: "A five-column Sears ad on the op-ed page and Jane Fonda vilified on the editorial page. . . . Ads that look like news stories. . . . News stories that read like ads. Pitiful Washington coverage. No investigative reporting at all."

Worst Magazine in the United States: The evils of *People*, Time-Life's drippy new nonmagazine, and the mindless outrages of *Cosmopolitan* are as nothing compared to *Kampfruf*, the official publication of the National Socialist League. Based in Los Angeles, the NSL is the official organization of Nazi homosexuals not only in twenty-five states throughout the nation but in several foreign countries as well. *Kampfruf* (which means battle-cry) is a monthly and its pages are adorned with lots of swastikas, pictures of naked men, and editorials which play up Hitler's admiration of noted gays like Frederick the Great and Richard Wagner. While its small

94

core of subscribers are generally euphoric ("How long we have waited, we Aryan homophiles, for someone with strength and daring to wrench the wheel from those who have steered Gay Liberation hard to the left," writes one reader), others are less enthusiastic, including the National Socialist White People's Party, in Arlington, Virginia. "On the question of homosexuality," they recently editorialized in the *Nazi Bulletin,* "the position of National Socialism is crystal-clear and unequivocal: Queerism is unnatural and a sick perversion of the life instinct."

Worst News Photo of the '70s: A serious diplomatic rift between the governments of Japan and South Korea in September 1974, prompted thirty-two Korean demonstrators to hack off their index fingers publicly and then present them at the Japanese embassy in Seoul, South Korea, wrapped in newspaper, like the remains of a fish-and-chips dinner. The fingers were photographed for publication in the Korean *Times.* Later reporters discovered that the South Korean government had paid handsomely for this "spontaneous" act of patriotism; demonstrators received anywhere from $125 to $375 for each finger they sacrificed.

Worst Public Opinion Poll: The *Literary Digest* Presidential Straw Poll of 1936. The *Literary Digest* had polled nearly 2.5 million voters and by the morning of November 1, just four days before Franklin Roosevelt's bid for reelection, the news magazine made its prediction: 370 electoral votes and a resounding victory over FDR for Kansas Republican Alfred M. Landon. But by election night, Roosevelt had been swept into a second term by the most overwhelming landslide in American history, winning 523 electoral votes to Landon's eight. Red-faced and miffed, the *Digest*'s editors vowed to do better next time. They never got the chance; the magazine went bankrupt and disappeared within a year.

Most Unusual Edition of a Newspaper: Editor-in-chief Mickey Carlton of the Richman (British Columbia) *Review* published a special edition of his paper in 1970 "designed to please everyone and offend nobody." Excised from the *Review*'s pages for one day was anything that could be even remotely construed as beyond the bounds of good news or good taste: reports of court proceedings, crime stories, pictures of indecently clad women, and angry editorials. The lead story on page one concerned a local farmer's purchase of a $4,000 heifer, which was photographed with objectionable parts of its anatomy airbrushed out. The paper sold miserably and provoked much criticism. Carlton apologized for the lack of "lively news" in the "special pink tea issue, dedicated to the minority who prefer to view the news through rose-colored glasses."

Most Unusual Press Conference: During his years in the White House, John Quincy Adams liked to rise before dawn, grab a towel, and slip out unseen through the back door for a quick dip in the Potomac before taking on breakfast and his presidential duties. One day, having cavorted in the water for an hour or so, he stepped up onto the bank to dry himself and, stark naked and dripping wet, found himself face-to-face with Anne Newport Royall, a noted investigative reporter of the day, sitting on his underwear. Adams quickly stepped back into the water to cover his privates and then demanded that Miss Royall leave, but she insisted on first asking him some rather pointed questions about his pet project, the Bank of America, which she heartily opposed. For all his anger, Adams had no choice but to grant the unexpected interview. In later years, the crusading Miss Royall was tried and convicted in the court of the District of Columbia for being a "common scold."

Sports

Best (Baseball) Batter: The best batter and probably the greatest all-around player in the history of the game was Tyrus Raymond "Ty" Cobb who played with the Detroit Tigers and the Philadelphia Athletics. Some of his records include:

Highest lifetime batting average .... .367
Most lifetime hits 4,191
Most seasons leading the major leagues in batting 11
Most consecutive seasons batting over .300 23

But Josh Gibson of the old Negro leagues may have been the best ever. From 1930 to 1946 he hit some 800 home runs, clouting as many as 89 one season and 75 in another. In one 1934 contest he hit the only home run ever to clear the roof of Yankee Stadium.

Rogers Hornsby of the St. Louis Cardinals batted .424 in 1924, the best season's batting average recorded in modern baseball.

James F. "Tip" O'Neill, of the old American Association's St. Louis club, hit .492 in 1887, when bases on balls were counted as hits.

The longest hitting streak ever achieved was by Yankee outfielder Joe DiMaggio in 1941. DiMaggio hit safely in fifty-six consecutive games that year between May 15 and July 16, finally going hitless in a night game against Cleveland on July 17. During that period he hit 15 home runs, drove in 55 runs, and batted .408.

The home run records of Babe Ruth, Roger Maris, and Hank Aaron are common knowledge: Ruth hit 60 in a 154-game season in 1927; Maris hit 61 in a 162-game season in 1961; and Aaron's 733 home runs to date are the most ever hit in a lifetime.

Among the more arcane home run records: Stan Musial

of the St. Louis Cardinals hit five home runs in a double-header in 1954; Dale Long of the Pittsburgh Pirates homered in eight consecutive games in 1956; Wes Ferrell of the Cleveland Indians hit nine home runs in 1931, the most ever hit by a pitcher in a single season. He also won 22 games that year.

Best (Baseball) Fielding Play: Willy Mays's catch off Vic Wertz in the opening game of the 1954 World Series. In the eighth inning of that game Cleveland Indian first baseman Vic Wertz walloped a towering drive to center field. Mays ran as fast as he could—which was *fast*—and caught up with the ball 450 feet from home plate, catching it one-handed, with his back to the diamond. Said Mays after the game, "I knew I had it all the way."

Al Gionfriddo, an obscure utility outfielder for the Brooklyn Dodgers, robbed Joe DiMaggio of a home run in the 1947 World Series with a running catch that many feel was greater than Mays's play in 1954. Arthur Daley of *The New York Times* called it "one of the most unbelievable catches ever seen anywhere."

Best (Baseball) Manager: John J. McGraw. In a 1939 poll, John McGraw was voted by sportswriters as the greatest manager ever. Hot-tempered and aggressive, McGraw was most famous as manager of the New York Giants from 1902 until poor health forced his retirement in 1932, just two years before he died. "McGraw was a scrapper who fought with umps and tongue-lashed players," according to sportswriter Ralph Hickok, but he was scrupulously honest, a brilliant tactician, and universally respected by his own players and by opponents. Under McGraw's tutelage, the Giants won ten pennants and four World Series.

The won-lost record of Connie Mack hardly compares with that of McGraw, but sheer managerial longevity may very well qualify him as McGraw's equal. From 1901–1950 he managed the Philadelphia Athletics, piloting them to nine pennants and five world championships. As brilliant a field strategist as McGraw, and as ruthlessly honest, he was otherwise McGraw's opposite. Quiet and circumspect, he dressed in street clothes when he managed and rarely if ever left the dugout to argue with an umpire. A man of boundless grace and patience, he was seldom called anything other than "Mr. Mack" by his own or opposing players.

Best (Baseball) Pitcher: The choice is traditionally between Walter Johnson, Christy Mathewson, and Cy Young, with the edge going to Johnson who pitched for the Washington Senators from 1907–1927, winning 416 games and turning in a 2.17 earned run average with perhaps the best fastball in the history of the game. But Satchel Paige, who played most of his career in the Negro leagues, joining Bill Veeck's Cleveland Indians in 1948 as a forty-two-year-old rookie, may well have outclassed them all. According to Dizzy Dean, who watched him pitch, and major league stars like Joe DiMaggio and Charlie Gehringer, who played against him, Paige was the best ever.

Best (Baseball) Player (Current): This is a category that inevitably evokes arguments. Our choice is Reggie Jackson of the Oakland A's, whom Ted Williams has called "the most natural hitter I've ever seen." In 1973 Jackson led the American League in home runs (32), runs batted in (117), runs scored (99), game-winning hits (18), and slugging percentage (.531). His .293 batting average was tenth best in the league. Jackson is fast—he does the 100-yard dash in 9.6 seconds—plays right field better than anyone in the major leagues since Carl Furillo, and is unquestionably the major force on the best team in professional baseball today.

Best (Baseball) Runner: James Thomas "Cool Papa" Bell. When he was voted into Baseball's Hall of Fame in 1947, baseball commissioner Bowie Kuhn called "Cool Papa" Bell "the fastest man ever to play baseball." Bell played twenty-nine years in the Negro leagues, the California Winter League, the Mexican League, the Cuban League, and in the Dominican Republic, but never in the major leagues. During a 200-game season in 1933 he stole 175 bases and in another year his remarkable speed was the major factor in a .480 batting average. Judy Johnson, a long-time friend and rival who played against Bell, says that an infielder could not afford to play at his normal depth when Bell was at bat. "If you played in your regular position," he says, "you'd never throw him out."

Best (Baseball) Season (Individual Athlete): Babe Ruth was baseball's greatest player and the best year he or anyone else in baseball history ever had was 1920 (and not, as you may have thought, 1927). That was the Babe's first year with the

New York Yankees, as Ruth's biographer Robert W. Creamer has pointed out, and the statistics tell the story: 54 home runs, 137 runs batted in, 137 runs scored, 9 triples, 36 doubles, 14 stolen bases, and a .376 batting average. His astronomical .847 slugging average that year surely ranks among the great achievements of Western man.

Best (Baseball) Team: The 1927 Yankees. "The 1927 Yankee team has been called the greatest of all time more often than any other club in the annals of baseball," notes Joe Reichler, baseball editor of the *Associated Press.* Babe Ruth hit 60 home runs that year, batting a lusty .356 and driving in 164 runs. First baseman Lou Gehrig was no less impressive with 47 homers, 175 runs batted in, and a batting average of .373. Left fielder Earl Combs batted .356, center fielder Bob Meusel batted .337—with 102 r.b.i.'s—and second baseman Tony Lazzerri batted .309, hitting 18 home runs and driving in 102 runs. Yankee pitching that season was equally superb: Herb Pennock posted a 19–6 record, Waite Hoyt was 20–7, Urban Shocker 18–6, and Wilcy Moore, one of the most reliable relief pitchers of all time, 19–7. The Yankees finished 19 games ahead of the second-place Philadelphia Athletics in 1927, and won 110 games—-an American League record that stood until the Cleveland Indians broke it with 111 victories in 1954. (The Indians were subsequently defeated in the World Series by the New York Giants, four games to none.) The Yankees went on to take the Pittsburgh Pirates in four straight games in the World Series. Those who were present say that Pirate morale was demolished during batting practice before the opening game; Pittsburgh players stared goggle-eyed as the Yankees' "Murderers' Row" rifled baseball after baseball into the grandstands.

Best (Baseball) Umpire: Bill Klem. Known as "the Old Arbiter," Klem was a National League umpire from 1905–1942. Early in his career he locked horns with John McGraw over a close call and incurred the Giant manager's unending wrath; or so it seemed. Within a remarkably short time McGraw became convinced of Klem's utter honesty—and skill—as did everyone else in the National League, and often insisted that Klem be behind the plate during crucial games for the Giants.

Best Basketball Team (College): The University of Kentucky Wildcats of 1948–49. This is the team, according to sports-

1948–49 basketball team at the University of Kentucky

writer Luke Walton, that is "generally acknowledged as the greatest college basketball team of all time," a tough five-man combination that worked like a well-oiled machine. After they graduated, the five—Alex Groza, Wallace "Wah-Wah" Jones, Ralph Beard, Joe Holland, and Clifford Barker (who could balance a basketball on one finger)—turned down most of the bids they'd received from the professional teams and bought their own franchise in Indianapolis instead, playing in 1949 as the Indianapolis Olympians—a team they represented not only on the court but in the front office as well, as owners and members of the board.

Best Dive: At Fort Lauderdale, Florida, twenty-six-year-old Mike King dove from a hovering helicopter into the water, 150 feet below. He did it, he said, to break the old high-diving record of 135 feet and it cost him two broken vertebrae.

Best Exercise: True believers in isometrics maintain that the best exercise is to push down on your office desk with all your strength, in an attempt to drive it through the floor. Others insist that bench-pressing 400-pound barbells is the way to get in shape. Still others have asserted that making love combines pleasure with excellent conditioning. Poppycock, says Dr. Kenneth H. Cooper, the physical fitness advisor to the Air Force and author of *Aerobics,* probably the most sensible book available on keeping fit. "I'll state my

Jim Thorpe

position early," he writes in *Aerobics*, "the best exercises are running, swimming, cycling, walking, stationary running, handball, basketball, and squash, and in just about that order." After carefully measuring a wide variety of exercises according to the energy each costs the body to perform, Dr. Cooper concludes that isometrics, calisthenics, and weight lifting are inferior to sustained activity. And while golf, tennis, and volleyball are better than nothing, you are fooling yourself if you think they are keeping you hale and hearty. Only exercises that make continuous demands on the lungs, heart, and blood system—that require a lot of oxygen over a long period of time—are sufficient to produce a significant training effect.

Best Football Player (College): Doak Walker. Walker played for SMU in the late 1940s and, according to sportswriter Dan Jenkins, "did more things well in football, including win—and win with a mediocre team—than just about anyone who ever played. He passed, ran, punted, caught, placekicked, blocked and defended." O. J. Simpson, while not as versatile as Walker, was perhaps the game's *best runner*. During the late 1960s, as a running back for USC, he gained over 3,500 yards and scored 36 touchdowns in 22 games.

Best Football Player (Professional): Jim Thorpe. He once punted a football 70 yards and the chief distinction of that punt was that it was his shortest kick of the day. Sports-

102

writer Walter Manning writes of Thorpe, "Anyone who ever saw him play agrees: Jim Thorpe was the best, the absolute best ever to pull on a pair of cleated shoes." A halfback who began playing professional football in 1915, Thorpe later joined the fledgling National Football League, playing with such now-defunct clubs as the Oorang Indians, the Toledo Maroons, the Rock Island Independents, and the Canton Bulldogs, finishing up in 1925 with the New York Giants. But it would be unfair merely to bill Thorpe as the best football player in the history of the game; he was also the greatest and most versatile athlete in modern times—a track and field star in the 1916 Olympics, a major league first baseman, and a star at basketball, lacrosse, wrestling, and soccer.

Best Football Punt: In an American Football League game in 1969, New York Jets' kicker Steve O'Neal punted practically the length of the field—98 yards—for the longest kick in the history of professional football. Said one sportswriter who was present, "It went further—literally—than a lot of home runs I've seen."

Best Football Team: The 1941 Chicago Bears. On December 6, 1940, as the National Football League season was drawing to a close, the Chicago Bears whipped the Washington Redskins 73–0 in a game that was not merely an embarrassment to the Redskins but a taste of things to come for the Bears. With top-seeded stars such as Clyde Turner, George McAfee, and quarterback Sid Luckman (whom coach George Halas claimed never called a wrong play), the 1941 Bears have been called the greatest team ever by *Sports Illustrated*. They capped a magnificent 10–1 season by demolishing the New York Giants 37–9 in the NFL playoff game.

Best Golfer: Bobby Jones. Jones was a star of the 1920s and his best year, ironically, was also his last as an active golfer—1930. That was the year he achieved the Grand Slam, or the Impregnable Quadrilateral as the pedants know it. Copping the Impregnable Quad meant winning both the American and British Open and Amateur championships, a feat that may well never be duplicated. Jones was something of a golfing Mozart, playing his first U.S. Amateur Open at the age of fourteen. He died in 1972 at the age of seventy.

Best Physical Fitness Freak: Alan Jones had polio when he was five years old, and when he was seventeen he was laid

103

up with a back injury so serious that doctors told him, "You'll never be able to do any heavy lifting and you'll probably be confined to a desk job the rest of your life." Were they ever *wrong!*

On August 17, 1974, Jones, a Marine Corps captain from Portland, Oregon, did 27,003 sit-ups in thirty hours to set a new world's record. Apart from a badly chafed bottom—which he tried to control during his sit-ups by dousing himself liberally with talcum powder—Jones suffered no ill effects from his record-breaking feat. In fact, the following morning he rose early and went on a camping trip with his wife and daughter.

Jones's reason for going after the world's sit-up record, or so he told his friends, was to make it into *The Guinness Book of World Records*. In fact, come July 4, 1976, he plans to go after another *Guinness* superlative by swimming the Mississippi River—lengthwise—in record time.

"The long-distance swimming record is 1,826 miles in 176 days," says the stockily built twenty-seven-year-old. "I know I can go farther and faster. I'll swim approximately from Minneapolis to New Orleans." Jones has also swum 100 miles down the turbulent Columbia River—in a wet suit—in thirty-five hours, and led a four-man relay team in running 310 miles nonstop across the entire state of Oregon.

"I was never all that good at traditional sports," he says of his collegiate days at the University of South Dakota, where he graduated in 1969, "so I decided to concentrate on endurance events. I want to see how far I can push myself, maybe go where no one has ever gone before."

Best Proof That Winning Is Not Everything, It's the Only Thing: The Aztecs of ancient Peru played a primitive form of basketball, the object of which was to shoot a solid rubber ball through a stone ring placed high on a wall. The winner was traditionally awarded the clothes of all spectators present. The loser was put to death.

Best Tennis Player (Current): Tops on the pro circuit today is twenty-two-year-old Jimmy Connors, who beat Ken Rose-wall in the men's singles at Forest Hills in 1974 and whom *Sports Illustrated,* among other respected voices in the sports world, calls the best player in the business today. Connors's forte is the two-handed ground shot—and running strength that is unique. Says veteran Jack Kramer, "The kid is unconventional in that he doesn't overpower anybody with serve or volley, or even quickness. His countershots, returns and passes are what beat people."

Best Tennis Player Ever: Bill Tilden. The greatest courtsman of them all, Big Bill Tilden of Philadelphia made his mark, predictably, during America's Golden Age of Sports—the 1920s—turning professional in 1930 and playing well into the '40s. (He died in 1953.) Equipped with a powerful backhand and forehand and probably the best service the game has ever seen; Tilden was an early master of what came to be known in later years as "the big game"—the smashing serve followed by an aggressive rush to the net for some jaw-smashing volleying. Sportswriter Allison Danzig calls Tilden the best ever, and so did an international poll of tennis journalists in 1969.

Best Unicyclist: Steve McPeak has the distinction of mastering the world's tallest unicycle—a one-wheeled vehicle thirty-two feet tall. On a modest little thirteen-foot unicycle, McPeak rode from Chicago to Los Angeles in six weeks in 1968.

Worst (Baseball) Batter: New York Yankee pitching star Lefty Gomez is unofficially regarded by many sportswriters and baseball buffs as the weakest hitter in modern times. But these other, less storied names are also immortalized in the record books:

Monty Cross, a shortstop with the Philadelphia Athletics, who batted .182 in 1904, the lowest season's batting average ever recorded in the major leagues; George McBride, Washington Senator shortstop, who hit an anemic .218 in 1,652 games between 1901–1920—the lowest lifetime batting average of any modern player. McBride also compiled the lowest lifetime slugging percentage—.264; Ed Brinkman, Washington Senator infielder, who made 82 hits in 444 times at bat in 1965; Bob Buhl, Milwaukee Brave pitcher, who went 0-for-70 in 1962; Charlie Pick of the Boston Braves, who went hitless in 11 times at bat in a 26-inning game against the Brooklyn Dodgers—the longest game ever played—in 1920; and pitching star Sandy Koufax, who struck out 12 consecutive times during his rookie season with the Brooklyn Dodgers in 1955.

Worst (Baseball) Fielder: Outfielder Babe Herman, of the old Brooklyn Robins, is said to have been struck on the head more than once by fly balls he'd intended to catch. There is also hard-hitting New York Giant third baseman Charlie Hickman, who muffed almost two out of every ten chances in 1900 for an .836 fielding percentage—the worst ever.

Many players have pulled five errors in a nine-inning game, but second baseman Andy Leonard of the Boston Braves made *nine* errors in a game in 1876, the National League's first year. And while four errors in one inning is a record held by many players, a feat by third baseman Mike Grady of the New York Giants is still unsurpassed; in an 1895 game he made four errors *on a single ball.* It happened this way: Grady bobbled an easy grounder long enough for the batter to reach first base safely: error number one. He then fired the ball across the infield high above the first baseman's outstretched arm for error number two. The runner scampered to second base and turned toward third; the first baseman's throw reached Grady in ample time to nail the runner, but he dropped it for error number three. And finally, as the runner headed for home, Grady threw the ball to the catcher and watched it sail into the grandstand: error number four.

Worst (Baseball) Team: The 1962 New York Mets. Question: What has eighteen legs and lives in the cellar? Answer: the New York Mets. Or so went a popular joke of the day. Paragons of ineptitude, the Mets in their first year of existence dropped their first nine games, slipped unobtrusively into last place, and remained there for the rest of the season, mathematically eliminating themselves from the pennant race by the beginning of August. Despite help from one-time Brooklyn Dodger stalwarts Duke Snider and Gil Hodges and from home run king Frank Thomas, the Mets ended the season with a laughable 40–120 record, 60½ games behind the pennant-winning San Francisco Giants. Mound star Roger Craig led the pitching staff with a 4.51 earned run average, winning ten games and losing twenty-four; Al Jackson also starred, with a 4.40 e.r.a. and an 8–20 record. Legend has it that after an especially devastating series of losses, the Mets were rained out and celebrated with a victory party.

The 1899 Cleveland National League ball club was, in its own fashion, even worse. After winning the first game, they lost the next seven. Team members began to desert, and by midseason the manager had resigned in disgust and was succeeded by Joe Quinn, an Australian undertaker. Under his aegis the team continued to flounder, losing 40 of the last 41 games and ending the season 20–134, 80 games out of first place. A hotel cigar clerk talked Quinn into letting him pitch the last game of the season in exchange for a box of his best Corona-Coronas. Why not? Quinn figured. The cigar clerk was beaten, naturally, and by the following season Cleveland had dropped out of the league.

Worst Exercise: An eye infection suffered as a youth permanently damaged Aldous Huxley's vision. Later, he became a follower of Dr. William Bates, a prominent physician who advocated a series of unusual exercises for improving eyesight. One that Huxley found especially valuable was "nose writing." If the myopic reader cares to practice a little nose writing, he should imagine that his nose, like Pinocchio's, is eight inches long. Focusing your eyes on the end of your extended nose, pretend it is a pen and move your head about as if to sign your name. "A little nose writing," Huxley says in *The Art of Seeing,* "will result in a perceptible temporary improvement of defective vision." A word of caution, though: We tried about five minutes of nose writing, scrawling such sentences as "Aldous Huxley had a prominent proboscis" in the air, without results.

Worst Football Defeat: The referees were kind to the Cumberland College eleven when that team locked horns with Georgia Tech in 1905. They stopped the game midway through the third quarter, with Tech leading 220–0. The Tech quarterback Leo Schlick, alone, had scored 100 points.

Cumberland's gridiron contingent that year may well have been the *worst football team ever fielded.* Actually, there hadn't been a team at the school to speak of until Tech invited Cumberland to play on Tech's home turf. The Cumberland coach scouted up enough players to make a team, and they included Gentry Dugat, who had played two games in his entire life (one in high school, the other in prep school) and had to have the meaning of "down" explained to him. On the way to play Tech, several of the players detrained at a stopover in Nashville, got lost, and missed the game.

Years later, fullback A. L. Macdonald recalled that he "had made our longest gain of the day when I lost five yards around right end." One team member is said to have fumbled

107

the ball behind scrimmage with the massed strength of the Georgia Tech line racing toward him. "Hey, pick it up," he yelled to a teammate nearby.

"You pick it up," said the teammate. "You dropped it."

Worst Football Strategic Blunder: Roy Riegels, a defensive lineman for the University of California, picked up a Georgia Tech fumble in the second quarter of the 1929 Rose Bowl and galloped 65 yards in the wrong direction. He was finally tackled on USC's own two-yard line by· teammate Bennie Lom. Appropriately, Riegels's error proved to be the margin of defeat for USC: On the next play Georgia Tech scored a two-point safety by tackling USC's punter in the end zone and went on to win by a score of 7–6.

Minnesota Viking lineman Jim Marshall repeated Riegels's miscue thirty-five years later in a game against the San Francisco 49ers at San Francisco. In the first quarter Marshall picked up a 49er fumble, spun around a few times à la Riegels, and then headed off toward his own goal line, crossing it unhampered and throwing the ball gleefully into the air. It was Bruce Bosley of San Francisco who broke the news to Marshall and none too gently, by throwing his arms around him and thanking him for the two-point safety he'd just scored for the 49ers. All the same, the Vikings went on to beat the 49ers 27–22 and Marshall came into demand after the season as an after-dinner speaker.

Worst Football Tackle: Rice University halfback Dicky Moegle was in the clear and racing toward a 95-yard touchdown run in the 1954 Cotton Bowl at Dallas. Suddenly, Alabama fullback Tommy Lewis jumped off the bench as Moegle was running past him and stopped the ball carrier with a flying tackle. Instantly horrified at his own misdeed, he crawled back to the bench cursing himself for his impulsiveness while 75,000 fans went slack-jawed with disbelief.

The referee himself picked up the ball and carried it the rest of the way to the Alabama goal line, giving Rice the touchdown that Moegle surely would have scored, and Rice went on to win 28–6. Years later, as a high school coach, Lewis watched in disbelief as one of his own players made the same mistake with his team ahead 12–7 and a minute left to play. They lost 13–12.

Worst Football Team (Current, College): The California Institute of Technology played its first football game in 1893,

108

taking a 60–4 drubbing from USC, and since then they've coasted downhill all the way, compiling a record of 105 wins and over 300 losses. Most of those wins came in Cal Tech's early years; they haven't had a winning season since 1957, and today they field what many consider the nation's worst college team, a gridiron contingent so relentlessly inept that these days they dare to play only against junior varsity teams and junior colleges.

Not that it should be any different. Cal Tech is a science and engineering school, perhaps the best in the nation; it's never been known for its athletic program. ("Cal Tech is about as well known for its football team as *The Wall Street Journal* is for its sports section," says Harold Brown, the school's president.) Barely 20 percent of the team members, who average about 160 pounds in weight, come to Cal Tech with any varsity high school experience; many must learn the game from scratch. "I only have two rules," says their coach, Tom Gutman. "Don't miss practice and wear your helmet at all times." However anemic their performances, the Cal Tech eleven "play closer to their potential than most kids," Gutman argues. After a 74–28 loss to Pomona College, Gutman had nothing but praise for his charges. "At halftime we led 28–27," he said. "But since our guys had to play both offense and defense, as usual we were physically worn down in the second half."

Most Unusual Archer: Mohamet II was an avid archer who insisted on practicing his art upon moving targets. Citizens straying too near the palace were frequently found studded wtih arrows, and it did not take pedestrians too long to learn to stay well out of the range of their mad sultan. Understandably, Mohamet was disappointed when he discovered that his people were avoiding him. Left with no alternative, he ordered the palace guard to round up a regular supply of Istanbullians for hazardous assignment as royal prey.

At last, the terrified Turks appealed to Sheik Ul-Islam, an influential man of the cloth, who was one of the few who still dared to approach the world's most imprudent archer. After patient and tactful negotiations, the sheik persuaded Mohamet to limit his practice to eight targets a day—restricting himself to prisoners of war.

Most Unusual Baseball Card: According to *Esquire* magazine, the people who make the dusty pink squares of bubble gum

109

never issued a baseball card of the immortal Solly Hemus. The object was to keep kids buying and buying, trying to get the picture of Solly that would complete their collection. The Hemus image remains untarnished by this scandalous revelation; there is no reason to suspect that Solly knew about the dastardly scheme.

Most Unusual Baseball Contract: In the years before the lively ball, when major league baseball was still a nickel-and-dime operation, players were often asked—and more often required—not only to room together but to share the same hotel bed as well in order to cut expenses. Rube Waddell and Ossie Schreckengost, a top-notch pitcher-catcher combo for the Philadelphia Athletics, were willing bedfellows until a nocturnal quirk of Waddell's almost severed their friendship. To prevent further friction, Schreckengost demanded from manager Connie Mack that a clause be written into his contract forbidding Waddell from eating animal crackers in bed. His demand was met.

Most Unusual (Baseball) Extra-Inning Game: On May 1, 1920, the Boston Braves and the Brooklyn Robins (Remember?) played to a 1–1 deadlock before the game was called after 26 innings on account of darkness.

Fidel Castro provided a good example of situation ethics when he was pitching a baseball game in Cuba in 1964. After the last out in the last half of the ninth inning, Fidel's team still found itself behind, but the never-say-die premier decreed that the game should go into extra innings.

Most Unusual (Baseball) Ground Rule: At Fenway Park, home of the Boston Red Sox, the pigeon-fly rule is observed. If a batted ball strikes one of the countless pigeons that make their home in the stadium, the ball (though not necessarily the pigeon) is ruled dead.

Most Unusual (Baseball) Home Plate: Cliff Carroll, who played professional baseball in the late 1800s, brought his pet monkey with him to every game. When Carroll's pet caught a cold and died the Pittsburgh team held a special ceremony and buried the monkey under home plate.

Most Unusual (Baseball) Home Run: "Doc" Cutshaw, who played infield for a variety of National League teams in the early years of this century, hit a sizzling ground ball at Ebbets Field in Brooklyn in 1913, that struck the outfield fence and then, miraculously, rolled up the fence and into the grandstand for what was then scored as a home run.

Most Unusual (Baseball) Ladies' Day: To boost their flagging attendance, the Washington Senators offered freebies to the ladies one day in 1897. George "Winnie" Mercer, a dashingly handsome pitcher, was on the mound for the Senators and argued with the home plate umpire, Bill Carpenter, on virtually every pitch. The women rallied behind Mercer, of course, growing increasingly angry at Carpenter as the game progressed. Apoplectic with rage, they stormed onto the field after the last out, chasing the umpire back to the clubhouse, mauling him savagely and tearing off his clothes. Having chased their quarry to safety behind closed doors, the women rioted outside the clubhouse, hurling bottles and paving stones at the door and rampaging through the stadium, digging up the infield turf and ripping out the seats. Some time later, Carpenter escaped through a rear exit.

Most Unusual (Baseball) Player: Pete Gray. He lost his right arm in a car accident at age six, but remained determined to make baseball his career. In 1943, his first year in professional baseball, he played for the Three Rivers Club in the Canadian-American League, leading the league with a .381 batting average. He batted .333 and stole 68 bases the following year, and in 1945 played center field with the St. Louis Browns. His batting average slipped to .218 that year, but he did manage to hit six doubles and two triples. Playing a cautious defense, he would field a ball with his gloved hand and then tuck the glove under the stump of his right shoulder and grab the ball with his left hand to throw it into the infield, all in one fluid motion.

In 1951, St. Louis Browns owner Bill Veeck signed Eddie Gaedel, a 3'7" midget as a pinch-hitter. Before 20,299 fans, Gaedel made his first—and only—pinch-hit apearance against the Detroit Tigers. With a strike-zone of perhaps twenty inches, he walked, naturally, and was replaced by a pinch-runner, never to be seen on a major league diamond again. Two days after his controversial appearance, the baseball commissioner's office banned all midgets forever from the field of major league play.

Most Unusual (Baseball) Stolen Base: Germany Schaefer, an infielder for the Pittsburgh Pirates and other National League clubs from 1901–1918, once reached second base on a double and then proceeded to steal first. He did it, he later said, to confuse the pitcher.

Most Unusual (Baseball) Team: Our candidates for this category are the Kids and the Kubs, the two teams that comprise the Three Quarter Century Softball Club, Inc., of St. Petersburg, Florida. Strong legs and a keen eye are important, but no one gets to play unless he's at least seventy-five years old. The Kids and the Kubs lock horns three times a week from November through March, and their stars include Jim Waldie, who is eighty-eight and plays left field for the Kids with the long-legged grace—if not quite the same speed—of a Ted Williams. He bats regularly over .400 and nails runners down consistently with a rifle throwing arm. Bill Davis, a triple threat as catcher, pitcher, and second baseman, is ninety-one and refuses to take a warm bath to soothe his bad back. One of the club's youngest players, seventy-six-year-old Ed Stauffer, used to pitch for the St. Louis Browns. One season he was barred from the mound after pitching a shutout. He also led the league in hitting, wtih an .835 batting average and a record-breaking 30 home runs.

Most Unusual Boat Race: The Todd River, in Alice Springs, Australia, is the site of an annual regatta in which two-member crews, standing inside bottomless boats which they grip by the gunwales, run a foot race along a course mapped out on the dry river bed. The races were canceled in 1973 when torrential rains flooded the Todd River, washing out the activities. The gods looked with greater favor and sunnier skies, however, on the elders of the Cowichan Bay Privy Council, of Cowichan Bay, British Columbia, and allowed them to hold their annual motorized outhouse races, one of the more popular sporting attractions in western Canada.

Most Unusual Boxing Match: In April 1893, Bowen and Burke fought 110 rounds to a draw for the lightweight championship of the South. Burke, a Texan, had both hands broken and was saved by the bell from a knockout count in the 48th round. Bowen, a hometown boy, kept insisting that he would put him away in just another round or two, but at midnight, according to *The Police Gazette,* the crowd began singing "Home Sweet Home" and by two in the morning much of the crowd was gone. Finally the referee called the

Mechanical chess player

fight, with Bowen protesting he would "send him to heaven in 111."

Most Unusual Chess Player: When the eccentric Austrian inventor Johann Nepomuk Maelzel decided there was no longer a market for his mechanical orchestras (see *Worst Beethoven Composition*), he purchased a mechanical chess player from the son of its late inventor, Baron von Kempellen, and went on tour with it in the United States in the 1820s. Dubbed "the Turk," the machine consisted of a massive and rather expressionless Turkish man carved of wood, turbaned, robed, bedecked with jewels, and seated behind a wooden chest, a chess-board carved into its top. The Turk, Maelzel would tell audiences up and down the East Coast, is not only the world's only mechanical chess player but more skilled at the game than any human on the face of the earth. Is there anyone among you, he would ask, who would care to challenge him?

The inevitable volunteer would then be seated facing the automaton. Maelzel, after opening all the doors of the chest to expose a whirring clockwork of coils, springs, cogs, rods, and brass fittings—and to demonstrate that its workings were totally mechanical—cranked up the machine and let it play. The Turk's hand slowly zeroed in on its piece, moved it, and then came to rest on a velvet pillow next to the board. When the volunteer completed his move, the Turk's arm mysteri-

113

ously reactivated itself and played move number three. It generally had the human opponent checkmated within an hour after the opening move.

What the audience didn't know was that despite Maelzel's candor in showing them the innards of the Turk, there really was somebody inside pulling the strings—a young French-woman at first, and then a chess expert whom Maelzel had imported from Europe. The internal structure of the chest allowed his assistant to move from one compartment to another rather quickly on a series of casters and skateboards, and with Maelzel opening only one door at a time, it wasn't difficult at all to escape detection.

A down-and-out former chess-playing associate of Maelzel's blew the impresario's cover in 1837, by telling the popular French magazine *Pittoresque* the secret of the Turk's success. The Turk's popularity soon waned and the once-wealthy Maelzel went broke, drinking himself to death the following year.

Most Unusual Combat Sport: Popular—but against the law —in Hong Kong, cricket fighting inspires heavy betting and is not unlike cockfighting. The spectators are seated around an inverted wooden tub that serves as the ring and owners pull out their fighting insects from under their shirts. After irritating the combatants' antennae with a small brush, the festivities commence, and by the time one cricket has had its ears pinned back—or worse—much violence will have been done. Not recommended, as they say in the movie review biz, for the squeamish.

Most Unusual Fishing Lures: Lobsters are scared to death of octopuses. Clever fishermen in New Caledonia fasten a dead octopus to the end of a long pole and dangle it in a pool filled with spiny lobsters. The crustaceans freeze in terror, and divers can easily harvest them by hand without fear of being pinched.

Some Japanese fishermen use cormorants as hunters use falcons. The cormorant is a large, voracious sea bird, with ducky-looking feet and a pouch under its bill like a pelican. The fishermen clip their wings and send out ten or twelve cormorants from their small boats, controlling them with leashes. They also fasten iron collars around the birds' necks to keep them from swallowing their catch. Even though their stomachs are getting no satisfaction for their efforts, the cormorants cannot control their impulse to dive for fish. They dive repeatedly, only to have the fishermen pull them in and shake the catch out of their pouches.

Most Unusual Football Coach: In October 1965, Dr. Gustave Weber, president of Susquehanna University in Pennsylvania, accepted with reluctance the resignation of head football coach Jim Garrett and his coaching staff, with two games left to the season. In the four years that Garrett had been coach he had led his charges to a remarkable 39–4 record, but this season they had yet to win a game and Garrett, frankly, was disgusted. With two games left and no coach in sight, Weber decided to coach the team himself. After all, he'd been a nine-letter man during his undergraduate days at Wagner College and felt he could make a passable job of coaching.

Sportswriters from all over the nation descended on the Susquehanna campus to get the real story behind the college-president-turned-football-coach, and Weber announced that he had a few strategic tricks up his sleeve that might cause Susquehanna's critics to think twice about downgrading the team again.

Unfortunately, Susquehanna lost both games.

Most Unusual Football Player (Current): Garo Yepremian, a top-rated field-goal kicker for the Miami Dolphins, broke into professional football in October 1966. Three weeks prior to his first appearance he had never even *seen* a football game, and four months before that he had never even seen a *football*.

Cypriot-born, he had lived most of his life in London and came to the United States for the first time in June 1966 to visit a brother in Indianapolis. Yepremian was a skilled soccer player with a strong, accurate kick, and his brother suggested that he remain in the United States and try for a football scholarship at a university.

He tried and it didn't work simply because he lacked a high school diploma. At his brother's suggestion, Yepremian sought tryouts with a number of professional teams and after seeing his stuff, both the Atlanta Falcons and the Detroit Lions offered him contracts. He signed with Detroit.

In his first few outings Yepremian failed dismally. Then, in a mid-November game against the Minnesota Vikings, Yepremian came into the game in the second quarter and

kicked three quick field goals to bring Detroit up from behind to a 12–10 lead over the Vikings. He went on to kick
a total of six field goals in that game, setting a new National
Football League record, and helping Detroit to edge out
Minnesota 32–31.

Most Unusual Football Team: Plainfield Teachers College
had just trounced Ingersoll 17–0 and the New Jersey school's
fast-talking PR man Jerry Croyden raced back to his office
to phone in the score and highlights to *The New York Times*
sports desk. It had been Plainfield's third shutout victory in
as many outings that 1941 season and while the *Times* had
buried its coverage of those games among the used car ads
and the birth announcements, people were beginning to sit
up and take notice with this third victory. In the coming
weeks Plainfield extended its unbroken string of wins, chewing up teams like Scott College and Chesterton, and with each
phone call the rewrite man on the *Times* kept Croyden on
the phone a bit longer, drawing out more color from him,
more background dope on the players, more comments from
Plainfield's up-and-coming coach.

The star of the team was John Chung, a Chinese-born
quarterback who was averaging a 9.3-yard gain on each
carry and had scored more than half his team's points.
Sportswriter Herbert Allan wrote in the New York *Post,*
just one of a number of big-city dailies in the Northeast that
were covering the team, that, "if the Jerseyans don't watch
out, Chung may pop up in Chiang Kai-shek's offense
department one of these days." As the season wore on and
Chung continued eating up the yards, Croyden let it be
known that "the prowess of Chung may be due to his habit
of eating rice between the halves."

Suddenly, the Plainfield eleven had the rug pulled out
from under them. On November 13, Croyden's office issued
this press release: "Due to flunkings in the midterm examina-
tions, Plainfield Teachers College has been forced to call off
its last two scheduled games with Appalachian Tech tomorrow and with Harmony Teachers on Thanksgiving Day.
Among those thrown for a loss was John Chung, who has
accounted for 69 of Plainfield's 117 points." It was a tough
break for the Plainfield team; a few more victories and they
would have commanded national attention for sure. The
Times sports desk was disappointed.

As it turned out, it wasn't failing exam scores that wiped
out the team. New York *Herald Tribune* reporter Cas Adams

was the one who broke the real story: There *was* no Plainfield Teachers College, no team, no rice-eating Chinese quarterback. The team and its winning record were a *hoax* cooked up by Morris Newburger, a senior partner at a Wall Street brokerage house. Each Saturday he and other employees at the firm took turns posing as Jerry Croyden to phone in the mythical ball scores. After some of the embarrassment among the *Times*'s sports staff had worn off, Cas Adams of the *Tribune* penned this tribute to the Plainfield Eleven, an anthem sung to the tune of "High Above Cayuga's Waters":

> Far above New Jersey's swamplands
> Plainfield Teachers' spires
> Mark a phantom, phony college
> That got on the wires.
> Perfect record made on paper,
> Imaginary team,
> Hail to thee, our ghostly college,
> Product of a dream!

Most Unusual Gladiators: Thais still bet on contests between Siamese fighting fish. When a particularly courageous fighter dies, admirers hold an elaborate funeral, complete with brightly dressed mourners, music, and dancing.

Most Unusual Physical Education Program: When students change classes at St. Helen's School in Newbury, Ohio, the halls are crowded with unicycles. Each student is required to learn unicycle riding in gym class and encouraged to ride at every opportunity. Believing that everyone should have at least one skill that is exceedingly daffy, Steve McPeak, the unicycle-riding headmaster of St. Helen's, originated the program. (See also *Best Unicyclist.*)

Most Unusual Rugby Rule Infraction: Almost anything goes in rugby, but Corporal George Wright of the British Commandos carried passion a bit too far during a Devon Rugby Football Union match in which he played during the 1974 season: He bit an opposing player on the ear, an act less affectionate than it may sound. For the offense he has been suspended from the Union until 1976.

Most Unusual Ski: How long have downhill racers been schussing along mountainsides at nearly 100 miles per hour?

Well, the Swedes found an ancient ski preserved in a peat bog that was carbon-dated at 3,000 B.C.

Most Unusual Track Meet: A tribe of South American Indians periodically conduct zany track meets called *bimiti*. The contestants run a long course toward a trough filled with the local brew (called *paiwari;* see also *Worst Beverage*). The runner who reaches the trough first has the honor of bathing in the intoxicating suds. Rarely, however, does anyone finish the race. Enthusiastic young girls line the sides of the course to cheer on their favorites and to throw red pepper and ashes at the others. With all the dust and pepper in the air, all the runners are soon coughing, sneezing, and rolling on the ground, much to the delight of the fans.

Most Unusual Track Record: Larry Lewis ran the 100-yard dash in 17.8 seconds in 1969, thereby setting a new world's record for runners in the 100-years-or-older class. Lewis was 101.

Government

Best Act of Diplomacy: The crafty French foreign minister Talleyrand had a flair for polite diplomatic evasion. When asked whether the ailing George III had died, Talleyrand replied, "Some say that the King of England is dead; others say that he is not dead; but do you wish to know my opinion?"

"Most anxiously, Prince," the questioner said.

"Well, then, I believe neither! I mention this in confidence to you; but I rely on your discretion: The slightest imprudence on your part would compromise me seriously."

Best Calvin Coolidge Story: When Will Rogers told them, stories about America's most taciturn president were reprinted in newspapers all over the country. This one is typical and true: Calvin Coolidge fell asleep at his large oak desk during the middle of the work day. After dozing for some time, he awoke with a start and inquired of his chief of staff, "Is the country still here?"

Best First Lady: Eleanor Roosevelt—who else? Neglected by her husband in matters connubial, she played a more central role in government affairs than did any other first lady in the nation's history. Said one anti-Roosevelt columnist, "FDR is 20% mush and 80% Eleanor."

Best Flag: Hudson's department store in Detroit displays its famous American flag every year on Flag Day, June 14. First exhibited at the 1939 World's Fair in New York City, the Grand Old Rag measures 235 by 104 feet and weighs nearly three-quarters of a ton; each of the stars is a full five and a half feet high. By the way, "Keep your eye on the Grand Old Rag" was the original last line of George M. Cohan's famous song. He later changed it when people reacted with horror at his overfamiliarity.

Best Imperialist: Homely, shy, and weighing just over one hundred pounds sopping wet, William Walker (1824–1860) realized every American boy's dream and became president— first of Sonoran Mexico, and later of Nicaragua. Justifiably, he has been called "the greatest American filibuster," in the old sense of the word meaning a meddler in foreign politics.

An unsuccessful physician and journalist, Walker was lured to California by the great gold rush, but he arrived too late to stake out a profitable claim. Turning his eyes southward, he and a band of armed irregulars crossed the Mexican border into southern California and seized control of a vast stretch of desert; on January 18, 1854, Walker proclaimed himself president of an independent republic. As soon as the Mexican government recovered from the initial shock, it sent troops to cut off the crazy adventurers from their supplies and reinforcements. On the verge of starvation, Walker's men retreated back across the border, but their leader's appetite for conquest and high office had been whetted.

In 1855, at the request of a small band of Nicaraguan revolutionaries, Walker and a fifty-seven-man private army launched an expedition to Central America, and within a year they had toppled the ruling government. Walker was inaugurated president of Nicaragua in July 1856, and his regime was promptly recognized by the United States. As head of state, he planned to establish "a southern republic founded on Negro slavery" and began plans to build a sea-level canal connecting the Atlantic and Pacific oceans. But the diminutive imperialist made the fatal error of opposing Commodore Cornelius Vanderbilt, who had a stranglehold on the Central American economy. Vanderbilt financed an armed contingent from El Salvador, Honduras, Guatemala, and Costa Rica to throw out the Yankee president.

Still claiming to be the legitimate ruler of Nicaragua, Walker attempted to regain power in 1860, but was apprehended by Honduran authorities. And on September 12 he was executed by a firing squad.

Best Orator of Modern Times: President Franklin D. Roosevelt. The Roosevelt image has fallen on hard times over the past few years, what with disclosures by his son Eliott of his father's marital infidelities and his vacillation in the face of the German military buildup in the 1930s. Nonetheless, no one can fault FDR's oratorical skill. His voice was magnificent, his style was spellbinding. Listen to a record of any

Thomas Jefferson

of his speeches—in particular, his Day of Infamy Address to Congress the day after Pearl Harbor and his First Inaugural.

Best Political Leader of the Twentieth Century: If it's beneficence and courage we're talking about then the choice is Winston Churchill, according to Jenkin Lloyd Jones, editor and publisher of the Tulsa *Tribune*. If we're talking about effectiveness, then Jones feels the choice is Josef Stalin. Our own candidate is Mahatma Gandhi, who, by demonstrating the power of passive resistance, changed the course of history not only on the Indian sub-continent but throughout the world.

Best President (U.S.): In a 1948 poll of fifty-five American historians and political scientists conducted by Harvard University historian Arthur Schlesinger, Sr., five past American presidents were designated "great": George Washington, Thomas Jefferson, Abraham Lincoln, Woodrow Wilson, and Franklin Delano Roosevelt. A similar poll in 1962 yielded identical results. But there is a difficulty in labeling any one president as the greatest of all time: each of the five "greats" in the two polls was marked by a Shakespearean "fatal flaw." That, anyway, is the opinion of Montana State University historian Morton Borden, who has added five other presidents to the "great" list in a study he made in 1962: John Adams, Andrew Jackson, James Knox Polk, Grover Cleveland, and

121

Theodore Roosevelt. All things considered, Lincoln and Jefferson are probably the all-time best.

Best Unsuccessful Presidential Candidate: Americans don't always elect the best man. Franklin Pierce beat Winfield Scott, Warren Harding beat James Cox, Dwight D. Eisenhower beat Adlai Stevenson, and, perhaps the greatest loss the nation has ever sustained in this regard, Calvin Coolidge defeated John W. Davis, the Democratic contender, in the 1924 presidential election. Historical novelist Irving Stone calls Davis a "thoughtful liberal" who might have had the intellectual tools Coolidge lacked and who "would have listened to the experts and put a curb on wild speculation and the pyramiding of paper wealth," thus averting the Great Depression. His ability to draw the best out of men of diverse views was great, and he never lost sight of the interests of both big business and the working class. Says Stone, "John Davis would have made the kind of president of whom Thomas Jefferson would have approved."

Worst Act of Diplomacy: During the Middle East war of 1948, Warren Austin, the then U.S. Ambassador to the United Nations, urged the Arabs and Jews to resolve their disagreements "like good Christians."

Worst Bureaucratic Verbal Obfuscation: The following clarification of terms is found in the California State Code of the Division of Consumer Services, Department of Consumer Affairs: "Tenses, Gender, and Number: For the purpose of the rules and regulations contained in this chapter, the present tense includes the past and future tenses, and the future the present; the masculine gender includes the feminine and the feminine the masculine; and the singular includes the plural and the plural the singular."

Worst Campaign Slogan: The Whig slogan "Tippecanoe and Tyler, too," first chanted during the presidential election campaign of 1836, was an attempt to capitalize on General William Henry Harrison's distinguished military record. The Democrats countered by ballyhooing the heroism of their vice-presidential candidate, Colonel Richard M. Johnson, who claimed to have killed the Shawnee Indian chief Tecumseh at the Battle of the Thames. Johnson's friends originated the slogan: "Rumpsey, dumpsey, Rumpsey, dumpsey/Colonel Johnson killed Tecumseh." Pulitzer Prize-winning historian Samuel Eliot Morison asserts that this couplet has never been surpassed for "electioneering imbecility."

Worst Case of Governmental Red Tape: *Esquire* magazine reported in 1963 that Mrs. Agnes Matlock of New Hyde Park, New York, had charged in a lawsuit that her house had burned to the ground while the two fire departments that had answered her call argued over which one had jurisdiction to put out the fire.

The town council of Winchester, Indiana, passed an anti-pornography law, but the editors of the town's only newspaper refused to publish it on the grounds that the statute itself was pornographic. Unfortunately, a law does not take effect in Winchester until it has been published in a newspaper.

Worst Congressional Study: In 1970, United States Representative Thomas P. "Tip" O'Neill, Jr., of Massachusetts, assigned a staff aide to prepare a detailed research report on the length of men's hair. "We discovered that since the time of Christ, the male species has worn long hair and beards about 90 percent of the time," the congressman reassured a hair-harried nation. "The western world turned to short hair and clean-shaven faces only after the Prussian victory over France. All the great heroes of America have worn long hair. It's nothing for Americans to get alarmed about."

Worst Event: Realizing full well the innumerable ghastly, base, vain, cruel, dishonorable, stupid, and vile actions perpetrated by mankind, it is with all humility that we nominate the following as a candidate for the exalted title "Worst Event of All Times."

Inez de Castro was secretly married to Don Pedro on January 1, 1347. Three years later she was assassinated by agents of Don Pedro's father, who was King of Portugal and a long-standing political foe of Inez. When Don Pedro heard of his wife's murder, he was overcome with rage and sorrow. Even when he captured the assassins and had them gruesomely tortured and executed it did his heart no good.

Not long afterward, the old king died, and Don Pedro ascended the throne as King Pedro I. His first royal act was to have Inez's body removed from the grave, carried to the palace in a magnificent procession, and placed upon a sump-

123

tuous throne. There she was crowned "Queen of Portugal." Don Pedro personally placed the orb and scepter of her office into her ghastly hands. Then, in a bizarre second funeral, Inez was returned to the grave.

Epilogue: Pedro ruled well for many years, earning the epithet Pedro the Just.

Worst First Lady: Mary Todd Lincoln. First ladies are supposed to stand to the side, quiet and demure, like Bess Truman, and avoid clogging up the machinery of statework—or else they should participate productively and imaginatively in their husband's administration, as did Eleanor Roosevelt. Mary Todd Lincoln followed neither route and, according to one biographer, made her husband's life "a hell on earth." In retrospect, historians and psychoanalysts agree that she was mentally disturbed and could have benefited from medical treatment. During her husband's first year as president, she overspent a congressionally approved appropriation of $20,000 for interior refurbishing of the White House by $6,700 and Lincoln hit the badly peeling ceiling. "It would stink in the nostrils of the American people to have it said that the President of the United States had approved a bill overrunning an appropriation of $20,000 for *flub dubs* for this damned old house, when the soldiers cannot even have blankets," he snorted.

Worst Mayor of a Big City: Richard Daley, say his supporters, gets things done in Chicago. The very thing for which he is so bitterly criticized by his opponents—his viselike grip on all facets of Cook County politics and government, which he has maintained for over twenty years—makes him a model of mayoral effectiveness.

Maybe so, but Mussolini also made the trains run on time. Chicago's police are still among the most corrupt in the nation, its public works system still among the most primitive. During the 1968 riots, Daley himself captured the essence of the situation as well as anyone: "The police," he said, "were not there to provoke disorder. They were there to maintain disorder." During uprisings in a black ghetto on Chicago's South Side, Daley issued his now-famous "shoot to maim" order, and at a city hall press conference, he once petulantly told a reporter, "Don't confuse me with the facts."

The East Coast's answer to Mayor Daley is Frank Rizzo of Philadelphia. A former chief of police, Rizzo once volunteered to take a lie-detector test in a supreme gesture of good faith. He failed. Chief executive of the nation's fourth largest city, he once telephoned the city editor of the Philadelphia *Inquirer,* one of several journalistic flies in the ointment of his political aspirations, and called him a "faggot."

Worst Political Action Group: The René Guyon Society, based in Alhambra, California, claims a membership of 670 conscientious parents dedicated to stopping "our kids' headlong plunge toward drugs and crime." Their novel solution to these problems—as well as suicide, divorce, alcoholism, and gambling—is to turn children on to "healthy sex." In the dispassionate words of the *Encyclopedia of Associations,* the Guyon Society serves as the voice for "those advocating child bisexuality protected with double contraceptives by age eight." This position is aptly summarized in their motto: "Sex by age eight—or else it's too late."

As a political action group, members work actively for the repeal of statutory rape laws and other legislation frustrating youthful sexual expression. The society proudly claims Freud, Wilhelm Reich, and Dr. René Guyon as its spiritual forebears. (For the uninitiated, the mysterious Dr. Guyon was a judge on the Thailand supreme court for thirty years and the author of a much-ignored volume entitled *Sexual Freedom.*)

Worst President (U.S.): Warren G. Harding or Ulysses S. Grant. The Schlesinger surveys drew the same conclusion in 1948 and 1962: As presidents go, Grant and Harding were the worst ever. "Both were postwar presidents who, by their moral obtuseness, promoted a low tone in official life," wrote Schlesinger, "conducting administrations riddled with shame and corruption." Schlesinger's remarks appeared in the July 29, 1962 edition of *The New York Times,* just three months before Richard Nixon swore he was leaving politics forever after being defeated by Edmund Brown for the California governorship.

Worst Presidential Election: Governor Samuel Tilden of New York ran against Rutherford B. Hayes in the election of 1876. Tilden, who had made a name for himself by busting up the corrupt Tweed ring, appeared to have won a clear victory from the preliminary returns. But three Southern states and Oregon submitted two sets of votes and there were reports that many Democrats had been turned away from the polls. A Congressional Investigatory Committee, composed of eight Republicans and seven Democrats, was set up to

125

Ulysses S. Grant

review the disputed returns. In a backroom deal, Northern Republicans apparently convinced a few Southern Democratic power brokers to accept Hayes's election in return for a promise to remove Yankee troops and to overlook violations of the Fourteenth Amendment. When the vote came, the Investigatory Committee divided on strict party lines, and the contested states were marked up in Hayes's column, giving him a 185 to 184 electoral college majority, even though Tilden received 250,000 more popular votes. In the *Oxford History of the American People,* Samuel Eliot Morison writes, "There is no longer any doubt that this election was stolen."

Worst Public Works Proposal: For years, sparrows and pigeons have made their nests above the main entrance of the massive marble building that houses the United States Supreme Court, carrying out frequent carpet-bombing attacks on the steps below. In 1975 the nine justices, having suffered too long in silence, unanimously requested a House appropriations subcommittee to back a $45,000 measure to "bird-proof" the building. Said Justice Harry Blackmun, "You are literally in danger, in going up those steps, of having bird droppings all over you."

Worst Senator (Current): William Scott (D-Virginia)—according to a poll of 200 congressmen, journalists, congressional staff members, and Capitol Hill regulars conducted by *New*

Times magazine. "The man is the most morally corrupt individual I've ever known," one former aide of Scott's told the Richmond *Mercury*. "There's nothing to admire. . . . He's irascible, uncooperative . . . and he chases women in the office. . . . A man like that needs a psychiatrist." Scott is the man who told the *Washingtonian* that "The only reason we need zip codes is because niggers can't read." When asked by a reporter to name the highlight of his freshman year in the Senate, he replied pensively, "Being sworn in was perhaps the highlight of the year."

Worst Senatorial Rationale: In 1970, Senator Richard B. Russell voted for the ABM (Anti-Ballistic Missile) because, "If we have to start over again with another Adam and Eve, then I want them to be Americans and not Russians, and I want them to be on this continent and not in Europe."

And Indiana congressman Earl Landgrebe—the man who was arrested for selling bibles to passersby on the streets of Moscow; who once snapped at reporters, "Don't confuse me with facts; I've got a closed mind"; who told a newsman on the day Richard Nixon resigned the presidency that he thought congressional favor was switching to Nixon—once explained that he had voted no on a bill to appropriate funds for cancer research because the cost was excessive and besides, discovering a cure for cancer would only change "which way you're going to go."

Worst Unsuccessful Presidential Candidate: William Jennings Bryan. Bryan had three stabs at the presidency—in 1896, 1900, and 1904—and had he made it any of those times the entire nation would have been crucified on a cross of cornstarch. This yammering, blathering religious fanatic was most true to form as the small-minded prosecuting attorney in the famous Scopes·Monkey Trial of 1925, and psychographic studies of his words and actions indicate that he was one of two bona fide psychopaths to run for the presidency. (The other was George McClellan, Lincoln's opponent.) Campaigning against McKinley in 1900, Bryan told a crowd, "Friends, tonight my little wife will be going to sleep in a cramped hotel room on the other side of town, but come next March she'll be sleeping in the White House!" He waited for the cheers, and then someone shouted, "Well, if she does, she'll be sleeping with McKinley, because he's gonna win." Irving Stone writes of Bryan, "His mind was like a soup dish, wide and shallow; it could hold a small amount of nearly anything, but the slightest jarring spilled the soup into somebody's lap."

Worst World Leader (Current): When Idi Amin, the strongman president of Uganda, went on a pilgrimage to Mecca, rain fell for the first time in fifty years. It was only a few drops, but Amin interpreted the unexpected shower as divine anointment. Since then he has been insufferable.

For instance, although Big Daddy (as he likes to be known) received his military training in Israel, he has recently become a virulent anti-Semite. "Hitler was right about the Jews," Amin wrote in a cable to Kurt Waldheim. "The Israelis are not working in the interests of the people of the world, and that is why they burned the Israelis alive with gas in the soil of Germany."

A 1973 speech he delivered in Brazzaville contained one of the most absurd statements ever uttered by a world leader, as measured against some mighty stiff competition: "Some Asians in Uganda have been painting themselves black with shoe polish. If anyone is found painting himself with black polish, disciplinary action will be taken against him." But to minorities in that African nation, Amin's policies are no joke; he deported 42,000 Asian citizens and resident aliens on just a few weeks' notice. A less malevolent but equally perverse presidential fiat established severe penalties for wearing miniskirts.

Big Daddy also has an uncanny ability to antagonize fellow heads of state. Since coming to power, he has precipitated a number of border wars with neighboring countries. And on July 4, 1973, he sent Richard Nixon a "get well card" from one statesman to another, wishing him "a speedy recovery from Watergate."

Most Unusual Campaign Song: Ferdinand Lop was a perpetual candidate for the French presidency and a much-beloved loser. A timid, leftist intellectual, he drew most of his meager support from students at the Sorbonne. Eventually his campaigns became a half-serious, half-satirical tradition, resembling the quadrennial efforts of Harold Stassen and Pat Paulsen in the United States. Lop dubbed his personal political party the "Front Lopulaire." And, according to *Horizon* magazine, his platform called for radical "Lopeotherapy," including the elimination of poverty after 10 P.M., the nationalization of brothels, and the relocation of Paris to some rural area where the air is fresher. Enthusiastic followers composed a catchy campaign song, to the melody of "The Stars and Stripes Forever": "Lop, Lop, Lop Lop Lop, Lop Lop Lop! Lop Lop Lop, Lop Lop Lop, Lop Lop LOP Lop!"

Most Unusual Country: The Sovereign Military Order of Malta, more commonly known by the acronym S.M.O.M., occupies a three-acre estate called the Villa de Priorato di Malta in Rome, Italy. S.M.O.M. still maintains diplomatic relations with several nations and is thus considered not only the world's tiniest country but also the most unusual. While its territorial holdings are slight, S.M.O.M. is governed under an impressive constitution ratified in 1957.

Most Unusual Election: In 1962, some 46,000 Connecticut voters wrote in the name of Ted Kennedy for United States Senator. Kennedy was running in neighboring Massachusetts.

Most Unusual Emperor: Joshua Norton was a wealthy San Francisco businessman who lost all his money and found himself living in a squalid rooming house, working in a Chinese rice factory. Depressed and idle, he began to fixate on the ills of the Union and soon came to be known among his friends as "the Emperor" for his loudly stated views on the need for an emperor to assume the reins of power. Then, having completely lost touch with reality, he dropped off this message at the offices of the San Francisco *Bulletin* on September 17, 1859:

At the peremptory request and desire of a large majority of the citizens of these United States, I, Joshua Norton, . . . declare and proclaim myself Emperor of these United States; and in virtue of the authority thereby in me vested, do hereby order and direct the representatives of the different states of the Union to assemble in Musical Hall, of this city, on the first day of February next, then and there to make such alterations in the existing laws of the Union as may ameliorate the evils under which the country is laboring and thereby cause confidence to exist, both at home and abroad, both in our stability and in our integrity.

Thereafter, Norton assumed—in his own mind, at least— full imperial powers. He appeared in public dressed in a secondhand officer's uniform with blue and gold trim. His proclamation appeared in newspapers and was widely read.

He abolished both major political parties, dissolved the Republic, scheduled a national convention and ordered that a new constitution be drawn up. His friends and former business associates humored him completely, giving the penniless emperor everything he demanded.

Norton's fame—and the willingness of people to cater to his bizarre fancies—extended far beyond the city limits of San Francisco. He dined in the finest restaurants, announcing himself to the headwaiter and being seated at the best table in the house. He had no qualms whatsoever about chewing out a delinquent waiter or sending back an overdone steak, and, of course, he never paid for his meal. Norton rode free in buses, lived free in a dingy room in a boarding house, and issued "Bonds of the Empire" to finance his government. These were printed gratis by a friend in exchange for a promise to appoint him Chancellor of the Exchequer. They bore Emperor Norton's likeness and were worth fifty cents.

He levied taxes too—twenty-five cents on small shopkeepers, three dollars or more on industrialists. A local paper noted that he would often accost a friend and "attempt to negotiate a loan of several million dollars, and depart perfectly contented with a two- or four-bit piece."

Norton died in 1880 at the age of sixty-two, and received an elaborate funeral, paid for by his friends and worthy of a legitimate state ruler. The headline in the San Francisco *Chronicle* the following day was LE ROI EST MORT.

Most Unusual Empress: Without repeating any of the racier stories about her life, Catherine the Great of Russia still ranks as the most unusual female monarch. It is said that she preferred water with gooseberry syrup to any other drink. Informed sources report that she delighted in having her feet tickled and her fanny slapped. During her reign, there were many who obliged her in this respect.

Most Unusual English Queen: Richard I, Coeur de Lion (Lion-Hearted), took Berengaria, the beautiful daughter of Sancho VI of Navarre, to be his bride; she thus became Queen of England and Richard's other realms. Richard, of course, became a legend in his own time. For the troubadours he was the very symbol of chivalry; but he was a lousy husband. Berengaria was willing to follow her lord, even to the battlefields of Palestine, yet Richard soon left her behind. Over the remaining nine years of his life, the crusading twelfth-century king saw Berengaria only once more, for a few short weeks. While Richard pursued Odyssean adventures, the Queen endured her loneliness in Italy and later in France, earning a small place in history as the only English monarch never to set foot on the island over which she reigned.

Most Unusual Example of Political Censorship in the Free World: Stare at a map of North America for 30 seconds and then turn away and say the first thing that pops into your mind. If it's "Nikolai Lenin," you may have more political savvy than you give yourself credit for: In 1974, a map of the North American continent that appeared on a newscast over Turkish television looked so much like a profile of Lenin to the public prosecutor that he conducted an investigation to determine whether it constituted illegal communist propaganda.

Most Unusual Explanation of the Watergate Affair: Bad diet makes for bad government, says Sir Dingle Mackintosh Foot, British elder statesman: "If the Americans had a substantial breakfast of bacon and eggs," he says, "they wouldn't have these problems. A proper breakfast adds to your judgments. You can't expect to start the day on cereals, shredded wheat, muck like that."

Most Unusual Holiday: Each year on March 17, Bostonians celebrate Evacuation Day—the day the British troops withdrew from their city. Though the date may have a familiar ring, there are probably a lot of Bostonians who have never heard of the holiday they observe. It seems the city's Irish politicians were looking for a nonethnic way to make St. Patrick's Day a legal day off from work, and a microscopic reading of the history books uncovered E-Day—an unlikely excuse for putting on the green.

Most Unusual King: As best we can determine, James Jesse Strang (1813–1856) was the only monarch ever crowned within the borders of the United States. Strang was an influential Mormon elder, and following the mob murder of Joseph Smith in 1844, he sought to assume the mantle of church leadership. Although Strang produced two gold tablets covered with strange writing, purportedly proving that he was the divinely appointed successor, Brigham Young commanded the allegiance of the majority of Mormons. Strang, along with several hundred loyal followers, withdrew to Beaver Island, a desolate romantic wilderness on northern Lake Michigan.

The sect named their rugged new home "Zion." And on July 8, 1850, Strang, dressed in a flowing robe that once belonged to a Shakespearean actor, accepted a base metal crown ornamented with glass stars, and assumed the title James I, King of Zion. The new monarch instituted an early model of the welfare state, providing social security and old-age pensions, as well as legalizing polygamy. At first this little kingdom seemed too weak and far away for the government to worry over, but when the king began to intercept "enemy" lake shipping and interfere with the profitable business of smuggling whiskey to the Indians, federal and state officials sprang into action.

James I was arrested on charges of treason and brought to Detroit for trial. But the government prosecutors had not reckoned with the soaring eloquence of His Highness. Strang argued persuasively that he was "being persecuted for religion's sake," and he was acquitted by the sympathetic frontier jury.

Ironically, the downfall of James I was not to come at the instigation of a foreign power, but rather through the treachery of a few of his own subjects. For some unknown reason, Strang decreed that all the women of the sect should adopt short skirts and pantaloons, in the fashion of Amelia Bloomer. The bloomers were exceedingly unpopular with men and women alike, and two disgruntled husbands who could not tolerate the sight of their wives in pants, assassinated the first, and last, King of Zion.

Most Unusual Political Essay: "The Demonstration of the Fourth Part of Nothing and Something; and All; and the Quintessence taken from the Fourth Part of Nothing and its Dependencies containing the Precepts of Sanctified Magic and Devout Incantation of *Demons* in order to find the origin of the Evils of France and the Remedies for them," by Demons, a sixteenth-century French attorney. The author of a work entitled *Eccentric Literature* elucidates Demons's work thusly: "Demons said that he had determined to bring to light a classification of the shades of his timid obscurity in the quintessence which he had taken from nothing and to give an explanation of the enigma of his invention."

Most Unusual Poll: A Birmingham, Alabama, newspaper polled its readers on the following question: "If you had one extra place in your fallout shelter, who would you give it to?" Politicians finished last.

Most Unusual Postal System: In 1877 a society was formed in Belgium to promote the use of cats to make mail deliveries. The theory was that since they have a wonderful sense of direction they could be used like homing pigeons to deliver small packets of letters. To demonstrate the feasibility of the program, thirty-seven cats from Liège were tied up in a gunnysack and transported to a spot twenty miles from town. One found his way home within five hours, and all the rest returned within twenty-four. Despite this impressive performance, the authorities never adopted the idea.

Most Unusual President (U.S.): At 12:00 noon on March 4, 1849, Zachary Taylor was scheduled to succeed James Polk as president. But March 4 was a Sunday and Taylor was a very religious old general who refused to violate the Sabbath by taking the oath of office. Thus, under the Succession Act of 1792, Missouri Senator David Rice Atchinson, as President Pro Tempore of the Senate, automatically became president of the United States. Atchinson is said to have taken his high office very much in stride. Tongue in cheek, he appointed a number of his cronies to Cabinet positions, then he had a few drinks, and retired to bed to sleep out the remainder of his administration. On Monday at noon Taylor took over the reins of government, but Americans can look back on the Atchinson presidency as a peaceful one, untainted by even a hint of corruption.

Most Unusual Republic: The oldest republic and one of the smallest is Andorra, nestled in the Pyrenees Mountains. Charlemagne ceded the 190-square-mile country to a handful of mountaineers in A.D. 805 in return for the assistance they had given his armies in battling the Moors. As part of the price for independence, Andorra pays $200 in tribute money to France and Spain biennially. They are also obligated to send the bishop of Urgel 12 capons, 12 hens, and 24 cheeses. The bishop traditionally returns the offering.

The Andorrans are careful not to develop their small but rich lead and silver deposits for fear working mines might make their powerful neighbors covetous. They have an annual defense budget of 300 pesetas—about $5—which they spend for blanks and fireworks to celebrate their independence day. Their last war was World War I, which lasted forty-four years. Andorra played such a minor part in that engagement that the Allies forgot to invite them to the Versailles Peace Conference and consequently the proud mountaineers did not formally terminate their state of belligerency against the Germans until 1958.

The Andorran economy is based on tourism and smuggling.

Most Unusual Socialist: Charles Fourier (1772–1837) was a utopian socialist with some sensible ideas and a lot of peculiar ones. (His sensible ideas are no concern of this book.) Fourier advocated that the world be divided into small communities called phalanxes in which everyone would eat seven meals a day—three or four of them salads. Fourier loved parades almost as much as he loved salads, so the members of a phalanx would be issued one set of work clothes and one set of parade clothes.

Each person would pursue the trade for which he was best qualified. Since children enjoy playing in the dirt, they would be dressed in bright uniforms and assigned to collect the garbage. Fourier loved the moon almost as much as he loved salads and parades, so he planned to put several new moons in the sky. Some people consider this scheme prescient in light of the space program; others still consider it silly.

Fourier recognized that sex was a fundamental human drive, but he felt that it interfered with more important things when people engaged in it all the time. Thus, he would set aside one week in the year when the phalanx could indulge in any and all sexual activities, while the rest of the year they remained celibate.

Most Unusual State Mottoes: The meanings of many state mottoes are far from self-evident. For one thing, many of them are in Latin, perhaps to disguise their insipidity. A personal favorite is the New Mexican slogan: *Crescit Eundo*, which means "It grows as it goes." The motto of Washington is *Alki* (Chinook Indian for "By and By").

Most Unusual Supreme Court Nominee: This is Senator Roman Hruska's (R-Nebraska) emotional tribute to Supreme Court nominee Harold Carswell, a man who was unusually usual: "Even if he were mediocre, there are a lot of mediocre judges and people and lawyers, and they're entitled

Cartoon of Victoria Woodhull

to a little representation, aren't they? We can't have all Brandeises, Frankfurters, and Cardozos."

Most Unusual Unsuccessful Presidential Candidate: Victoria Woodhull was a distinctive nineteenth-century hybrid of genius and charlatan. As a young girl, she traveled with her family's medicine and fortune-telling show. Her enthusiasm for mesmerism—healing with magnets and hypnosis—eventually brought her to New York where she made the acquaintance of Cornelius Vanderbilt. Vanderbilt set her up as a stockbroker, and soon she was financially independent. Ms. Woodhull began to develop an active interest in the women's suffrage movement and founded a newspaper in which to voice her unorthodox opinions. Among the innovations she endorsed were short skirts, an end to capital punishment, legalized prostitution, birth control, free love, and vegetarianism. She was the first publisher of the "Communist Manifesto" in the United States. On April 2, 1870, Ms. Woodhull became a candidate for the presidency, running on the ticket of the National Radical Reformers. The vice-presidential nominee was Frederick Douglass, the famous black orator and abolitionist. When she showed up at the polls on election day, she was, predictably, denied the right to vote for herself. She ran for the presidency four more times, until she married a wealthy banker and emigrated to England.

She admitted to living with two men at the same time, which could have done her political ambitions no good. But there is little doubt that Victoria Woodhull was the most colorful and original presidential candidate in American history.

Most Unusual Vice-President: Until Spiro Agnew became a household word, there was no such thing as an unusual vice-president. Wilson's VP, Thomas Marshall, showed unusual promise when he said, "What this country needs is a good five-cent cigar!" but he never said or did anything else that anyone can remember.

Spiro Agnew made vice-presidential history when he emerged from colorless anonymity and became one of the most controversial men in America. His phrase-making alone would assure him a status even greater than Tom Marshall. Who can forget "nattering nabobs of negativism," "effete corps of impudent snobs," "fat Jap," or "If you've seen one slum, you've seen them all"?

And, finally, there was Agnew's untimely departure from office to begin a new career writing spy novels. Only one other man ever resigned from the vice-presidency—John Calhoun—and that was in a pique over states' rights.

The Law

Best Executioner: In Thailand public executions are still fashionable, often drawing large crowds, and an aggressive law and order campaign in recent years has brought many convicted felons face-to-face with Nai Mui Juicharoen, Thailand's official executioner. Aficionados of capital punishment have admired the style and efficiency with which Nai Mui dispatches his victims, and Thai newspapers have built him into something of a folk hero. One journal featured two photographs of Nai Mui on its front page. One depicted him in the line of duty—about to blast out the brains of a condemned man—and the other showed him in a lighter moment—dandling little children on his knees.

Each execution earns Nai Mui $17.50 and business is booming. In the fashion of Wild West gunslingers, he memorializes each man he has killed with a notch in his rifle stock; at last count there were over 120 notches. But most importantly, Nai Mui seems to delight in his work and is eager to take on increased responsibilities, if necessary, to stem Thailand's rising crime rate. "I could manage to execute 100 a day if I had to," he boasts.

At least one politician wants to bring back the good old public execution in the United States. Odell McBrayer, a recent Republican candidate for governor of Texas, not only came out in favor of restoring the death penalty but he also advocated live television coverage from the death house. There was one proviso, however: "I favor televising executions only if not done offensively," he said.

Best Policeman: A headline in *The New York Times*, February 5, 1970: SAIGON POLICEMAN CITED FOR HONESTY. It seems the young officer was offered a ten-dollar bribe and turned it down. The South Vietnamese government thought this was such an exceptional act of character that they awarded him a medal of honor.

Worst Form of Disorderly Conduct: Dick Hyman quotes the following judicial opinion in *It's Still the Law,* his comprehensive collection of peculiar old laws still on the books: "It is disorderly conduct for one man to greet another on the street by placing the end of his thumb against the tip of his nose, at the same time extending and wriggling the fingers of his hand." (*The People* v. *Gerstenfeld,* 1915, 156 New York City, 991)

Worst Form of Revenge: In Sicily it was once a customary act of revenge to bite off your spouse's nose if he or she was unfaithful. Nose-biting was also a bizarre part of the vendettas—or blood feuds—for which Sicily was long famous. This practice resulted in a thriving rhinoplasty business, as various medical men and quacks attempted to create replacement noses; these were the first serious experiments in plastic surgery.

Worst Punishment: Here is proof that Richard the Lion-Hearted was not a nice guy. Holinshed reports that Richard issued the following guidelines for punishing murderers: "Who kills a man on shipboard, shall be bound to the dead body and thrown in the sea; if a man is killed on shore, the slayer shall be bound to the dead body and buried with it." Richard is also credited with institutionalizing tar and feathering as a punishment for thievery.

When one noble miscreant appeared before Empress Anne of Russia she at least gave him a choice: death by hanging or sitting on a nest of eggs and clucking like a chicken.

Worst Tort Suit: When twenty-five-year-old Gloria Sykes was hit by a cable car in San Francisco, it appeared on first examination that she had merely suffered a few cuts and bruises. Only later did she discover that the accident had caused her serious psychological and neurological damage. She filed suit, claiming that because of her run-in with the cable car she became a nymphomaniac, engaging in sexual relations with nearly one hundred men. The court found in Miss Sykes's favor and awarded her $50,000 in damages.

Her lawyer, Marvin Lewis, has become something of a specialist in this odd field. In 1974 he took the case of a forty-seven-year-old mother of seven from Santa Ana, California, who was suing a health club for $1 million. The woman charged that she was trapped in a sweltering sauna for ninety minutes—a traumatic experience which compelled her to pick up twenty-four men in barrooms.

Most Unusual Alibi: Not every revolutionary group has the police making excuses for them, but when a women's collective claimed credit for the bombing of Harvard University's Center for International Affairs, in October 1970, the Cambridge police gallantly defended them. "This was a very sophisticated bomb," a police spokesman said. "We feel that women wouldn't be capable of making such a bomb."

Most Unusual Arsonist: Nine Houston firemen confessed to setting a series of fires in southeastern sections of the city to relieve their boredom. U.P.I. quoted one investigator as saying, "They liked to see the red light and hear the siren."

Martin C. Reilly of Pittsfield, Massachusetts, had an even more ironic career as an arsonist. In 1962 he burned down his eighteen-room house to avoid paying property taxes. With the home in ashes, the town of Pittsfield sought to collect back taxes nonetheless.

Most Unusual Court Case: Case #7595 in the records of the District Court of western Pennsylvania is listed as *The United States* v. *350 Cartons of Canned Sardines*. At issue was whether or not the cartons had been improperly marked for interstate commerce. At the conclusion of the jury's deliberation, the foreman announced, "The jury find a verdict in favor of the United States and recommends the mercy of the court." To which presiding Judge Gibson replied with equal levity, "We will take your recommendation of mercy under consideration."

Most Unusual Defense: In 1821, long before the *Miranda* decision, a man named Desjardins was apprehended as an accomplice in the murder of the Duke de Berri. While in custody, he abjectly confessed to the crime. Shortly after, however, he repudiated his confession. In court, Desjardins defended himself by claiming to be a notorious liar, and he called dozens of witnesses to his bad character and complete unreliability. The court was persuaded and Desjardins was found not guilty on the basis that no one could believe a word he said.

139

Most Unusual Execution: Two classic stories about the condemned cheating the hangman.

Joseph Samuels of Sydney, Australia, was accused of stealing a bag of gold and silver coins, killing a policeman in the process. He was duly convicted and sentenced to be hanged in September 1803. Up to the last moment, Samuels protested his innocence. The real murderer, he said, was a spectator in the crowd gathered to watch the execution—a rogue named Isaac Simmonds. Simmonds and Samuels exchanged curses, and the crowd grew uneasy, but the marshals, intent on getting the dirty business over with, slipped the noose around their prisoner's neck.

Samuels stood silently on the cart; the driver snapped his whip above the horses; the team pulled away. Samuels dropped, hung for a moment, then fell to the ground. The hangman's knot had come undone, and Samuels lay in the dust unconscious, but alive.

He was too stunned to stand again, so the marshals sat him on the end of the cart the second time. Again, the cart pulled away. This time the rope unravelled, leaving Samuels dangling with his feet barely touching the ground. Crowds at executions are not notably sentimental, but they could not stand to watch a man die the hard death of strangulation; they screamed for the marshals to cut him down.

They tried and failed a third time to hang Joseph Samuels, but the rope snapped cleanly. He was returned to jail and later released. Simmonds—the man in the crowd—was eventually implicated in the murder, brought to trial, and routinely executed. In a made-for-television movie, Samuels would have reformed and married Suzanne Pleshette, but, in fact, he remained a thieving drunk to the end of his days.

The other story is similar: Will Purvis was convicted of murder, a crime his friends said he could never commit. They tried to hang him on February 7, 1894; as in the Samuels story, the knot slipped loose. The crowd intervened and would not allow the executioners to try again. Later, when the governor refused to pardon Purvis, his friends broke him out of jail and hid him until a new governor was elected. The new governor commuted his sentence to life imprisonment, and finally he was released altogether.

Twenty-two years later another man confessed on his deathbed to the crime Will Purvis had been accused of.

Most Unusual Felon: A talking crow was arrested in Myzaki City, Japan, in 1972 for pecking children and using obscene

140

language in public. Refusing to answer questions at the police station, the bird was released and appeared on Japanese television a few days later.

In 1963, a rather mulish donkey owned by Osorio Fernandez, a Brazilian farmer, was arrested and charged with the murder of a young boy whom it had kicked in the head.

Most Unusual Hijacking: It sounds almost too pat to be true, but police in Santa Fe, Argentina, arrested a man who boarded a city bus, drew a revolver, and demanded to be driven to Cuba.

Most Unusual Jail Break: While seventy prisoners and visitors watched, Mrs. Cynthia Knell removed the screws from a glass partition in a Santa Ana, California, prison. She then put the window to one side, and she and her convict-husband calmly walked out of the building.

Most Unusual Judge: Sir Francis Page's reputation as the most severe jurist in eighteenth-century England earned him the moniker, "The Hanging Judge." He also had a weakness for limericks and bad jokes. When he was nearly eighty and quite feeble, a friend asked him how his health was holding up. "My dear sir," Page replied, "you see I keep hanging on, hanging on."

Most Unusual Kidnapping: At the tender age of two, W. S. Gilbert was kidnapped from his parents in Naples, Italy. He was ransomed on a pound sterling per pound baby basis—twenty-five pounds in all. When baby Gilbert grew up and became Arthur Sullivan's famous collaborator, he made use of the kidnapping in two of his operettas.

Most Unusual Laws: When will society quit trying to outlaw the victimless crime? According to James Terry Taylor, Jr., there is an old law, still on the books, in Lexington, Kentucky, against carrying an ice cream cone in one's back pocket.

Paul Steiner mentions an earlier regulation imposed by Emperor Joseph of Austria forbidding nuns to wear corsets.

Still further back in history, Roman prostitutes were required by law to wear yellow hair. This piece of legislation was responsible for a fad among the amorous of the upper class. Bales of blond hair were imported from Germany and made into wigs for the rich; hairdressers made fortunes on

141

bleach jobs. The emperor Claudius's less than faithful wife Messalina was one of the first fine ladies to set the towhead trend.

Most Unusual Law School Textbook: *The Criminal Prosecution and Capital Punishment of Animals,* written by E. R. Evans in 1906. Suing a giraffe for defaulting on his refrigerator payments? Want to get an exhibitionist fruit fly away from innocent women and children and behind bars where he belongs? This is your book. For the more numerically inclined, there is *The Problem of the Law of Justice Solved by Arithmetic: Statement of What Passed for Many Years Between Dr. John Dee and Some Spirits,* published in England in the eighteenth century.

Most Unusual Lawyer: A French lawyer, Bartholomew de Chassenie, launched his distinguished legal career in 1510 by defending the rats of the village of Autun against the charge that they had stolen the barley crop. De Chassenie was merely a court-appointed counsel (since the rats had not bothered to secure their own), but he pleaded the case with imagination and conviction.

When the case was first called, the bailiff failed to produce any rats. De Chassenie leapt to his feet; his clients, he argued vigorously, could not be tried *in absentia* unless the state could show that it had made a genuine effort to inform them of the serious charges against them and to bring them to the bar. What's more, since every rat in Autun had been named in the charges, every rat had a right to be present in the courtroom. The judge sustained the defense's objection and ordered a delay.

In a second appearance in court, de Chassenie produced a bombshell: A number of his clients (who had a right to be presumed innocent) had been attacked by vicious cats on the way to the court. Certainly the state could not expect them to appear unless it could guarantee their safety. Again, the judge was persuaded and he issued an injunction prohibiting the cats from molesting rats on their way to the trial.

Unfortunately, the records of the case that have been preserved are incomplete and do not tell us the final verdict. But it is known that Bartholomew de Chassenie, after the conclusion of this *cause célèbre,* was involved in many more animal trials, both as a defense lawyer and as a prosecutor. In fact, de Chassenie was involved in the historic cases establishing that animals are subject to anathema and excommunication by the Church as well as civil prosecution.

Most Unusual Oath: Since the Romans had no Bibles on which to swear, it was the custom to place one's right hand on one's testicles when swearing to tell the truth. The English word "testimony" is derived from this practice.

Most Unusual Ordeal: Once upon a time, the judicial process was much simpler. Instead of haggling for years over points of law and agonizing through appeals, people simply passed the question of guilt or innocence along to "the Great Judge." Trial by ordeal was for the most part a *Catch-22* proposition: You threw a suspected witch in the pond—if she floated she was guilty, if she drowned she was innocent. In contrast, the Chinese developed a comparatively sensible method of lie detection—the ordeal of chewing rice. The accused was given a handful of dry rice to eat. A guilty person, the theory went, would be so nervous that his mouth would go dry, leaving him unable to swallow; in contrast, an innocent person, theoretically, had less on his conscience and more saliva in his mouth.

Most Unusual Racket: An article in the June 28, 1967, issue of *The New York Times* carried the following headline: GARBAGE CARTING IN GRIP OF MAFIA.

Most Unusual Recidivist: When his wife ruined dinner by undercooking the roast, Noel Carriou grew livid and fumed silently. In the middle of the night he kicked her out of bed and she suffered a broken neck, dying shortly thereafter. Carriou, a Parisian night watchman, received a twelve-year prison sentence. He was released after seven years for good behavior and remarried. This time his wife burnt the roast and Carriou screamed, "You cook like a Nazi," stabbing her to death. He received an eight-year prison term.

Most Unusual Rehabilitation Program: In the *Ignorance Book*, Webb Garrison describes a unique rehabilitation program in the Illinois state prison system. With all the controversy over behavior modification in prisons, it is surprising that more people have not heard of Dr. John Pick's facial modification approach. Operating on the theory that a new face makes a new man, Dr. Pick has performed plastic surgery on hundreds of inmates who have requested it. Statistics show that prisoners with new mugs have a much lower recidivism rate than the prison population as a whole.

Most Unusual Rip-off: If you saw *The French Connection*, you have some idea what the "good guys" went through to confiscate all that heroin. The New York Police Department locked nearly $3 million worth away in its vault for use as evidence. When next they bothered to check on the contraband, they found that someone had replaced nearly $1 million worth of the potent white powder with sugar. All signs pointed to an inside job, and as of this writing the process of finding out which of the "good guys" are "bad guys" is still underway.

Most Unusual Traffic Fine: Run a stop-sign in Fargo, North Dakota, and it will cost you *either* a twenty-five-dollar traffic fine *or* a pint of blood. This unusual choice was offered to minor traffic violators in 1974 by municipal court judge Thomas Davies, who figured it was a good way of dealing with a long-standing blood shortage in Fargo. He was somewhat concerned, however, that the unconventional fines "would screw up the courts' bookkeeping."

Most Unusual Traffic Violation: In Jackson, Mississippi, in 1972, police flagged down a car that was zigzagging randomly through traffic and discovered that the driver was blind. He was being directed by a friend in the seat next to him who said he was too drunk to drive himself.

Most Unusual Warrant: During an archaeological dig in the ancient city of Aquila, an engraved copper plate was discovered in an antique marble vase. The first sentence on the plate (found in 1810) in Hebrew characters reads: "Sentence rendered by Pontius Pilate, acting Governor of Lower Galilee, stating that Jesus of Nazareth shall suffer death on the cross." On the back is written: "A similar plate is sent to each tribe." Exactly who had the plates engraved, or what their purpose was, is not known, but what appears to be the death warrant of Jesus is now preserved in the sacristy of the Chartem in Naples.

The Military

Best Weapon: Nippon Oils and Fats Co., Inc., a Japanese firm, has developed a new explosive called Urbanite that demolishes rock, concrete, and steel with little noise and less violence. The explosive is so safe, in fact, that it can be detonated at rush hour in the middle of a busy city without threat to life or limb.

The secret, says a spokesman for the company, is Urbanite's slowness to burn. While the basic ingredient is nitroglycerin, the political terrorist's friend, several "secret ingredients" have been added to reduce its burning speed to about a fourth of dynamite's and the resultant noise to about one-third that of a jackhammer. The price, however, is about four times that of dynamite.

Worst Court-martial: Seabee Leon L. Louie made naval history as the first person ever to be court-martialed for pie throwing. A group of bored sailors at Port Hueneme, California, devised a slapstick plan "to boost morale," and Louie was elected to do the pitching. At the morning muster of the 700-man battalion, Louie dutifully withdrew a chocolate cream from a paper bag and squashed it in the face of Chief Warrant Officer Timothy P. Curtin.

Navy prosecutors didn't think it was funny, and in December 1974 the young Seabee was brought to trial. Louie's attorney called Soupy Sales as an expert for the defense, who testified that he has been on the receiving end of "more than 19,000 (pies) since 1950. It's the thing you can really do to relieve tension without hurting anybody."

Most Humiliating Defeat: It was the law in the Greek city of Amyclae to hold one's tongue. The Amyclaeans had often panicked when they heard rumors that the powerful Spartan army was coming, and to put an end to defeatism, a law was passed forbidding rumors. Violators were to be executed.

When the Spartans actually did appear, no one had the courage to report it, and the city was overcome without a fight.

Worst Intelligence Report: The English of King Harold's day wore their hair cut about shoulder length, and only the priests had shorter locks. Receiving reports that a party of Normans had landed on English soil, Harold sent out a spy to estimate their numbers and the potential threat they posed. When the secret agent observed a thousand close-cropped Norman soldiers, he mistakenly reported to the King that the French had sent an army of priests across the Channel to "chant masses." This miscalculation of William the Conqueror's forces was one factor contributing to Harold's defeat at Hastings.

Worst Military Regulation: In an effort to maintain military discipline "in and out of uniform" during the last days of the American presence in Vietnam, Major Paul M. Boseman, operations officer of the 377th Security Police Squad, issued the following order: "Salute when you recognize an officer, even though you both, officer and non-commissioned officer, are nude."

Most Unusual Aircraft Carrier: During World War II, Geat Britain established what was commonly referred to as "the Department of Bright Ideas" to review suggestions submitted by ordinary citizens for new weapons and other schemes to aid the war effort. Most of the plans were egregiously impractical: perpetual motion machines, a design for a rubber raft the size of England that would float in the North Seat and confuse German pilots, and so on. But Project Habbakuk was different, says astronomer Patrick Moore who screened suggestions for the DBI. The idea was to carve a suitable iceberg off the North Polar cap, blast and bulldoze it into shape, tow it into the English Channel, and use it as an aircraft carrier. Should the iceberg be hit by enemy bombs, one would simply fill the holes with water which would soon freeze back into a level and usable landing strip. This giant effort at ice sculpture was never actually undertaken, but for a while,

Netherlands' army soldiers

Moore says, Project Habbakuk had "the full backing of the War Cabinet."

Most Unusual Army: The army of the Netherlands is like no other. Recently it became the first fully-unionized fighting force in the world, and the aggressive young union, known as the VVDM, has instituted some remarkable changes in military life. The union experiments have made the Dutch army "more humane" or "a laughing stock," depending on whom you listen to.

For one thing, the Dutch army *looks* different. There are few crew cuts among the troops. The union insists on a soldier's being able to wear his hair in any style he pleases; the only requirement is that long-haired men wear hairnets when operating heavy machinery. When out on maneuvers, most recruits have shed those nasty, heavy, combat boots in favor of sneakers.

The union also frowns on saluting—"a strange way of contact between people"—and only on ceremonial occasions is this primitive custom observed. Other innovations include

147

a new abbreviated twelve-month stint of service for draftees, and overtime pay for such undesirable assignments as KP and weekend guard duty. There is one important issue on which the union has yet to develop a position: war. But since the VVDM has close ties with Dutch pacifist organizations, there is little reason to fear that the Netherlands will launch an unprovoked attack on France, Germany, or even Luxemburg.

In charge of this gentle army is the new Socialist Minister of Defense Vredeling (whose name, loosely translated, means "peacenik"). Recently a newspaper reporter spoke to him about the Netherlands's role in NATO: "Frankly I know nothing about it," he said. It seems the Minister had been promised another, more prestigious Cabinet post, and he received the job in the Defense Department as a kind of consolation prize. "And I have an allergy to uniforms," he complained.

Most Unusual Cannon: The *Chemical and Engineering News* recently hailed the development of a pneumatic cannon that can fire dead chickens at speeds up to 620 miles per hour. The National Research Council of Canada devised this unique piece of artillery to test airplane parts likely to be struck by birds. The cannon will accommodate either the standard four-pound chicken, for testing windshields, or the rugged eight-pound bird, for testing tail assemblies. The big gun will also fire synthetic chickens.

Most Unusual Cannonballs: During a naval battle between Brazil and Uruguay in the middle of the nineteenth century, the Uruguayan vessel ran out of shot. Captain Coe, the commander of the ship, ordered the cannons loaded with Dutch cheeses. "They were too old and hard to eat anyway," he reasoned. In a few minutes Coe's ship opened fire again. According to William Walsh, the first two cheeses went sailing over the mark, but finally one crashed into the mainmast of the Brazilian ship, shattering into thousands of pieces. Cheese shrapnel killed two sailors standing near the Brazilian admiral. After taking four or five more cheeses through the sails, the prudent admiral ordered his ship to retire from the engagement.

Most Unusual Cause of a Major War: Militantly Catholic, King Ferdinand of Bohemia vowed to crush the Reformation.

But his repressiveness provoked a revolt, and in 1618, angry Protestant nobles stormed his castle in Prague and hurled two royal councillors from the window. They fell seventy feet to the ground, later claiming that they were saved only because they prayed fervently to the Virgin Mary as they plummetted earthward. However, history records that they survived the fall by landing in a pile of horse excreta. In any event, the Defenestration of Prague was the immediate cause of the Thirty Years' War.

On the minor war level: Grease was the cause of the Sepoy Rebellion, an uprising of colonial troops in India between 1857 and 1858. A rumor that some newly issued cartridges for the regulation Enfield rifles were greased with pig and cow fat touched off a mutiny among Hindu and Moslem soldiers. At that time, rifle shells had to be uncapped in one's mouth, and the mutineers believed that this was a mortal sin, since it violated their religions' dietary laws against eating pork and beef.

Most Unusual Cavalry: Contending they were the "ideal mounts" for the Southwestern cavalry, Jefferson Davis, as Secretary of War under President Pierce, persuaded Congress to authorize $30,000 for the purchase of eighty one-humped camels. A skeptical Lieutenant Edward F. Beale took delivery of the first thirty-four dromedaries at Indianola, Texas, in 1856.

At first the experiment did not go well; horses bolted in terror whenever they saw the strange creatures; soldiers were afraid to ride them. Worse yet, the army hired a Turkish veterinarian as its camel expert, solely on the basis of his Near Eastern ancestry. Having no experience whatsoever with camels, he once tried to cure a sick animal by tickling its nose with a chameleon's tail.

It wasn't long, however, until the camels began to demonstrate their merits. They could carry 1,000-pound loads, travel thirty or forty miles per day, and go without water for six to ten days. Lieutenant Beale was won over by their performance. "My admiration for the camels increases daily with my experience of them," he reported to the War Department. The lieutenant even learned Arabic in case the animals were homesick.

Forty-six more joined the stable in 1857, and the War Department officially declared the experiment a success, asking the Congress for permission to import an additional 1,000 camels for cavalry service. But the government was preoccupied with the threat of civil war, and the noble plan was forgotten.

Most Unusual Cavalry Engagement: In 1794 French General Charles Pichegru led the French revolutionary forces in their invasion of the Netherlands. It was the dead of winter when the French entered Amsterdam. There, Pichegru learned from informers that the Dutch fleet was stationed nearby, off the town of Den Helder. A cavalry brigade was sent north to report exactly on the vessels' whereabouts. Arriving in Den Helder, the French discovered the Dutch ships frozen fast in the bay; urging their horses out on the ice, the French cavalry managed to surround and capture the entire Dutch fleet.

Most Unusual Chemical Warfare: Abandoning their lands before the advancing armies of Pompey the Great, ancient Spaniards left behind great tubs of azalea honey. When the delighted troops discovered the sweet booty, they immediately took to eating great globs of it with their fingers. Soon most of the men were deathly ill, the victims of toxic impurities in the honey. The Spaniards, who had been waiting patiently in the hills, then swooped down on the disabled legions.

Most Unusual Draft Dodger: During the Civil War, Grover Cleveland hired a substitute to fight in his place. It was a common and perfectly legal practice, if something short of heroic. During the presidential campaign of 1884, however, it appeared that the charge of draft dodging might prevent him from ever occupying the White House. Cleveland was saved when it was discovered that his Republican opponent, James Blaine, had also evaded the draft by hiring a substitute.

Most Unusual General: General Richard S. Ewell, who fought gallantly for the Confederacy at Winchester and Gettysburg, sometimes hallucinated that he was a bird. For hours at a time he would sit in his tent softly chirping to himself, and at mealtimes he would accept only sunflower seeds or a few grains of wheat.

Most Unusual Intelligence Operation: In his fascinating book *Of Spies and Stratagems,* Stanley P. Lovell, the wartime director of research and development for the OSS, describes how the leaders of the intelligence community planned to wage glandular warfare against Adolf Hitler. In the midst of World War II, the OSS commissioned a wide-ranging study of the health and habits of the Führer. Among other interesting findings, the report suggested that Hitler was not so virile as he would have liked the world to believe. In fact, in Lovell's words, Hitler was "close to the male-female line. A push to the female side might make his mustache fall out and his voice become soprano." This, the OSS believed, would destroy his charismatic appeal for the German people, drive him from office, and bring a more reasonable leader to power.

To give Hitler that little push, the OSS hoped to capitalize on his well-known fondness for vegetables. They bribed his personal gardener to inject large quantities of estrogen into carrots headed for the Führer's table. But, alas, this ingenious (not to say absurd) "destabilization program" failed. Lovell speculates that either Hitler's official tasters noticed something funny in the carrots or, more likely, the gardener was a double-crosser who kept the bribe and threw away the hormones.

Most Unusual Lieutenant Colonel: The Portuguese army honored Anthony, its patron saint, by bestowing upon him the honorary rank of lieutenant colonel. (One wonders what Saint Anthony could have done to make major general.)

Most Unusual Pilot: Russian scientists were looking into the possibility of training cats to pilot air-to-air missiles in 1970. Their research was presumably based on a B. F. Skinner proposal to use pigeons as bombardiers that the noted behaviorist had offered to the United States Navy during World War II.

This isn't to suggest that the military conscription of animals was unheard of before Skinner. Earlier in the war, a Swedish scientist had developed a program for training baby seals to plant mine charges on ships. The seals fared better as frogmen than cats would later fare as airplane pilots for, as Skinner has noted, felines get airsick quite easily. Aware of this complication, the Soviet researchers have also considered using the severed brain of a cat in the pilot's seat rather than the whole animal.

Most Unusual Siege: Nothing was sacred to King Cambyses I of Persia. Herodotus speaks of him "opening ancient tombs and examining the dead bodies." The lowest blow of all occurred when Cambyses laid siege to the Egyptian city of Memphis in the sixth century B.C. The Persian knew that Egyptians held cats to be sacred. (Perhaps he learned this in the tombs; see also *Most Unusual Auction.*) He ordered his troops to gather up all the cats they could find, and then heave them over the walls of the city. The horrified defenders immediately surrendered rather than risk further injury to the animals.

Most Unusual Submarine: Leonardo da Vinci was quite willing to put aside his painting and anatomical studies and apply his genius to military engineering when called upon by the pope or his patron Ludovico Sforza. A few of his inventions may have been put to use on the battlefield, but many, including his designs for tanks, diving suits, helicopters, and parachutes never got off the drawing board even though they were technically promising.

Of all his machines of war, Leonardo was most enthusiastic about his design for a submarine. The idea was simple: He sketched a small boat propelled by a pedallike apparatus that could handle a crew of one or two. The submariners would sneak up on enemy vessels and use a large drill device to bore holes below the water line of their wooden hulls, sending the foes to Davy Jones's locker. Indications are that he was well on his way to developing a unique system for delivering air to his crew. At least he was excited enough about the process to scribble a cryptic note to himself (Da Vinci usually wrote from right to left) to "choose a simple youth" as his assistant in making a scale model—a dolt who would be unable to leak, or even comprehend, the secret.

Ultimately, however, Leonardo abandoned the project, apparently on humanitarian grounds. He was reluctant to make his design known to politicians "on account of the evil nature of men." Although Leonardo felt the submarine could morally be used against the infidel Turks, he feared that once it was in the possession of the doge of Venice or the pope they might also turn it against their European enemies. This prospect was intolerable to Leonardo, who felt that drowning was far too horrible a death to bring upon any Christian.

In order for any submarine to cruise underwater, it must carry a certain amount of ballast. In its day, the USN *Trout* transported some fabulous dead weight. It was February 1941 and the *Trout* had finished unloading its cargo of munitions and supplies on embattled Corregidor. Ordinarily the

152

crew would have made up for lost weight by taking on gravel, but with the Japanese pressing their offensive, gravel was urgently needed for the construction of fortifications. The navy was faced with a problem.

Then someone suggested gold; compact, heavy, and easily loaded, it would make ideal ballast. The Philippine government and private mining companies were anxious to move their assets out of the country for safe keeping, and after some hasty negotiations the crew of the *Trout* began loading the hold with 583 gold bars, valued at $9 million. For additional weight, eighteen tons of silver pesos, worth over $300,000 were brought on board, as well as crates and trunks filled with negotiable securities.

Weighted down with a cargo worthy of the Spanish galleons, the *Trout* fought its way back across the Pacific and safely delivered every glittering brick to authorities in San Francisco.

Most Unusual Uniform: On the battlefield during the Mexican War, General Zachary Taylor wore a "hickory shirt," made of heavy twilled cotton with blue pin stripes, a civilian sack-cloth coat, and a straw hat. At the opposite extreme, and equally in violation of army regulations, was George Armstrong Custer, of last stand fame, who often wore a dandy blue velvet uniform.

Most Unusual War: We mention two ridiculous wars, but there are certainly others. In 1739 Captain Jenkins insisted that the members of the British Parliament examine a jar containing what he claimed was his ear. According to Jenkins, a Spanish scoundrel had removed it with a saber. While some historians have challenged Jenkins's story, there was no doubt that he *had* lost his ear somewhere, so the British fought the War of Jenkins's Ear. Fortunately, no one else could work up as much enthusiasm over the ear as Jenkins, and the war came to an early end after a few inconclusive naval battles.

One of the briefest wars on record was the skirmish between Honduras and El Salvador in 1969. The two nations had been engaged in an ongoing border dispute and had broken diplomatic relations with one another. However, the immediate cause of the war was El Salvador's 3–0 victory over Honduras in the World Cup soccer playoffs. The two sides exchanged fire for about thirty minutes before cooler heads prevailed.

Most Unusual Weapons: In 1972, the Committee to Re-elect the President assembled thousands of "Democracy kits" to be dropped over North Vietnam in a renewed effort at winning the hearts and minds of the people. The kits consisted of diamond pins and handsome pen-and-pencil sets—the latter decorated with the presidential seal and the signature of Richard Nixon—of the sort presented to generous political contributors. They had been left over from the campaign.

On a smaller scale, a group calling itself the Aliens of America sent postcards to all nine Supreme Court justices in 1974, concealing a tiny packet of nerve gas beneath each stamp. No injuries were reported.

Also, scientists in Great Britain have developed an antiriot device that emits sound and light waves which produce vomiting, nausea, and epileptic convulsions.

Most Unusual Weapon (Ancient): A man named Callimachus defended Constantinople against the naval assaults of the Saracens with a substance called "Greek fire." The mysterious concoction, probably containing naphtha, sulphur, and pitch, could be extinguished only with wine or vinegar—water made it spread. Invented in the seventh century, it was extremely effective, and several times saved Constantinople for the Greeks. The ingredients were a closely guarded secret for 400 years, but finally the Mohammedans duplicated the formula. Greek fire continued in use until the advent of gunpowder.

Archimedes, the great Greek scientist and mathematician, is said to have invented a mirror that focused sunlight on the sails of the Roman fleet, causing them to burst into flames. The ingenious machine could not save the city, however, and Archimedes died in the sack of Syracuse (212 B.C.).

Finally, in a war against the Greeks in ancient times, Jewish soldiers were armed with very stale potato pancakes to hurl at enemy infantrymen.

Most Unusual Weapon of the Future: The navy has disappointedly abandoned its top-secret Project Aquadog. The goal of that hush-hush research had been to teach dogs to swim underwater and attack enemy frogmen. But apparently navy scientists are going ahead with experiments to establish the feasibility of using dolphins to retrieve spent torpedoes that have missed their mark.

Most Unusual Women's Corps: Women now play an active role in the armed forces of Israel and other nations, but in the 1800s this was unthinkable. Thus the "Army of Wives" makes the rebellion of T'ien-wang all the more unusual.

T'ien-wang was a religious fanatic who believed he had a holy mission to overthrow idolatry. No ascetic holy man, he had a harem of thirty wives, and many of his followers were also polygamists. When the fighting got tough, the wives of T'ien-wang's sect were formed into a women's militia commanded by women officers. Altogether, half a million women garrisoned the city of Nanking in 1853. The Army of Wives held the city until 1864 when the uprising was finally crushed by the central government. In a cinematic conclusion, T'ien-wang committed suicide amid the flames of the palace he had usurped.

Religion

Best Grace: Oliver Cromwell, the Puritan Lord Protector of England, often said this prayer before dinner: "Some people have food, but no appetite; some people have an appetite, but no food. I have both. The Lord be praised!"

Best Shrine: The Kailasantha shrine of Ellora, India, was once just an ordinary mountainside. Throughout the eighth and ninth centuries, sculptors cut away the exterior rock, leaving a beautiful temple—built from the top down. A wonder of advanced planning, the pillars, statues, ornaments, and foundation had to be anticipated practically from the first cut.

Worst Church: The All Saints Church of Sedlac, Czechoslovakia, was looted of all its fine ornaments in 1600. Undeterred, the worshippers of Sedlac set about redecorating their house of worship with human bones. They exhumed the remains of nearly 10,000 people for what is surely the most macabre interior in all of Christendom. The highlights are a bony chandelier, made predominantly of femurs, and hundreds of skulls piled in the shape of the Schwarzenberk family crest. *Fodor's Czechoslovakia* calls it a "ghastly fascination."

Worst Crucifix: The commercialization of Christ offers endless potential for human debasement. The worst crucifix we've ever seen is sold in Venice and features a plastic Jesus glued by his Roman captors to a cross of colored seashells. A milk chocolate cross sold at Easter time in the United States runs a very close second and is our undisputed favorite as the *tastiest* crucifix ever marketed, filled to its hollow center with real chocolaty goodness—an Easter-time treat for the whole family.

Bone chandelier in All Saints Church, Sedlac, Czechoslovakia

Worst Deity: If you are smitten by the red-robed bitch goddess Shitala, the best you can do is get plenty of bed rest, pray fervently, and don't pick the scabs. The most dreaded deity in Indian mythology, Shitala is said to ride through the countryside atop a donkey, thrashing her victims with reeds until their bodies are covered with purulent, running sores.

157

The victims all go delirious with pain and die within a few days.

Shitala is the goddess of smallpox.

Worst Miracle: In Bombay, India, in 1966, a Hindu yogi named Rao announced his intention to walk on water. Six hundred prominent members of Bombay society were invited to witness the spectacle, with tickets going for as high as $100 each.

Garbed in flowing robes, the snowy bearded mystic stood majestically on the side of a five-foot deep pond, prayed silently, and then stepped boldly into the void. He sank immediately to the bottom.

Worst Pope: Boniface VIII may have been the most impious pope. He once said that a man has about as much chance of enjoying life after death as "a roast fowl on the dining table." If his metaphysics were in error, Boniface is surely occupying the position deep in Hell that Dante assigned him.

For wickedness and incompetence, however, no pope can quite compare with John XII, a man whom Church scholar E. R. Chamberlin called "the Christian Caligula." A member of the outrageous Theophylact line, John served both as religious leader of the Western Church and temporal ruler of Rome. To maintain his power he recruited armed gangs from among the Roman mob and terrorized the honest citizenry. He was an avid gambler who constantly invoked the names of foul demons to bring him luck, and as Chamberlin documents "his sexual hunger was insatiable." He depleted the wealth of the papacy by giving away Church lands and holy relics to his favorite mistresses, and it is not an exaggeration to say that he turned the Lateran into a brothel. There may even have been truth to the charge that he was a rapist.

As a moral leader, John couldn't have been worse, and he was no better at politics. He enlisted the support of Otto I, the king of Germany, against Italy's King Berengar II; soon, however, he double-crossed Otto, and the German promptly conquered Rome, called a synod to depose John, and installed the antipope Leo VIII. In 964 John regained power only to be murdered within the year.

Worst Shrine: The president of Toyota Motors in Japan is planning a shrine that promises to be somewhat less than sublime. He has set aside $445,000 to erect an edifice to honor the souls of persons killed in Toyotas throughout the world.

Worst Synod: The Council of Constance, convened from 1414 to 1418, removed the scandalous Pope John XXIII from office and was supposed to institute a general house-cleaning.

John XXIII was accused of poisoning his predecessor and then bribing his way into office. Before the council finished its investigation, they had also charged him with atheism, adultery, and incest. John was later declared an antipope, but no prelate would take his soiled title until the saintly Angelo Giuseppe Roncalli chose to be called John XXIII in 1958.

As far as the council was concerned, they were hardly in a position to cast the first stone. Gebhard Dacher, a con-temporary chronicler, reported that there were 18,000 priests, 83 wine merchants, 346 clowns, dancers, and jugglers, and 700 harlots in attendance. Another source places the number of harlots at closer to 1,500.

Worst Theological Dispute: Whenever artists set out to de-pict Adam and Eve in their innocence, they run into a theo-logical problem that has been acrimoniously debated for centuries. The subject of this ongoing controversy was "that tortuosity or complicated nodosity we usually call the Navell," as Sir Thomas Browne put it in 1646. Browne contended that since Adam and Eve were created and not born, they should be portrayed with smooth, unindented abdomens. Then, in 1752 Dr. Christian Tobias Ephraim Reinhard published the definitive work on the issue—*Untersuchung der Frage: Ob unsere ersten Uraltern, Adam und Eve, einen Nabel gehabt (Examination on the Question: Whether Our First Ancestors, Adam and Eve, Possessed a Navel).* Dr. Reinhard argues the pros and cons interminably, siding ultimately with the anti-navel forces.

In actual practice, artists vacillated for many years, and an examination of Adam and Eve portraits from the Middle Ages and Early Renaissance shows some with and some without. By Reinhard's time, however, the immaculate stomach was a hopeless cause. On the Sistine ceiling Michel-angelo boldly asserted the legitimacy of picturing the um-bilicus and greatly influenced subsequent navel tradition. In his incomparable panel of Adam receiving the spark of life from the fingertip of Jehovah, the new creation sports an inny belly button.

The navel controversy was unexpectedly revived in 1944 by the House Military Affairs Committee. Representative Durham, a North Carolina Democrat, loudly opposed distribution of a government pamphlet entitled *The Races of Mankind* to American servicemen, ostensibly because in some of the illustrations "Adam and Eve are depicted with navels," an insult to fundamentalists everywhere. There were, however, some cynics who maintained that the congressman was really more concerned about a statistical table in the pamphlet showing that the average IQ for blacks in some Northern states was higher than the average for Southern whites.

Most Unusual Biblical Essay: In 1663 a noted orientalist presented to the French Academy a paper in which he concluded that Adam was 140 feet tall, Noah, 50 feet tall, Abraham, 40 feet tall, and Moses, 25.

Most Unusual Church: The largest active salt mine in the world is located in Zipaquirá, Colombia. Contained within the mine, 800 feet deep in the mountainside, is the great Salt Cathedral. Never has there been a place of worship so magnificent and so earth-bound. The three main corridors, with ceilings arching 73 feet high, supported by columns of solid salt, took six years to excavate. The sanctuary seats nearly 5,000 people.

Most Unusual Communion: When Lord Strothallan, a Jacobite hero, received a mortal wound at the Battle of Culloden Field, on April 15, 1745, a priest administered the last rites and offered him a Eucharist of whiskey and oatcake, there being no bread and water available. (A less romantic source agrees that it was oatcake, but insists that Strothallan washed it down with water.)

Most Unusual Deity: Known as "that fat boy" among the holymen of the Upper Ganges, Guru Maharaj Ji claims to be a true avatar—a living incarnation of God. One of the sixteen-year-old perfect master's devotees is the antiwar leader Rennie Davis, who was quoted as saying, "I would cross the planet on my hands and knees to touch his toe."

Apparently even a deity must suffer the vicissitudes of

modern life. His physician reports that the young guru has a duodenal ulcer, and in Detroit Maharaj Ji endured the indignity of a nonbeliever smacking him in the face with a shaving cream pie. But then there are the good things in a god's life: the $100,000 town house in London, the Telex machines, the private jets and yachts and his recent marriage to an airline stewardess, to mention just a few. Perhaps the highlight of this incarnation came at the Houston Astrodome in the fall of 1973 when Maharaj Ji kicked off the "Millennium," billed as "the most holy and significant event in human history."

Abbie Hoffman is not so fond of the guru as his fellow Chicago Seven defendant. "If the Guru Maharaj Ji is God," he groused, "he's the kind of God America deserves."

Most Unusual Devotional Book: A book published in Oliver Cromwell's time bore the title: *The Spiritual Mustard Pot, To Make the Soul Sneeze with Devotion.*

Most Unusual Exorcism: The Hittite people of the Middle East practiced an unusual form of political exorcism. As they prepared to lay siege to a city, the warriors invited the enemy gods to come over and join the Hittite pantheon. They were not beyond a little bribery, too: The Hittites set up large vats of beer as an enticement to undecided deities and even strung red, white, and blue streamers from the city walls to show the turncoat gods the way to the free brew.

Most Unusual Heretics: The Ophites were an early Christian sect who felt that the temptation of Eve brought knowledge and revolt into the world, and hence was a positive rather than a sinful event. Therefore the Ophites highly revered serpents and thought the Devil was all right, too. They required that the bread of the Eucharist be licked by serpents before serving it to communicants.

Another heretical group, the Cataphiggians, were followers of a man named Montanus. While praying, they made it a habit of putting their index and middle fingers in their nostrils, as a symbolic gesture of faith.

Most Unusual Hermit: In the *Decline and Fall of the Roman Empire,* Gibbon recounts the life of Simeon Stylites, a Syrian shepherd who became an anchorite monk. After his novitiate, during which he repeatedly had to be rescued from "pious suicide," Simeon chained himself to the top of a column 60 feet high. There he remained for the rest of his life—through thirty summers and winters—a record that no flagpole sitter ever approached. To while away the decades, Simeon prayed a great deal and did sit-ups.

Most Unusual Pilgrimage: In her prayers Catherine de Medici asked a favor of the Lord, and when that favor was granted she made good on her promise to send a pilgrim to Jerusalem. But Catherine had asked for a big favor, and the pilgrimage she promised in return was not an ordinary one. She said that for every three steps forward her appointed representative would take one step backward. The man she hired did just that all the way from France to the Holy Land. For his service he was made a nobleman.

Most Unusual Pope: Over seventy historians of the papacy have insisted that a woman—Pope Joan—served for two and a half years after the death of Leo IV (855) and before Benedict III came to power. As a young girl, Joan fell in love with a less-than-celibate priest in Athens who tutored her in Latin and theology as well as romance. Her aptitude for these subjects was so astounding that she decided to pose as a man and make a career of her own in the Church. From Athens she moved to Rome, distinguishing herself for her learning and her ability to survive the rough and tumble Church politics of the ninth century. When Leo died, the unsuspecting synod elected her pope. Little is known about her actions in office, although it seems that at least one of her colleagues discovered that she was a woman. In 857, as she was entering the Lateran Church, Joan went into labor and died.

It is a great story, and several years ago Hollywood made an atrocious movie out of it starring Liv Ullmann. The only problem is that despite the word of seventy historians of the papacy, Pope Joan almost certainly never existed. No contemporary source mentions her reign, and the myth seems to have originated with a single monastic document written centuries later that shows the name Joan inserted with a caret between the names of Leo and Benedict in a roster of the popes. After the Reformation a number of Protestant propagandists gleefully latched onto the story, embellished it, and reported it as gospel—confounding reputable historians for several centuries.

In *The Bad Popes* E. R. Chamberlin does mention a woman who controlled the selection of the pope and influenced his decisions, although she did not wield power directly. Marozia was the lady's name and she had a reputation for sensuality and a penchant for Roman mob politics. As the most powerful figure in the house of Theophylact, she arranged for the election of her son, Pope Leo VI. With Leo as a figurehead, Marozia controlled the Church and the city of Rome for seven tumultuous months in 926. It is possible that the true stories about Marozia, exaggerated by successive generations of gossips, are one source of the Pope Joan legend.

Most Unusual Relic: In 1247 Emperor Baldwin II sent to Saint Louis a small vial purportedly containing a few drops of milk from the breast of the Virgin. Nearly thirty European churches have claimed to have similar relics.

Most Unusual Religious Allegory: The seventeenth century in England gave rise to some of the most imaginative religious writing ever produced, including such allegorical essays as "Eggs of Charity, Layed by the Chickens of the Covenant and Boiled with the Water of the Divine: Take Ye and Eat," "Spiritual Milk for Babes, drawn out of the Breasts of both Testaments for their Souls' Nourishment: A Catechism," and "High-heeled Shoes for Dwarfs in Holiness." Perhaps the most bizarre was "A Wordless Book." While devoid of words, the book is not without its message: there are eight pages, the first two of which are black, the second two red, the next two white, and the last two gold. They symbolize, in succession, the evil of man, his redemption, the purity of his soul, "washed in the blood of the Lamb," and finally, eternal bliss.

Most Unusual Steeple: Billy Graham and members of the Jesus movement frequently flash the "one way" sign—the right hand raised with the index finger pointed heavenward. Though the specific symbolism is new, the gesture has been a favorite as long as there have been pulpits. An especially well-liked preacher of the First Presbyterian Church in Port Gibson, Mississippi, frequently used that very gesture over 120 years ago. In 1859, the communicants of First Presbyterian erected a steeple in his memory, and on top, instead of a cross, they placed a cast hand with the index finger pointing up.

Psychology

Best Idiot Savant: Tom Wiggins was a feebleminded fellow from Georgia with the uncanny ability to imitate any piano performance after hearing it only a single time. His keyboard work was identical to that of the master he copied, down to the subtleties of interpretation. Following the Civil War, Wiggins toured Europe, performing before enthusiastic crowds. Gradually, however, his talent began to fade.

A similar phenomenon was Kyoshi Yamashita, a very popular Japanese artist, who was totally unable to care for himself and depended on his government-appointed guardians. More than once, Yamashita was found half-naked in the streets, unaware of his own home or name. But his art shows no signs of his mental deficiency.

Best Madman: Not all lunatics are dribbling, unproductive wastrels who do nothing but talk to themselves on the subway and frighten people. Colin Martindale of the University of Maine studied the lives of fifty-two French and English poets recently and found that nearly half of them were psychotic and 15 percent were psychopaths. Percy Shelley, for example, hallucinated frequently and was haunted by visions of a man attacking him with a revolver. (The man in his fantasies could have been the equally unbalanced Lord Byron, who was a textbook paranoid and always carried a pistol with him.) John Keats often alarmed his friends with alternating fits of weeping and hysterical laughter, and the nineteenth-century French poet Édouard Joachim Corbière spent much of his time constructing scale-model ships and then destroying them.

Most Unusual Anal Compulsive: According to the catty Miss Gertrude Stein, the tidy French poet Guillaume Apollinaire always made love on an overstuffed chair because he did not want to mess up his ever-so-neatly-made bed.

Most Unusual Cure for Kleptomania: If you're a storeowner beleaguered by shoplifters, the people at Rent-a-Thief Canada, Ltd., a Toronto-based firm, may have the remedy you've been looking for. For $100 a day, they'll send over one of their carefully screened and trained free-lance thieves (who are mostly students and out-of-work actors) who will go through the motions of filching merchandise and getting caught and berated publicly while he's unceremoniously hauled off to the store office and the police are called. Says Les Cohen, general manager of Rent-a-Thief, "The whole thing is a put-up to show everyone present what's in store for shoplifters." The company is a subsidiary of College Marketing and Research, Ltd.

For the kleptomaniacs among us: Lady Cork (1746–1840) was wealthy enough to indulge her kleptomania without ever having to fear a prison sentence or a trip to Bedlam. Whenever she "shopped" at a London store, the proprietor would routinely assign a clerk to make notes of the items she swiped. When Lady Cork returned from a visit to friends, the maid went through her Ladyship's handbag and returned all the valuables she did not recognize. Once she filched a pet hedgehog from a neighbor and stowed it in the bottom of her carriage. Soon discovering that the prickly little animal made an uncomfortable traveling companion, she traded him to a baker for a sponge cake. "A hedgehog," she said, "is just what you need to rid your bakery of black beetles." The baker had no black beetles, but he was a man of principle and never turned down a hedgehog proffered by a Lady.

Most Unusual Delusion of Grandeur: In his prime Wilhelm Steinitz was one of the world's most brilliant chess players, but as he grew older he slowly went insane and was enslaved by the delusion that he could make telephone calls without a telephone and move chess pieces from one square to another without touching them. He possessed, he claimed, a unique ability to emit electric signals from his fingertips that could move objects.

Steinitz also claimed to be on speaking terms with God, and in one Icarian burst of *chutzpah*, he challenged God publicly to a game of chess. Worse yet, he offered Him a one-pawn handicap!

Most Unusual Erogenous Zone: According to Freud, the human nose contains tissue which becomes erect when sexually stimulated.

Most Unusual Fantasy: Apparently even those who are constantly called upon to make speeches must deal with butterflies in their stomachs. Winston Churchill found that a simple fantasy helped him to conquer his stage fright. Whenever he stood before a crowd, he tried to imagine that every man and woman he was addressing had a hole in his sock.

President Eisenhower is said to have taken his fantasies one step further and formed a mental picture of his audience sitting before him as naked as worms.

Most Unusual Foot Fetish: Probably the most unusual was the Chinese practice of binding girls' feet in early childhood. Bound feet became a symbol of sexual oppression.

According to a *Life* magazine article, the ancient Greeks had a gentler fetish. They considered a longer second toe aristocratic—a longer first toe, base and plebian.

Most Unusual Phobias: Mercifully, psychiatrists have not given names to every fear troubling mankind. Perhaps the most unusual phobia with a name of its own is amaxophobia, the fear of riding in vehicles. Other unlikely aversions include skokophobia (fear of spies) and triakaideaphobia (dread of the number 13).

Thomas Hobbes was afraid of the dark and always slept with a lighted lamp.

Degas suffered from nausea whenever he was in the presence of flowers or perfume.

Napoleon, whose name seems to pop up frequently in these pages, suffered from aelurophobia (the fear of cats). Once in the Palace of Schönbrunn his aide-de-camp heard a great ruckus in the general's chamber. He entered to find "mon commandant" half-dressed, lunging with his saber at a terrified kitten cowering behind a wall hanging. King Henry III of France was another swashbuckling political leader who felt faint at the very sight of a cat.

Erasmus, the Dutch scholar and humanist, came down with a fever anytime he smelled fish.

While perhaps not a phobia in the clinical sense, Winston Churchill's professed dislike of toilet seats was certainly a full-blown aversion. At his home in Hyde Park Gate, London, all of the toilets for house guests were equipped with seats, but Sir Winston's personal commode had none. When a plumber suggested that one be installed, Sir Winston answered testily, "I have no need of such things."

(For His Royal Highness Prince Philip, the Royal Consort, the superfluity of toilet seats is as nothing when compared to the unjustified extravagance of modern plumbing in general. "This is the biggest waste of water in the country by far," he once said. "You spend half a pint and flush two gallons.")

Most Unusual Psychological Test: *Link,* a weekly newspaper published in New Delhi, India, quoted color specialist Max Luscher as saying that a person may offer clues about his *real* personality and innermost feelings by the way he adjusts his color television set. If he makes the picture too red, says Luscher, he is probably too lustful; if he makes it too blue, he overeats; too yellow, he is too hopeful. A picture too dominated by magenta may indicate homosexuality.

Health and Death

Best Anesthetic: You're going to have a nose job, an event for which you've been readying yourself emotionally for years, but a disagreement with your doctor threatens to mar the joy of it all. He would like you awake during the operation and thus wants to administer a local anesthetic. You, on the other hand, find the thought of hearing your own cartilage and bone being chipped, sliced, and hacked less than appetizing; you'd prefer to sleep through it all.

It's a common dilemma, and one that may be resolved in the near future by a drug called Lorazepam. Developed by anesthesiologists David Heisterkamp and Peter Cohen, of the University of Colorado Medical School, Lorazepam deadens sensation locally while the patient remains awake. However, it also induces postoperative amnesia, permanently blocking the patient from ever remembering the process.

Best Blood Donor: As of September 1974, sixty-one-year-old Joseph Kerkovsky, of Moline, Illinois, had donated 189 pints of blood—that's a bit under twenty-four gallons, or more than a Chevrolet gas tank will hold—since World War II, at hospitals and Red Cross chapters.

Best Cure for Cramps: Queen Victoria's physicians prescribed *Cannabis* (marijuana) for the relief of her menstrual pains.

Best Cure for Hiccups: There are scads of folk remedies for the hiccups: a sudden fright, standing on your head, breathing into a paper bag, holding your breath, drinking ten swallows of water, or inhaling and exhaling like a panting dog. In severe cases doctors may prescribe strong tranquilizers. But alas, all these sure-fire cures only work for some of the people some of the time, and thus we are pleased to report that Dr. Edgar Engleman of the University of California

Medical Center in San Francisco has hit upon a highly reliable hiccup medicine—a teaspoonful of sugar swallowed dry.

Dr. Engleman first encountered this bit of folk pharmacy when the host of a party he attended recommended a dose of sugar for Engleman's hiccupping wife. Her hiccups stopped immediately. This inspired a series of carefully controlled laboratory experiments in which Dr. Engleman tested the sugar remedy on two groups of hiccuppers. The first group was composed of seventeen people who had been suffering from this dread affliction for only a few hours; upon swallowing a spoonful of sugar, fifteen immediately overcame their glottal contractions. The second sad group was made up of chronic hiccuppers who were in the midst of attacks that had lasted anywhere from eighteen hours to six weeks. Sugar provided immediate relief for twelve out of twenty-two in this group, and additional doses suppressed the hiccups of four more.

Dr. Engleman theorizes that sugar irritates the nerves at the back of the throat, counteracting the hiccup reflex. Salt, sand, or any gritty substance would be equally effective, but most people find sugar the most palatable.

Best Dying Words: The most comprehensive guide to dying utterances that we have seen is *Famous Last Words* compiled by Barnaby Conrad. In an introduction to this book, Clifton Fadiman singles out his favorite, "Though I have weighed many curtain lines, the perfect one still seems to me Lady Mary Wortley Montagu's 'It has all been very interesting.' " (Lady Montagu, 1689–1762, was an English wit, letter writer, and victim of Alexander Pope's satires.)

Henry David Thoreau also died with grace. When a friend, attending him at his death bed, asked whether he believed in an afterlife, Thoreau replied, "One world at a time." Then, shortly afterward, he spoke two final, dreamy words: "Moose . . . Indian." The tombstone over his grave in Concord, Massachusetts, bears the concise epitaph, "Henry."

We mention three other notable candidates here, although there are certainly many others that are deserving.

As Gertrude Stein lay dying, she hoped for some foreknowledge of the Beyond. Over and over again she asked, "What is the answer? What is the answer?" When Alice B. Toklas and the others gathered around her remained silent, Miss Stein suddenly sat up in bed and called out, "What is the question?" then fell back dead.

169

Not long before his fatal collapse, Dylan Thomas sat drinking in a New York bar celebrating his thirty-ninth birthday and the success of his *Collected Poems*. A friend recalled his last boast: "I've had eighteen straight whiskeys. I think that's the record."

Finally, we mention William Palmer (1824–1856) who is far less well known, and deservedly so; he was hanged for poisoning his best friend. As he stepped out on the shaky gallows trap, he looked nervously at the executioner and asked, "Are you sure it's safe?"

Worst Cure for Hiccups: In *English Eccentrics*, Dame Edith Sitwell relates the woeful history of Squire John Mytton (1796–1834). Mytton took to drink at age ten and for many years he downed eight quarts of port a day. Because of his tremendous capacity for alcohol, his friend and biographer Nimrod dubbed him "Mango, the King of the Pickles." Constantly tipsy, Mytton was forever falling off his horse, racing his carriage recklessly through the streets, even riding on a brown bear in a mood of drunken hilarity. And like many heavy drinkers, Mytton occasionally suffered from the hiccups.

Nimrod describes one dizzy evening when Squire Mytton tried a novel but unfortunate cure. " 'Damn the hiccup,' said Mytton as he stood undressed on the floor, apparently in the act of getting into bed, 'but I'll frighten it away.' So seizing a lighted candle, he applied it to the tab of his shirt, and, it being a cotton one, he was instantly enveloped in flames." Two servants, hearing his shouts, rushed into the room, tore the fiery nightshirt from his back, and smothered the flames. Mytton was painfully burned, but before falling into bed he managed to observe that "the hiccup is gone, by God."

Worst Disease: The Foré tribe of New Guinea is afflicted by epidemics of kuru, a very rare disease characterized by trembling, dizziness, and a gradual decline into insanity. At one stage of the illness, the victim is subject to fits of excessive laughter, and in fact kuru is sometimes referred to as "the laughing death." As far as doctors have been able to ascertain, there is only one way that the slow virus that causes kuru can be transmitted from one person to another— by eating portions of infected brains. The Foré are one of the few tribes in New Guinea still practicing ritual cannibalism of their own dead.

Worst Doctor: For a mere $1,500 Dr. John R. Brinkley of Kansas would implant young goat glands in men who were feeling their age. According to Brinkley, the effects were miraculous; his patients supposedly enjoyed a return of their youthful energy and a sexual renaissance. (And there was no problem with bleating or other side effects.) It was a sore disappointment when patients discovered that goat glands were about as effective as Dr. Brinkley's own patent medicine—a mixture of blue dye and hydrochloric acid.

But quacks do not need results. Good public relations and a little help from the placebo effect has made many a charlatan rich, and Brinkley did well enough to buy his own high-powered radio station in Mexico, along with limousines, yachts, and a private plane. In fact, his popularity was so great that he ran for governor of Kansas three times, once narrowly losing to Alf Landon. True to form, Brinkley's politics were as bad as his medicine. He was the sugardaddy of the Silver Shirts, who, though better dressed, shared the philosophy of Germany's Brown Shirts.

Worst Epitaph: Pity the poor woman doomed to eternal sleep beneath this epitaph in an East Hartford, Connecticut cemetery:

> Hark! she bids all her friends adieu;
> An angel calls her to the spheres;
> Our eyes the radiant sun pursue
> Through liquid telescopes of tears.

However, this inscription found on a gravestone in a churchyard in Kent, England, is even worse:

> The wedding day appointed was
> And wedding clothes provided.
> But ere the day did come, alas!
> He sickened and he die did.

Worst Hemorrhoids: An article published in *The Wall Street Journal* on August 10, 1973, offers hindsight on the Battle of Waterloo. An overlooked factor in the French defeat was the health of Napoleon Bonaparte. According to medical historian Rudolph Marx, the emperor spent much of the day resting in his tent, laid low by an excruciating case of swollen hemorrhoids. Lack of sleep and opium administered by his physicians left him too groggy to mount his horse and take advantage of a breach in Wellington's flank.

Worst Operation: Japanese women are caught between two worlds. On the one hand there is the liberated life-style of the cities and universities and on the other there is the traditional, conservative sexual ethic which makes Victorianism seem like swinging sin. Many Japanese men would not consider marrying a woman who was not a virgin, but fortunately, modern medical science has come up with a way for an experienced young woman to return to the state of innocence. In only half an hour, and for the modest price of $150, Japanese plastic surgeons will create a new hymen. Thousands of *jinko shojo* (artificial virgin) operations are performed each year.

Americans need not titter: In 1973, at least 300 men and women in this country received lipectomies of the buttocks—also known as bottom lifts.

Worst Remedy for a Sore Throat: Repeated X-ray treatments for cancer of the larynx rendered Robert Hopkirk's throat more sensitive than if it had been trampled by a herd of elephants wearing cleated shoes. Unable to swallow easily, he now lives on seventy-two raw eggs a week—and nothing else.

Hopkirk, a retired painter from Sydney, Australia, estimated in January 1975, that he had consumed over 4,500 eggs since beginning the treatment two years earlier. "It's a bit monotonous," he said, "but I feel great."

Worst Seasickness: By way of excuse for Napoleon (see also *Worst Hemorrhoids*), it has been reported that Lord Nelson was seasick at the Battle of Trafalgar.

Worst Suicide: A forty-year-old man in Biella, Italy, set himself afire and then, experiencing a sudden change of heart, threw himself to the ground and rolled around on the grass in an attempt to extinguish the flames. Onlookers gasped as he rolled off a cliff and fell to his death.

Worst Suture: When Honduran Indians receive a severe wound, they close it with live soldier-parasol ants. Each ant

172

is held up to the laceration; it bites down, drawing the edges of the flesh together. This process is repeated as many times as is necessary to stop the bleeding. Once the ants have locked their jaws, the patient breaks off their bodies. The heads remain in place and will not relax their hold until the wound is healed and the formic stitches are cut out with a knife.

Most Unusual Autopsy: André Bazile, a French convict from Nantes serving as a galley slave, died September 10, 1774 after complaining of violent stomach cramps. When an autopsy was performed with fifty incredulous medical students in attendance, the coroner discovered in the stomach of the deceased a knife, pewter spoons, buttons, and miscellaneous pieces of glass, iron, and wood. (In his report, the coroner concluded that "it must have been something he ate.")

Most Unusual Birth Control Campaign: In Budapest they control the pigeon population by mixing birth control chemicals with birdseed.

Most Unusual Cemetery: If one wishes to rest in peace alongside the greats, he should arrange to be buried in Père-Lachaise Cemetery. Chopin is interred in the high-class Paris boneyard and so are Wilde, Balzac, Rossini, Daumier, Corot, Molière, Sarah Bernhardt, and Bizet. But if we could express a personal preference, it would be to be buried next to Rin Tin Tin. Yes, Rinny is there beneath a stone which reads:

Ci Gît
le Bon Chien
Rin-Tin-Tin Au Cinema
Grande Vedette
Passant, Songe à la Brave Bete
Qui Fut Moins Chabot Que Plus Dieu

A loose translation: Here lies the honorable dog Rin Tin Tin, a great movie star; passerby, think about the good animal who was less of a ham than most.

Most Unusual Contraceptive: As late as the early years of the twentieth century it was traditional for a Muslim peasant woman in upper Egypt to terminate an unwanted pregnancy by lying face-down on the railroad tracks and allowing the next scheduled train to pass over her. Conversely, a woman who had difficulty conceiving would lie on her back on the tracks and allow the passing train to impregnate her.

It wasn't only in Egypt that the steam-driven locomotive was considered the embodiment of the male propulsive force. In India, women desirous of impregnation would rush to the tracks as a train approached, and as it passed, they would lift their skirts high in the hope of being made pregnant.

Most Unusual Cure: Israeli scientists reported in 1972 that freezing the big toe was one possible way of curing the common cold.

Most Unusual Disease: When the normally decorous seventeenth-century noblewoman the Marquise de Dampierre was seized on several occasions with an uncontrollable urge to scream obscenities in public, she became so thoroughly mortified that she lived a hermit's life for the next seventy years. Today, physicians know that the Marquise was the first recorded victim of what later came to be called the Tourette syndrome, a rare and understandably embarrassing nervous ailment.

Tourette sufferers invariably manifest their first symptoms—uncontrollable tics and twitches—during early to middle childhood. According to Dr. Arthur K. Shapiro, of New York Hospital's Payne-Whitney Clinic, the symptoms ultimately become verbal in nature as the patient finds himself hissing sharply at inappropriate moments, barking like a dog, shrieking, or echoing the words of others. Many patients, like Mme. Dampierre, find themselves swearing compulsively. Dr. Shapiro has treated some seventy cases of the Tourette syndrome and says that drug therapy has been highly effective in reducing its symptoms.

Most Unusual Death: Browsing pretentiously through the classics, we turned up a rare account of a politician smothered with affection, and a case history of terminal giggling:

The Athenian legislator Draco designed an early legal code that was, needless to say, draconian; he was nevertheless quite popular with his fellow citizens. In 590 B.C. there was a testimonial in his honor at the theater of Aegina. As Draco entered the open-air arena, thousands of well-wishers showered him with their hats and cloaks. Draco was smothered to death in the pile of clothing.

The most talented of the Greek soothsayers during the Trojan war was a man named Calchas. One day, as he was puttering around in his vineyards, a fellow prophet specializing in doom approached him and warned that he would never live to taste the fruit of the vines he was planting. Months later, after the grapes had been harvested and pressed and the wine had matured, Calchas invited his colleague to join him at a feast of thanksgiving. As the dinner commenced, the relieved host was about to raise his cup in a toast, when he allowed himself a moment of unprofessional gloating. "Repeat your prophecy of last summer," he ordered, and his guest obliged. Calchas began snickering, broke into an uncontrollable horselaugh, choked, spilled the contents of his cup, and died.

(Admittedly the ironist's art is detectable in both stories, but when faced with a choice of believing or disbelieving 2,000-year-old sources, why not choose the more interesting alternative?)

Most Unusual Doctor's Fee: Dr. Thomas Dimsdale received a $50,000 flat fee plus an annual pension of $2,500 for giving a half-dozen shots. Catherine II had summoned the famous physician to inoculate the royal family against smallpox and she expressed her gratitude with this prodigious shower of rubles. Other nobles also rewarded him handsomely for injections—one presenting him with a $15,000 ruby.

Most Unusual Epitaph: It has been widely reported that W. C. Fields's tombstone is inscribed "I'd rather be here than in Philadelphia," and at least one authority claims these were his last words. The original source of this quip, however, was a 1924 magazine article. *Vanity Fair*—now long deceased itself—invited fifty celebrities to compose their own epitaphs. The precise words of Fields's contribution were slightly less insulting to the City of Brotherly Love: "Here lies W. C. Fields. I would rather be living in Philadelphia."

Several others also came up with good lines:

"Ci Git: Alexander Woollcott [the reviewer and radio commentator] who died at the age of ninety-two. He never had imitation fruit in his dining room."

"Here lies the body of George Gershwin, American composer. American? Composer?"

And best of all: "Ci Git: Dorothy Parker. Excuse my dust."

Most Unusual Funeral: When His Most Gracious Majesty the Lord Grimsley of Katmandu died of a drug overdose in 1974, he lay in state for three weeks on a silken bed amid opulent surroundings before being buried in a casket bedecked with 1,000 carnations. The funeral orations consisted, in part, of readings from the poetry of Wordsworth and Shelley. At a cost of $3,600, it was probably the most expensive funeral ever given a parrot. Lord Grimsley was owned by David Bates, an antique dealer in London.

Most Unusual Grave: Hans Wilhelm von Thummel, a noted romantic poet, was laid to rest in the hollow of an oak tree March 1, 1824 in Noebdenitz, Germany. The tree still lives and it has long since enclosed the poet's body in an organic sarcophagus.

More familiar, perhaps, is the story of Ben Jonson who once jokingly told James I that he would like a square foot in Westminster Abbey. When the poet passed away, James obligingly had him buried standing up.

As an example of contemporary eccentricity in these matters, Edward Faber of Mansfield, Massachusetts, was buried on the eighteenth green he loved so well at Stowe Acres Country Club.

Most Unusual Gravestone: Chukche tribesmen of Siberia decorated the graves of their dead with piles of reindeer antlers, adding a new pair each year.

Most Unusual Heart: There was nothing particularly unusual about the heart of Giuseppe De Mai except that there was another just like it in his chest. In 1894 he signed a contract with the London Academy of Medicine, and was paid $15,000 for permission to study his two hearts after his death.

Today, such a person exists, courtesy of Dr. Christiaan Barnard, who surgically implanted a second heart in one of his South African patients in December 1974. This advance opens up wondrous new possibilities; now there is nothing standing in the way of men and women having three, four, or more organs of every description.

Most Unusual Home Remedy: Psalm 56:8 reads, "Put thou my tears into thy bottle." The reason for this peculiar statement is that throughout history tears have had a reputation for miraculous healing powers. Even today there are places in Afghanistan and Turkey where priests hand out small sponges before a funeral so that the mourners can collect their tears. Following the burial, the sponges are collected and the tears are wrung out and bottled.

Most Unusual Hypochondriac: Samuel Jessup died in 1817 at the age of sixty-five, but no one said that he should have taken better care of his health. Shortly before his decease, Jessup was summoned to appear in court to settle his accumulated apothecary's bill. Between 1791 and 1816, Mr. Jessup popped a total of 226,934 tablets and capsules. In the last five years of his life, as if in anticipation of the end, he averaged seventy-eight pills a day. His finest year was 1814 when he downed 51,590 altogether or over 140 per day. Also on Mr. Jessup's bill was a charge for 40,000 bottles of emulsions, juleps, syrups, and eluctuaries.

Most Unusual Mortuary: Before the energy crisis, it seemed like a promising undertaking. In 1968 Hirschel Thornton of Atlanta, Georgia, celebrated the grand opening of the world's first drive-in mortuary. Resting peacefully, the deceased was displayed behind a glass wall, while the motorists could file by and pay their last respects without ever having to leave their cars.

Most Unusual Pain Relievers: Dr. M. B. Greene, a New York anesthetist, made medical history in 1938. Until that year, the only known relief from the pain of abdominal cancer was injections of addictive morphine. After years in the laboratory, he discovered a nonpoisonous painkiller derived from cobra venom.

Galen, the most highly respected physician of the second century A.D., recommended that a good jolt from an electric fish was ideal for curing headaches. The learned Greek's remedy would have been dismissed as foolishness only a decade ago, but recent experiments with low amplitude electricity indicate that it *can* be useful in the treatment of migraines and chronic pain.

As long as we are on the subject of eels, we should mention a demonstration that took place at the 1939 World's Fair. A most unusual telegram was sent from the fair grounds to Eleanor Roosevelt in Washington, with electric eels providing the current for transmission.

Most Unusual Pregnancy: An Indonesian woman reported in 1969 that she had been pregnant for over eighteen months and that her unborn child could recite lengthy passages of the Koran from memory. She said she had tape recordings to prove her claim, but she was ultimately declared a fraud by the government.

In Sydney, Australia, that same year, a fifteen-year-old girl became pregnant after swimming in a public pool, although physicians swore that she was still a virgin. Nine months later, when she gave birth to a baby boy, the courts ruled that she had been impregnated by male sperm in the swimming pool water.

Madwoman Mary Tufts gave birth to rabbits two centuries ago—or so she claimed. In any event several pamphlets were published about the claim and the ensuing controversy. Many were bound in rabbitskin.

Most Unusual Resurrection: The wife of the mayor of Cologne fell victim to the Plague and was buried in 1571. As he helped with the interment in the morning, the gravedigger noticed a beautiful diamond on the lady's finger. That night he stole back to the grave and dug up the coffin. As the ghoul was removing the lid, the "dead woman" moved and groaned; it seems she had merely lapsed into a very deep coma, and the doctors, in fear of the contagion, had not checked too closely for vital signs. Delivered by a would-be graverobber, the mayor's wife lived on for many years.

Most Unusual Suicide: A Shrewsbury Englishman, William G. Hall, ended it all in 1971 by boring eight holes in his head with an electric power drill. There would have been an angry legislature to contend with had he been a resident of the ancient island-state of Cheos, where a person contemplating suicide had to announce his intention to the Senate. The senators would then debate the pros and cons, and either grant or deny permission to the citizen to do himself in.

Most Unusual Syndrome: Physicians Eulogio Rectra and Warren Litts of Lewis County General Hospital in Lowville, New York, recently ministered to a woman complaining of a tingling paralytic sensation in her hand. A neurological examination showed that she had pinched two nerves—the radial and the median—near her elbow. Significantly, she had first noticed the pain and numbness two days earlier after struggling home from the supermarket with two heavy bags of groceries. "Grocery-bag neuropathy" is what the good doctors dubbed the syndrome in an article in *The New*

England Journal of Medicine. "It seems that in our present day-to-day living," they wrote, "the average shopper is faced not only with the problems of inflation but also with the weight of his purchase." They related "grocery-bag neuropathy" to such other present-day ailments as "toilet-seat neuropathy," "gunbelt neuropathy," and "ski-boot neuropathy."

Most Unusual Tomb: In Pompano Beach, Florida, a person with a penchant for electronic immortality can purchase a talking tombstone from the Eternal Monument Company. Before he dies—and, presumably, long before death has become an imminent possibility—a customer must make an appointment to visit the firm and have himself filmed and his voice taped for the tombstone.

Most Unusual Undertakers: When a Spanish king dies (of course, there has not been a monarch for decades), the members of the Espinosa family, who have been royal undertakers for many generations, perform a unique ritual. Dressed in traditional mourning costumes hundreds of years old, they head the funeral procession to the Palace of Escorial, the burial place of the royal family. They stop for the night at a place about halfway; they could make the trip all in one day, but it is traditional to stop.

The next morning, the eldest male Espinosa knocks on the coffin and asks the king if he wishes to continue. Since the answer is never no, the cortege continues on to Escorial, arriving just after dark. There they find the doors of the church securely shut, even though everyone is expecting the arrival of the procession. The Espinosas rap loudly on the doors, but the monks within refuse to admit them, crying "How do you know the king is dead?" After a ceremonial argument, the monks grudgingly admit the unusual undertakers and their charge. A high mass is performed, then the king is finally laid to rest in a beautifully carved pantheon below the church.

Nature and Science

Best Drinking Water in the World: Residents of Bydgoszcz, Poland, turned on their water taps one morning in 1973 and got beer instead of water. A damaged valve in a brewery there had diverted several thousand gallons of the foaming brew into the city's water supply.

Best Invention: Thomas Crapper, a London-born sanitation engineer, invented the Valveless Water-Waste Preventer, the prototype of the modern flush toilet.

Crapper was a child of the Victorian age, when waste disposal was at best a primitive art. His business completed, a Victorian flushed his toilet simply by pulling a chain that sent the wastes, along with water from a cistern, sluicing into a pipe that emptied, ultimately, into the Thames. Queen Victoria, on viewing the Thames at a public ceremony, is said to have asked, "What are all those pieces of paper floating in the river?" Mustering up all the tact demanded by the age, one of her aides answered, "Your majesty, they are notices that swimming here is forbidden."

The excrement explosion brought England to a crisis point in the 1870s and the British Board of Trade spearheaded a drive to produce a solution. Crapper took up the call and came up with his valveless wonder, using the moveable metal float that is still the driving force behind many toilets today. The float greatly improved the efficiency of waste disposal, made real the miracle of indoor plumbing, and stemmed the huge outflow of water that threatened England so direly. At the 1884 Health Exhibition, Crapper proudly demonstrated the efficacy of his invention by disposing of a sponge, three wads of grease-laden paper stuck to the bowl, and ten large apples.

Flushed with victory, Crapper went on to develop several highly marketable spinoffs from his original invention, including a prison model in which the plumbing pipes were inaccessible to violence-prone convicts, and Crapper's Chainless Seat Action Automatic Flush. (A lift of the seat and the toilet is flushed. Chain optional.) In later years, as president and owner of T. Crapper & Co., Chelsea, he was commissioned to install toilet facilities in the country home of King Edward II at Sandringham.

Best Meteor Shower: Skywatchers say the most interesting meteor shower occurs annually on December 13, when the Geminids burn themselves out in the earth's atmosphere at a rate of about fifty per hour. Every thirty-three years or so, however, those who bother to look up on mid-November evenings witness heaven's most spectacular fireworks. An estimated 300,000 shooting stars per hour fell in the Leonids showers of 1799 and 1833, and on November 17, 1966 some 2,500 meteors per minute spilled out of the constellation Leo and blazed across the northern Arizona sky.

The largest known meteorite also fell on northern Arizona, near Winslow, about 27,000 years ago. The iron-nickel fireball struck the earth with the force of a thirty-four megaton atomic bomb and blasted a crater 4,150 feet across. But probably the most unusual meteorite is the Black Stone of the Ka'ba—the most sacred shrine of Islam. Western scientists have never had an opportunity to examine it, since nonbelievers are forbidden to enter Mecca under penalty of death, yet descriptions suggest to some that it is three shattered pieces of burnt-out space scrap. The legend is more romantic. The Angel Gabriel is said to have presented the stone to Abraham, and centuries later Mohammed ascended into heaven from it. According to tradition the rock was originally pure white, but it has turned black as it absorbed the sins shed by pilgrims to the Ka'ba.

Thomas Jefferson was one of many who preferred the legends about shooting stars to the facts. When informed in 1807 that astronomer Benjamin Silliman had established that meteors do indeed come from outer space, the president replied, "I would rather believe that a Yankee professor would lie than believe that stones fall from heaven."

Best Method of Preserving Documents: Pepsodent may purge the yellow from your teeth, but a similarly effective agent to prevent newsprint from yellowing and ultimately crumbling into nothingness has only recently been discovered, and its main ingredient, surprisingly, is good old club soda.

Richard Smith, an assistant professor of librarianship at the University of Washington, offers this recipe for preserving newsprint for generations yet unborn: Dissolve one milk of magnesia tablet in a quart of bottled club soda, mix well, and let the stuff chill for eight hours or so in a refrigerator.

Next, pour it out into a shallow pan and soak your document—or documents—in it for an hour. Remove the papers and pat them dry as well as you can before allowing them to dry more fully. The effect of this soaking, says Smith, is to counteract the processes which eat away at the cellulose fibers of the paper, causing it to turn yellow and brittle with age. Having timeproofed them with your favorite brand of bottled club soda, you'll be able to keep your documents intact and readable for as long as 300 years—not bad when you consider that the normal lifespan for a page of untreated newsprint is no more than a century. However, you must remember to have the papers resoaked every fifty years.

Best Star: The brightest event ever seen in the heavens appeared on the morning of July 4, 1054 A.D. The great nova, as Oriental astronomers describe it, was six times brighter than Venus and was only outshone by the sun and moon. For twenty-three days the nova could be observed in broad daylight.

Worst Cold Wave: At Verkhoyansk in eastern Siberia the temperature occasionally plunges to 90° below zero. If a traveler ventures out without a mask or an air-warming apparatus, his breath freezes in the air and falls to the ground with a soft crackling or whispering sound. Should he inhale, his lungs will immediately be coated with frost.

Worst Comet: "It may well be the comet of the century," Harvard astronomer Fred Whipple predicted. Other experts forecast that by January 1974, when Comet Kahoutek was to make its closest approach to the sun, it would be by far the brightest object in the sky. Its fifty-million-mile long tail would stretch one sixth of the way across the sky and its vaporized head would have five times the luminosity of the full moon. Kahoutek, everyone agreed, would be the kind of comet that caused the people of the Middle Ages to start saying their prayers and swelled the ranks of monasteries. Telescope and binocular sales boomed as would-be comet watchers prepared to get a good look.

But when Kahoutek kept its appointed rendezvous with the sun, it turned out to be, in *Time* magazine's words, "a faint smudge." Diehard fans in their Kahoutek sweatshirts stared in vain at the southwestern horizon, still hoping to catch a glimpse of the celestial disappointment, but few could pick it out with the naked eye. Venus and Jupiter far outshone it. As for the experts, they went skulking back to their observatories, like weathermen wearing raincoats on a sunny day.

So Halley's retains the unchallenged title of best comet. It is not the brightest ever seen, but it has the virtue of reliability. The earliest recorded sighting was in 467 B.C., and it has appeared regularly every seventy-six years since then. The superstitious say it was an omen of the destruction of the temple of Jerusalem, Attila's invasion of Western Europe, and the Norman conquest of England. You can wager confidently that it will appear in the sky at 9:30 P.M. (GMT) on February 9, 1986.

Worst Drinking Water in the United States: The nation's worst drinking water is in Lawrenceville, Illinois, and unless you've got relatives there or have a weakness for oil refineries, your chances of avoiding this south-central Illinois town are better than even. Large quantities of sulfur have evidently found their way into the city's water supply, because the filmy gonk that comes out of the water taps there has a decidedly eggy taste. Residents of Lawrenceville have inured themselves to the daily indignities of brushing their teeth, but short-term visitors invariably make do with bottled water, Coca-Cola, or gin.

Living Wilderness magazine recently carried a story about a barge containing 264,000 bottles of Scotch that foundered and sunk to the bottom of the Detroit River. A salvage crew had no difficulty raising the vessel and every bottle was recovered undamaged. But as soon as the liquor was brought to shore the Food and Drug Administration impounded it, spilled out the Scotch, crushed the bottles, and buried it all in a landfill. The owners were outraged. Why did the government destroy their perfectly good, unopened spirits? An FDA spokesman replied firmly, "Anything that has been submerged in the Detroit River is contaminated."

Worst Interplanetary Communications System: Astronomers are convinced that somebody is out there. When radio telescopes first picked up mysteriously regular signals from deep space, a number of sober scientists entertained the idea that intelligent beings from some distant civilization might be trying to communicate with us. As it turned out, pulsars—those strange, gigantic collapsing stars—were the source of the unusual radio patterns. But the odds, they say, are overwhelmingly in favor of life somewhere else in the universe and recently earthlings made their first serious attempt to contact aliens.

On the side of the Pioneer 10 spacecraft, which sent back the first close-up pictures of Jupiter and will become the first man-made object to leave our solar system, NASA scientists engraved a stylized picture of a man and woman with their right hands raised in a gesture of peace and greeting. (At least they hope that's the way the gesture will be interpreted.) And should extraterrestrial beings happen on the NASA probe, engraved symbols will tell them where we are so they can write back or pay us a visit.

While admittedly this method is about as crude as putting a message in a bottle and throwing it in the ocean, at least it is friendly, whereas the mode of communication proposed by Frenchman Charles Cros in the 1870s could have led to a terrible misunderstanding with the Martians.

Cros spent years trying to persuade the French government to construct a colossal magnifying glass that would focus the sun's rays on the Martian desert. The lens might then be manipulated slightly, burning letters and words into the planet's surface. Patrick Moore describes this scheme in *Can You Speak Venusian?*, a book about eccentric astronomers, and he poses an excellent rhetorical question: "I wonder what words Cros proposed to write?"

Worst Invention: The files of the United States Patent Office are filled with descriptions of inventions that might just as well have been left uninvented. One example is patent #560,351, held by Martin Goetz, "A Device for Producing Dimples." In the muddy prose of patent applications, this is how it works:

"The apparatus consists principally of two revolving arms which are pivoted and hinged together after the manner of a pair of compasses, the upper part being connected to a brace.

"When it is desired to use the device for the production of dimples, the knob of the arm must be set on the selected spot on the body, the extension put in position, then while holding the knob with the hand, the brace must be made to revolve on its axis."

Worst Science: The torture of political prisoners is no longer the primitive, hit-or-miss operation it was up until the last century. According to a recent article in *New Scientist,* the prestigious British publication, the systematic torture of individuals for political purposes is a growing technology that incorporates the latest advances in electronics, physics, behavioral psychology, biochemistry, and pharmacology. In fact, the governments of some thirty nations have hired specially trained scientists specifically to establish and carry out torture programs.

In Brazil, for example, scientists have perfected the *piquada,* which resembles a hatpin, packs an electric shock strong enough to cripple a horse, and is inserted beneath the fingernails. Also popular in Brazil these days is the Mitrioni vest, rumored to have been invented by a United States AID administrator. The vest is inflatable and is wrapped tightly around the victim's midsection and then pumped, blood-pressure-machine style, until the subject cries uncle. If he doesn't the vest can easily crush him to death.

Perhaps the worst of the "new wave" of torture methods, and certainly one of the most novel, is Aminazin, a drug that causes its victim to grow intensely hyperactive and uncontrollably restless. It has been used with great success to interrogate enemies of the state in the Soviet Union.

Worst Scientific Project: *Esquire* magazine reports that Dr. R. J. White of Cleveland expressed the following aspiration for his profession at a meeting of organ transplant specialists in Fiuggi, Italy: "We must, we want to think of transplanting the head."

Another gentleman who dares dream great dreams for science is J. V. Walker, a public health officer in England. He has suggested that researchers develop a pill that will postpone puberty until after students complete college.

Worst Smell: Ethyl mercoptan (C_2H_5SH) is one of the most powerful of smells and, to most noses, the worst. The odor is said to resemble that of rotting cabbage or sewer gas, except that it is somewhat purer and more revolting.

185

Worst Substance: The researcher who discovered it knew it was good for something. After all, you could shape it, stretch it, snap it, or roll it into a ball and bounce it. Later, it was accidentally discovered that you could flatten it and take an impression of newsprint. But what was it? Why, it was Silly Putty, of course.

Kids loved it and parents hated it. Mom and dad soon found that the original Silly Putty formula had a delightful way of fusing with the fibers of the living room carpet when left out of its container overnight, making it as difficult to remove as old chewing gum. Though this quality was later corrected, the original formula is still regarded with loathing by thousands of unforgiving parents.

Like the Blob, Silly Putty oozed inexorably over the nation. Some 32 million plastic eggs filled with the devil's goo were sold in the first five years of production, and its success inspired the invention of at least one other despicable substance—Flubber.

Worst Theory of Evolution: Kiss Maerth, the Yugoslavian-born author of *The Beginning Was the End: Man Came Into Being Through Cannibalism—Intelligence Can Be Eaten,* accepts Charles Darwin's premise that our ancestors were apes, but that is about the *only* similarity between his theory of evolution and that of the great nineteenth-century naturalist.

According to Maerth, the apes fed primarily on each other's brains. Since brains are an aphrodisiac, the apes' dinner-table preferences increased their sex drive, an effect which in turn whetted their appetite for more brains.

The major result of this gluttonous ingestion of the brains of their contemporaries was to swell the size of their own brains and make the apes more intelligent. However, this enlargement of their brains took place at a faster rate than the enlargement of their skulls, producing (a) presumably, some pretty fierce headaches and (b), for the apes, an inflated sense of their own importance in the universe. And that, Maerth suggests, is why we're in the mess we're in today.

Worst Valley: In the high Andes between Peru and Chile there is a valley through which people only dare pass in the daylight. Thousands of people who have tried the crossing at night have fallen victim to what is now known as Carrión's disease—a fatal anemia. Only those who have survived the illness and developed an immunity venture to live in the deadly valley.

A Peruvian medical student named Carrión first identified the disease which is carried by a sandfly so small that it slips through mosquito netting. The insects have an aversion to light, but millions swarm out of their hiding places after sundown. Chileans had done most of the research on the disease, but the War of the Pacific had just ended and the chauvinist Carrión wanted the medical credit to go to Peru. To make a positive identification of the anemia's source, he injected himself with serum from the sandflies; the injection proved his point but also caused his death.

Worst Weather in the United States: Among American cities, Bismarck, North Dakota, is the least tolerable—in the winter months, that is. According to records kept by the National Climatic Center of the United States Department of Commerce, the average daily temperature range for Bismarck in January is between 20° and −0°F. (They've recorded temperatures there as low as −43°.)

The most infernal town on the map—during the summer—is Phoenix, Arizona, where daily temperatures in July generally hit 105°F. In all fairness, however, Phoenix did have 219 clear days in 1973, the most of any United States city.

Most Unusual Almanac: The oldest known almanac dates back to 1200 B.C. Written in red ink on a papyrus scroll, it offers the standard daily advice based on astrological parameters, including such wisdom as "Do nothing at all this day."

A famous English almanac was published by Francis Moore. According to William Walsh, Moore would dictate his weather predictions off the top of his head—snow, sleet, rain, dry, cloudy, cold, and so on—as fast as his secretary could write them down. One unusual prediction secured Moore's reputation for accuracy. He was sleeping one afternoon when his secretary foolishly woke him up to inquire, "What weather shall I put for Derby Day [June 3] 1867?" Half asleep, Moore replied irritably, "Cold and snow, damn it!" As it turned out, it did snow on June 3, 1867. From then on, no matter how many times Moore was wrong, people would forgive his saying, "Ah, but remember Derby Day!"

Most Unusual Fire: Throughout the first half of this century a fire burned in a coal mine near Straitsville, Ohio. Smoldering underground for fifty-two years, the fire was finally put out only after it had caused $50,000 worth of damage and threatened hundreds of homes in the area.

Most Unusual Foundation: Roger Ward Babson was a stock market tycoon and a friend of Thomas Edison. One day the inventor said off-handedly, "Babson, you should look into gravity," or something of the sort, and Roger took up the challenge with a passion. He established and endowed the Gravity Research Foundation which now "serves as a free clearinghouse for everyone seriously interested in the causes and possibilities of gravity."

The *Anti*-Gravity Foundation might be a more accurate name, since most of the organization's efforts and funds have gone toward researching and developing a functional flying carpet. Specifically, the foundation sponsors an annual essay contest, offering $1,000 for the best paper of approximately 1,500 words on 1) a gravity insulator or reflecting device; 2) an alloy whose atoms are agitated by gravity, thereby offering a means of propulsion; or 3) any other means of harnessing the power of gravity. In recent years, Babson's followers have devoted most of their efforts to discrediting the theory of relativity, which, if correct, would make a gravity reflector or propulsion device an impossibility.

It is perhaps noteworthy that the foundation maintains an exhibit of 5,000 birds originally collected by Thomas Edison.

Most Unusual Glacier: In the Beartooth Mountains of Montana there is a glacier imbedded with millions of grasshoppers. Two centuries ago the immense swarm made a forced landing on the ice and was quick-frozen by a snowstorm. Today the grasshoppers are still excellently preserved, and when the glacial surface melts birds and bears gather to feed on the two-hundred-year-old insects. A vivid description of the Grasshopper Glacier appears in James L. Dyson's *The World of Ice*: "So numerous have these insects been at times that the odor of their putrefaction has been detected a quarter of a mile away."

A similar grasshopper graveyard has been reported at 16,000 feet on Mount Kenya in Africa.

Most Unusual Heat Wave: A freak heat wave hit the central coast of Portugal on July 6, 1949, sending the temperature up to 158°F for a period of two minutes. Moments later the mercury slid back down to the mid-120s. No satisfactory explanation for this fleeting swelter has ever been put forward.

Most Unusual Laser Beam Application: The greatest advance since the knife: A physicist at the University of Maryland has developed a technique for opening oysters with a laser beam.

Most Unusual Mountains: Consult a topographical map of Alaska and you can locate a pair of twin mountains officially known as the Jane Russell Peaks. In the same spirit, people in the South of France are now using a melodious adjective to describe a rolling, knobby landscape: (Gina) *lollobrigidienne*. In truth, this metaphor is as old as the hills. According to *A Dictionary of Americanisms,* the word Teton as in "Grand Tetons," is derived from the French word téton, meaning a woman's breast.

Most Unusual Rain: About nine o'clock in the evening on July 25, 1872, a dark cloud appeared over Bucharest, Rumania. Moments later it began to rain. The ladies and gentlemen in their evening clothes were surprised not only by a shower of water but also by thousands and thousands of black worms, about the size of honey bees, that fell from the sky.

Frequently, red and green rains have been reported, apparently caused by algae or other small plants somehow caught up in a cloud. Animal storms are less frequent, but there are a number on record. For example, Padeborn, Germany, experienced a storm of snails in August 1892; their shells shattered all over the streets from the velocity of their fall.

Most Unusual River: The comingling of two tributary streams in Algeria forms a river of ink: One brook contains iron; the other, which drains from a peat swamp, contains gallic acid. Swirled together, the chemicals unite to form a true black ink. (Black Brook in upstate New York is formed by a similar chemical blend.)

Most Unusual Science: Among the rarer "ologies" are argyrothecology, the branch of learning devoted to money boxes, and dendrochronology, the science of determining how old a tree is by its rings. The time-honored science of beer-making is known as tegestology. And finally, this book is an example of morology—the study of foolishness.

Most Unusual Smell: To a sizeable portion of the male population in America, there is one fragrance that is more pleasing to the nose than roses or lilacs or orchids—the smell of a new automobile. Now, the chemists of Frank Orcadi Company in Long Island City, New York, have done our olfactories a great service. They have synthesized "new car smell," making that delightful odor available to dealers selling foul and musty used cars.

Most Unusual Substance: Ordinary atoms are composed of electrons whirling around protons and neutrons. Recently physicists have discovered a complete set of antiparticles, so that, theoretically at least, there can be "looking-glass atoms" with electrical charges that are completely reversed. Separated from regular matter, this "antimatter" would be perfectly stable. But if matter and antimatter were brought together, each substance would annihilate the other in a tremendous, total-energy explosion. Some cosmologists speculate that for every particle in the universe there may be a corresponding antiparticle. In other words, somewhere there may exist antiworlds populated by antibeings—in an entire antiuniverse.

Most Unusual Value for Pi: According to R. Horwink's *Odd Book of Data,* a nineteenth-century Danish schoolmaster calculated the value of π out to 800 decimal places, an effort that stretched over his entire lifetime. A computer programmed to perform the same task took just a few hours to check his figures—and he was right. But to the Kansas Legislature of an earlier year, it was all wasted effort. Kansas once passed a law rounding off the value of pi from 3.14159265 . . . (and so on) to an even 3.

Most Unusual Volcano: At 19,344 feet above sea level, Mount Cotopaxi near Quito, Ecuador, is one of the highest active volcanoes in the world. When its blew its snow-capped top in 1877, there was only a modest lava flow, but the accompanying heat melted the nearby glaciers and caused flooding throughout the area. The flooding, in turn, created a tremendous mud flow that spilled down the mountainsides at speeds up to fifty miles per hour and devastated villages over 150 miles away. Even the writers for Hollywood catastrophe movies would have difficulty imagining a more freakish natural disaster.

Most Unusual Water: Lithium is a light metallic salt used in the treatment of manic depressives. Recently, Dr. Earl Lawson, a biochemist from the University of Texas, discovered that there is enough natural lithium in the water supply of El Paso, Texas, to keep the entire city happy and a little high. In the same way that natural fluorides prevent tooth decay, Dr. Lawson believes that lithium in the water supply is a factor in the city's low incidence of mental illness.

Most Unusual Waterfall: In the Koolau Mountains of Oahu, Hawaii, waterfalls spill over the high cliffs; the waters are caught by powerful updrafts, evaporated into a soupy mist, and blown back up over the cliffside. From a distance the waterfall appears to flow upward.

Most Unusual Weather Forecaster: Mrs. Fanny Shields of Baltimore, Maryland, owned a cat named Napoleon back in the 1930s who could predict the weather with an accuracy that was deadly.

During an especially severe dry spell that gripped Baltimore in 1930, when human meteorologists were offering no hope for relief, Mrs. Shields phoned the Baltimore newspapers and told them that rain would fall within twenty-four hours. How could she be so sure? the papers asked. Easy, she told them. She had just seen her cat Napoleon sitting with his front paws extended before him and his head on the ground, his own way of indicating that it was going to rain. The papers, needless to say, took her for a madwoman.

The following day, it rained.

In the ensuing months, the papers published Napoleon's forecasts regularly. They were accurate more often than not.

Plants and Animals

Best Insect Repellent: According to the Canadian national parks service, the most effective insect repellents are those containing diethyltoluamide, a pungent chemical that disgusts mosquitoes, blackflies, and ticks. A superpotent repellent containing a similar polysyllabic ingredient was developed by the U.S. Army to repel Vietnamese bugs; it also works well on domestic varieties and is now available at many army surplus stores. Caught without your diethyltoluamide, you might try rubbing orange or lemon peel on your skin for temporary protection. Garlic is also an effective repellent if you can stand it yourself. In fact, garlic juice can be lethal to mosquitoes and scientists are investigating its usefulness as a biodegradable substitute for DDT.

Best Parents: The temperature during the long Antarctic night may plunge to −80°F. Under these inclement conditions it is only through a heroic combination of patience and acrobatics that emperor penguins manage to hatch their eggs. Two-thirds feathers, the emperors are magnificent birds, standing nearly four feet tall. The female lays a single egg in midwinter and immediately departs on a long fishing trip, leaving her mate with the responsibility for incubation. In the bitter cold the egg would freeze almost immediately if it touched the ground. To protect it, the male stands for sixty days on one foot, holding the egg next to his warm underbelly with the other. Occasionally he switches feet, but throughout this period he eats nothing at all. Finally, when the chick is about ready to hatch, the female returns to take over the child-rearing tasks, and the famished male waddles off to the ocean for some fishing of his own.

Best Pet: A number of New York City pet stores are importing gecko lizards from the South Pacific for sale to apartment dwellers. The gecko, which comes in a number

Emperor penguin holding chick on its feet

of attractive pastel colors, makes an excellent pet. During the day he sleeps peacefully behind the refrigerator or stove, but at night he prowls the kitchen in search of his favorite prey—cockroaches. The shy and soft-skinned lizard is voracious, consuming hundreds of roaches a week; once a pet gecko has devoured all the insects in the house, he makes a wonderful gift for a neighbor with a vermin problem. Geckos are clean, quiet, and require no grooming, although they have been known to shed their tails when frightened.

The gecko played a role in a complex ecological crisis in Malaysia leading up to the world's most unusual airlift. In its efforts to control disease-carrying mosquitoes, the Malaysian government sprayed infested areas with DDT. The poisoned mosquitoes were devoured by roaches, which in turn fell prey to geckos. The residual poison was not enough to kill the hardy lizards, but it did affect their central nervous system, slowing them down and making them easier targets for hungry cats. The cats, however, were more vulnerable to DDT, and they began dying by the hundreds. With the cat population dwindling, the number of rats skyrocketed; parts of Malaysia were thus threatened with a serious rodent problem.

At this point, the World Health Organization stepped in and recommended an end to the use of DDT. Then, to restore the ecological balance, they airdropped whole planeloads of cats into remote areas where rats roamed fearlessly.

Gecko lizard

Worst Animal: Don't invite a sloth to your next dinner party or get stuck sitting next to one on an airplane. Apart from their maddening laziness, sloths are unquestionably the biggest bores of the animal kingdom.

Biologists Theodore Bullock and James Toole, fascinated by the sloth's inborn gift for doing nothing for hours on end—and doing it at a snail's pace—studied the animal's physiology in depth to determine what makes it tick. Or, more precisely, what makes it not tick.

For one thing, they found that its nervous system is depressingly sluggish and its reflexes all but nonexistent. Sloths will not so much as flinch, much less jump, at a sudden noise, and if a sloth is dropped from a height, it will remain in the position in which it lands and sag to the ground like a sack of flour, rather than set itself aright.

Moreover, only female sloths can maintain constant body temperatures, and they do that only when they're pregnant. Sloths can turn their breathing off and on at will without

194

Three-toed sloth

suffering any physical damage, and ingested food takes a good two weeks to make its way from one end of the alimentary tract to the other.

Indeed, ennui oozes from the sloth's very pores. In the words of the seventeenth-century naturalist Nehemiah Grew, the sloth is "an animal of so slow a motion, that he will be three or four days, at least, in climbing up and down a tree."

Worst Flower: There was a great deal of excitement at the New York Botanical Gardens on June 8, 1937; at long last, the giant Sumatran calla lily *(Amorphophallus titanium)* had burst into blossom. Its flower was the largest ever recorded, measuring eight and a half feet in height, four feet in diameter, and twelve feet in circumference. More precisely, the huge stalk was inflorescent containing thousands of small flowers. Regrettably, however, the distinctive fragrance somewhat dampened public enthusiasm for the calla lily; it smelled like rotten meat. Indonesians call it the "corpse flower."

195

Giant Sumatran calla lily

Worst Insect Repellent: The Canadian national park service is the source of this invaluable warning: "If you eat bananas, your skin will exude an odor which is very attractive to mosquitoes."

Worst Pet: While visiting in Tunis, Alexander Dumas, author of *The Three Musketeers* and *The Count of Monte Cristo,* was very much taken with "a superb vulture, a bird without fault." Jurgutha was the bird's name, and his Tunisian owner was anxious to sell since it devoured "everyone and everything that came near," most recently the tail of a pet dog that strayed too close. Dumas was satisfied with the price, and after having a muzzle made for the powerful beak, he arranged to have Jurgutha shipped back to France. Under Dumas's care the animal became quite tame, frequently offering its bald head to be scratched. The eccentric author's only dissatisfaction with his new pet was that, despite diligent efforts, he could not teach it to say "Scratch pretty Polly's head." On the Champs Elysées in Paris, Dumas occasionally terrified poodles and pedestrians as he strolled along with Jurgutha hopping in tow on a silver leash.

On the subject of pets, *Newsweek* magazine reported in 1974 a growing market in tarantulas in the United States. Pet shop owner Doris Mahalek of Detroit said that she had sold several hundred of the venomous creatures over the past three years and that "everybody—longhaired kids, doctors and attorneys—is buying them."

Worst Toad: The *Bufo marinus* is an especially ravenous species of toad which Australia imported from South America in the 1930s to eradicate the cane beetles that were ravaging crops in Queensland. The Aussies had undersold the toads' voraciousness, however, because after the beetles were gone, the toads, now grown to as much as eight inches in length, reproduced wildly and took to devouring garbage, Ping Pong balls, dogs, cats, and cattle, killing their prey with a poisonous glandular secretion. By the early 1970s the *Bufo* explosion had become something of a biological nightmare in Australia. The National Wildlife Department was offering a $30 reward for each toad brought in. "Wanted: Dead or Alive" posters proliferated throughout the continent, and, as a public service, at least one radio station was broadcasting tape-recorded mating calls of male *Bufos* in an attempt to lure love-starved females to destruction.

There is also a variety of clawed frog from Africa that is especially dangerous. A bunch of them escaped from a biology laboratory at the University of California at Davis recently and threatened to upset the ecological balance in the area by devouring the fish in nearby Putah Creek.

Duckbilled platypus

Most Unusual Animal: No book of wonders would be complete without a tribute to the duckbilled platypus. When the first specimen was brought to England from Tasmania in 1880 the zoologists were perplexed. Its two-foot-long body was covered with thick gray-brown hair (definitely mammalian); it had a broad, flat tail (not unlike a beaver); it had webbed feet and a wide rubbery bill (ducky); the brain was a single hemisphere (positively reptilian); behind the rear ankles were two spurs that secrete poison (like a snake). Most improbably of all, this freakish animal was reported to lay eggs. Most zoologists agreed there was only one explanation: *Ornithorhynchus anatinus* was a hoax!

Soon, however, the hoax theory had to be discarded when a team of scientists discovered a whole pond full of platypi in New South Wales, and they turned out to be even more marvelous than a preserved specimen could suggest. They growl like dogs; they live most of their lives in the water, but are also able tree climbers; they dine mostly on worms, which they store in pouches at the sides of their mouths like chipmunks. The females do indeed lay eggs—two at a time—and they also give milk. Lacking true nipples, the milk is simply secreted from the mammaries through primitive slits; babies lap the milk from their mother's hair.

Ultimately zoologists defined a completely new order, Monotremata, (most primitive living mammals) in which to classify the platypus. Recent studies of the way its spinal cord is attached to its brain have offered new evidence that the platypus is, in effect, the missing link between reptiles and mammals.

Most Unusual Arboriculturist: John D. Rockefeller and Kubla Khan shared a passionate fondness for trees. Whenever either of the great men saw a particularly nice specimen, he would buy it, have it pulled up, roots and all, and transplant it in the grounds of his own estate.

Most Unusual Bedfellow: There is an old nursery rhyme that begins, "Barber, barber, shave a pig." It sounds like nonsense, but pig-shaving was once a common practice in parts of northern China. On winter nights rural Chinese would bring pigs to bed with them for warmth, and they soon discovered that a porker makes a more pleasant bedfellow when its sharp and muddy bristles have been shaved off.

Most Unusual Conversations: The French philosopher Descartes once speculated that monkeys and apes actually have the ability to speak but keep silent to avoid being put to work. As it turns out that may not have been so far from the truth. Consider these unusual conversationalists:

A chimpanzee named Gua, raised by Winthrop and Luella Kellogg during the 1930s, could understand over 100 words though it never learned to speak. The first chimp ever to utter human words was Vicki, trained by Keith and Cathy Hayes; she could say and correctly apply the words "momma" and "poppa" (referring to the Hayeses) and "cup" as well as comprehend many more expressions.

The mouth, tongue, teeth, and central nervous system of chimps are apparently not well designed for handling human language and that seems to be the main obstacle standing in the way of their becoming politicians (or orators of another kind). But when Allen and Beatrice Carter taught American sign language to a chimp named Washoe, he immediately became quite talkative. Washoe uses his naturally dexterous fingers to signal out complete sentences. He can understand and form 140 different words and his favorite expression is "Give me fruit juice." In an even more unsettling development, Bruno and Booee, two chimps at the University of Oklahoma, have also mastered sign language and now use it *to converse with each other*. Oklahoma scientists are particularly anxious to discover whether Bruno and Booee will try to teach sign language to their children.

And finally, Lana, a chimp at the University of Georgia, uses a computer keyboard with one hundred symbols to communicate with *Homo sapiens*. There is no doubt among scientists that Lana is capable of using language abstractly and forming syntactically correct sentences. As yet she has not said anything much more profound than "Lana wants a tickle." But then, as Descartes suggested long ago, she may just be holding out on us.

Most Unusual Corsage: On his first voyage to the New World, Christopher Columbus was intrigued by the corsage-like ornaments worn widely by both men and women in the West Indies. They were made of popcorn.

Most Unusual Dog Fancier: Francis Henry Egerton, the Eighth Earl of Bridgewater (1756–1829) was one of the most eccentric dog fanciers of all times. He dressed all of his high-class canines in well-made leather boots, and each night he hosted a favored dozen at his own dinner table. While the dogs sat in armchairs with napkins primly tied around their necks, butlers in formal dress dished out the food from sterling serving pieces. But the earl would not tolerate a breach of good manners. A sloppy eater would be dismissed from the table and sent to dine alone in disgrace.

Queen Victoria kept as many as eighty-three dogs at one time in Buckingham Palace, and could call them all by name.

In *Useless Facts of History*, Paul Steiner records that after her coronation Victoria's first royal act was to wash her favorite dog.

Most Unusual Dog Story: Charles Burden of Missouri had a black and tan hunting dog named Old Drum whom he loved with a passion that bordered on the unnatural. On the morning of October 29, 1869, after a sleepless night waiting for Old Drum to return home from a day of romping in the woods, he found his canine cohort lying in a creek quite dead, his belly full of buckshot. Old Drum, it appeared, had been the victim of a gangland execution.

Burden suspected his neighbor and brother-in-law, Leonidas Hornsby, of the misdeed. Hornsby, a short, foul-tempered man with bad breath and a congenital scowl, denied the accusation vehemently. Nonetheless, it was well known that his dimwitted nephew, Dick Ferguson, had a standing order to shoot to kill any dogs who trespassed on his uncle's land, and that in the past, he had done a lot of shooting to kill.

Burden decided to sue. He hauled Hornsby before a jury who voted in his favor. Hornsby, however, had the decision reversed on appeal, but Burden claimed he had found some new evidence, and so the case went to a third court, and finally a fourth.

It was this fourth and final trial—the longest, most dramatic, and most skillfully argued of all—that decided the case, and a nation of dog lovers, legal buffs, and sensation-seekers followed it avidly.

Representing the plaintiff was the noted attorney George Graham Vest, who later became a United States senator. Representing the defendant was yet another senator-to-be, Francis Marion Cockrell, assisted by Thomas T. Crittenden, a future governor of Missouri.

Oratory flew like shrapnel across the courtroom, and Vest's summation was the height of wretched excess. ("Gentlemen of the jury, a man's dog . . . will sleep on the cold ground where the wintry winds blow . . . if only he may be near his master's side. . . . He guards the sleep of his pauper master as if he were a prince. . . . When riches take wings and reputation falls to pieces, he is as constant in his love as the sun in its journey through the heavens. . . .") As bathetic as it was, it was just such oratory that saved the day for Burden and the court ordered Hornsby to pay damages of fifty dollars to the appellant. A great moral victory had been won and a grateful nation rejoiced.

In the ensuing years, songs and sonnets were written about Old Drum, a mythology based on his life and untimely death arose, and he was memorialized by dog lovers everywhere. On the wall of the Warrensburg, Missouri, courthouse where the trial was held, there is a bronze plaque commemorating Burden's—and Old Drum's—victory. There is a monument to him on the banks of Big Creek, where he met his end, made from stone sent from most of the states of the nation, the Great Wall of China, the White Cliffs of Dover, France, Germany, Mexico, Jamaica, South Africa, the West Indies, and Guatemala. Yet another memorial—this one a statue created by the noted sculptor Reno Gastaldi—was unveiled in Warrensburg in 1958. The attorney-general of Missouri and Captain Will Judy, editor of *Dog World,* dedicated the work.

Most Unusual Elephant: Pink elephants exist. Pachyderms are fond of taking dust baths, and in some areas of Africa, where the soil is rich in iron, the dust caked on their skin gives them a bright pink color.

Most Unusual Exterminator: If you can judge the quality of exterminators by the quality of their clientele, then the Messrs. Tiffin and Son of London were topnotch. In 1851 they were appointed "Bug Destroyers to Her Majesty and the Royal Family." Robert Mayhew's *London Labor and the London Poor* includes a candid interview with the elder Mr. Tiffin, who described what it was like plying his trade in Princess Charlotte's bedroom: "Just at that moment I did happen to catch one, and upon that she [the young princess] sprang upon the bed, and put her hand on my shoulder, to look at it. . . . She said, 'Oh, the nasty thing! That's what tormented me last night; don't let him escape.' I think he looked all the better for having tasted royal blood."

Most Unusual Insect: The aweto (*Hipialis vivescens*), found in New Zealand, behaves like a cross between a caterpillar and a vegetable. Found at the foot of a large myrtle tree, the aweto buries itself among the roots a few inches below the ground and lives there peacefully until it is full grown. Then it undergoes a strange metamorphosis: The spore of a vegetable fungus fastens itself to the aweto's neck, and from the spore grows an eight-inch-high stalk resembling a cattail. Gradually the vegetable takes over the living aweto, filling up all the space within its skin, but leaving the external body unchanged. When the vegetable has completely replaced the caterpillar, both become hard and dry, then die. Dried awe-toes are gathered and burned to produce a dark pigment. In its curious life cycle, it is not fully understood how, when, (or why) the aweto reproduces itself.

Another interesting bug story: It is a little known fact that bedbugs bark enthusiastically when they smell human flesh. With this in mind, United States Army scientists devised a scheme to conscript the tiny *Cimex lectularius* for service in Vietnam. Their plan was to pack bedbugs in capsules rigged with miniature radio transmitters. The capsules were to be dropped on suspected Viet Cong hideouts; if a radio man overheard their hungry barks, the brass would order in the jets and artillery.

American participation in the war ended before the bugs could see active duty, but, as *Newsweek* magazine reports, scientists continue to find *Cimex* an interesting study. It seems that the little critters have an amazingly high sex drive and are polymorphously perverse in the extreme. When a male sees other bedbugs copulating, he becomes very excited and immediately joins in the affair with a partner of either sex. Moreover, according to Jacques Carazon of the National Museum of Natural History in Paris, a male bedbug no longer deposits his sperm in the female's reproductive tract. Whereas ancient bedbugs found preserved in the Pyramids made love in the conventional way, today's swinging *Cimex* punctures the female's abdomen for insemination. Miracu-lously, the female, in what by evolutionary standards is a very short time, has developed a special tube which carries the sperm from her stomach to her ovaries.

Xylocoris maculipennis is a cousin of the *Cimex* which also has peculiar sexual habits. Males of this species often copulate with other males, and their sperm becomes inter-mingled. When a male has sexual relations with a female, the sperm he transmits is a combination of his own and that of his male partners. This remarkable sex life would seem to frustrate the process of natural selection, leaving the paternity of young bedbugs almost wholly to chance.

Most Unusual Mermaids: The dugong is a relative of the manatee living in the Indian Ocean and Australian waters. Both species are members of the order *Sirenia*, so named because at a distance they vaguely resemble women floating with their heads and shoulders out of the water, giving rise to the myths about sirens and mermaids. Of the two, the grayish dugong is the more womanly; the female's breasts are placed high on its torso, like a woman, and she has a habit of holding her young to her breast in a very human posture. A Madagascar fisherman must perform an elaborate religious rite before selling a dugong; among other obligations, he must take an oath that he has not had unnatural relations with his strange and gentle captive.

Like men and elephants, the dugong cries, shedding real tears, when it is in pain or distress. A dugong on exhibit in a Ceylon zoo cried almost daily for years, as if pining for its freedom. Zookeepers collected the tears and sold them as a love potion.

Hunted for their hides, tusks, oil, and palatable flesh, dugongs are now rarely seen.

Most Unusual Mule: A mule is by definition the sterile hybrid of a jackass and a mare, as distinguished from a hinny, which is the offspring of a stallion and a jenny. Old Beck, a she-mule owned by Texas A & M University, was an exception. Displaying the legendary stubbornness of her breed, Old Beck defied convention and gave birth to two baby mules— one by a jack and one by a stallion.

Most Unusual Pet: An article in *American Horseman* reports that kings and millionaires have discovered a new house pet: midget horses. The foremost breeder of these miniatures is Julio César Fallabella who operates a ranch fifty miles south of Buenos Aires. Forty generations of selective breeding have produced what looks like a throwback to the eohippus —a full-grown pony smaller than a German shepherd. His smallest *enano* or dwarf measures only fifteen inches from ground to withers and weighs twenty-six pounds. The average is more like twenty inches in height; the price—$1,000 and up.

Most Unusual Protozoan: The Swedish botanist Linnaeus must have thought he had been peering through his microscope too long. But when a second squint confirmed what he had seen before, Linnaeus realized that he was in the presence of an animal like no other; he named his discovery *Chaos chaos*. In 1975 we celebrate the two-hundredth anniversary of the discovery of *Chaos,* which scientists have recognized only about fifty times since Linnaeus first made its acquaintance.

As this freakish organism is the terror of the one-celled world, it must be a comfort to other tiny animals that *Chaos* is so rare. Fifty times the size of an average paramecium, it hunts in vicious packs of three, completely surrounding entire schools of smaller protozoa and devouring them without mercy. Moreover, unlike any other one-celled creature, *Chaos* has three distinct nuclei; when it gets lonely it simply wrinkles and divides into three separate animals exactly like itself. Because of its tripartite personality, the *Chaos* is often handicapped by indecisiveness. Each nucleus sets out in its own direction, stretching out a long streamer of protoplasm. An internal tug-of-war follows. Eventually, one nucleus overpowers the others, forcing them to slither along after it.

Some biologists believe *Chaos chaos* or other organisms like it may have been the link between single and multicelled animals.

Most Unusual Retriever: English sportsmen used to train hunting pigs to fetch their game.

Most Unusual State Insect: That a state would bother to honor an insect is the unusual part. Once that decision has been made, California's choice of the dog-faced butterfly seems a fine one.

Most Unusual Stuffed Animal: Tufts University's P. T. Barnum Museum houses Jumbo, who was once the world's largest elephant; now he is not even the world's largest stuffed elephant, since the Smithsonian Museum acquired an even more elephantine specimen. Nonetheless, Jumbo remains the most unusual stuffed elephant because, as anyone who ever saw him perform will attest to, he had personality.

Business and Finance

Best (Lowest) Cost of Living in the World: If money means everything to you, you'll find Montevideo, Uruguay, to be just about the most inexpensive major city in the world in which to live, according to a study done by the United Nations Statistical Office in 1973. The study arbitrarily assigned New York City a cost-of-living index of 100 and gauged the indices of other cities in relation to it, taking into account standard prices on some 120 different consumer items. Montevideo's index is 52.

Best Entrepreneur: Phineas Taylor Barnum first gained fame with his American Museum in New York, where he exhibited Tom Thumb—the world's smallest man—and other freaks. Perhaps his greatest triumph was the discovery and publicity of the woman he called George Washington's wet nurse.

Joice Heth, an elderly black woman, was already making the rounds of the sideshows as "the living mummy" when P. T. first encountered her. Though she was toothless and nearly blind, Barnum saw something in her carriage and manner that suggested gentility and greatness. He immediately signed her up for his museum, billing her as the 161-year-old woman who had mothered the father of our country. She was an immediate success. Thousands of weeping suckers came to hear her relate memories of little George and firsthand anecdotes about the Revolutionary War.

Gradually, however, the crowds began to decline. Barnum responded with another brainstorm. Under a pseudonym, he contributed a series of muckraking columns to a local newspaper claiming that Joice Heth was not a woman at all, but actually a sophisticated automaton. The crowds came back for a second look, and Barnum offered undeniable proof that this wonderful old lady was, in fact, a living, breathing human being.

FOR ONE DAY ONLY!!!

JOICE HETH,

Now on her return to the SOUTH, where she must arrive before cold weather, will, (at the urgent requests of many ladies and gentlemen) be seen at

CONCERT HALL
FOR ONE DAY ONLY.

This is positively the LAST OPPORTUNITY, which can ever be afforded to the citizens of New England, of seeing this most wonderful woman.

JOICE HETH is unquestionably the most astonishing and interesting curiosity in the World! She was the slave of Augustine Washington, (the father of Gen. Washington,) and was the first person who put clothes on the unconscious infant who in after days led our heroic fathers on to glory, to victory and freedom. To use her own language when speaking of the illustrious Father of his country, "she raised him." JOICE HETH was born in the Island of Madagascar, on the Coast of Africa, in the year 1674 and has consequently now arrived at the astonishing

Age of 161 Years!

She weighs but *forty-six ponnds,* and yet is very cheerful and interesting. She retains her faculties in an unparalleled degree, converses freely, sings numerous hymns, relates many interesting anecdotes of *the boy* Washington, the red coats, &c. and often laughs heartily at her own remarks, or those of the spectators. Her health is perfectly good, and her appearance very neat. She was baptized in the Potomac river and received into the Baptist Church 116 years ago, and takes great pleasure in conversing with Ministers and religious persons. The appearance of this marvellous relic of antiquity strikes the beholder with amazement, and convinces him that his eyes are resting on the oldest specimen of mortality they ever before beheld. Original, authentic and indisputable documents prove however astonishing the fact may appear, JOICE HETH is in every respect the person she is represented.

The most eminent physicians and intelligent men in Cincinnati, Philadelphia, New-York, Boston and many other places have examined this *living skeleton* and the documents accompanying her, and all *invariably* pronounce her to be as represented 161 *years of age!* Indeed it is impossible for any person, however incredulous, to visit her without astonishment and the most perfect satisfaction that she is as old as represented.

☞ A female is in continual attendance, and will give every attention to the ladies who visit this relic of by gone ages.

She was visited at Niblo's Garden New York, by *ten thousand persons* in two weeks.———Hours of exhibition from 9 A. M to 1 P. M. and from 3 to 6 and from 7 to 9 P. M.—Admittance 25 cents—Children 12½ cents.

☞For further particulars, see newspapers of the day.   ☞Over

Advertisement for P. T. Barnum's Joice Heth. (Chicago Historical Society)

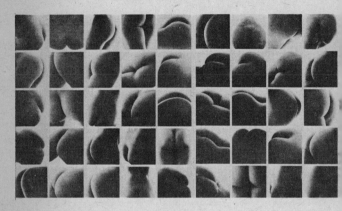

Furniture ad, first run in *Paris-Match*

The controversy over Joice Heth continued even after her death. Doctors who performed the autopsy estimated that the venerable performer was only eighty-four years old. Barnum, of course, vigorously denied this charge, maintaining that they had operated on the wrong woman.

Much of Barnum's career is now legend: the founding of his circus "The Greatest Show on Earth"; importing Jumbo the first white elephant Americans had seen; purportedly observing, "There is a sucker born every minute." He continued to float outrageous schemes throughout his life. In a gesture typical of his taste and sensitivity, one of Barnum's last acts was to telegraph the great Sarah Bernhardt when he heard that her leg might have to be amputated. Phineas offered her a flat fee of $1,000 for the severed limb. Miss Bernhardt never bothered to reply.

Best Way to Face the Specter of Spiralling Inflation: Secretary of Agriculture Earl Butz was seen at a Capitol Hill Club party pilfering food from the buffet table and wrapping it in napkins to take home.

Worst Advertisement: In Mexico, no one puts down Emiliano Zapata and gets away with it. In 1970, a magazine advertisement for Elgin watches made note of Zapata's notorious watch-stealing campaign and his much-bandied threat to kill any railroad conductor who tried to pull a fast one on the revolutionary hero by wearing an inferior timepiece. Said the ad, "It's a good thing Zapata's gone. He'd be stealing Elgins as fast as we could make them."

Sociologist José de Fonseca of Mexico City saw the advertisement and bridled, doubly piqued by the crass commercialism of an offer to readers of a "handsome Zapata poster" for one dollar. He retaliated by producing a poster ad for a mythical "Darkie Beer" that was deliberately and consummately tasteless. Under the heading WASHINGTON EN ONDA CON LAS NEGRAS ("Washington Swung with the Darkies") was a crumpled dollar bill and this legend: "George Washington, United States secessionist, had an excessive fondness for black slaves, according to legend. He used to sneak out of his home silently at night and head for the slave quarters, where he would abuse them.

"For us, Darkie is not a person, but a beer. We know you'll enjoy it."

Across the Atlantic, European journalism really touched bottom in 1969 when *Paris-Match* ran a furniture ad featuring fifty bare derrieres covering a two-page spread. The copy: "Yes, that's where it's at. We agree with Madame de Sevigne, who wrote, 'Most of our troubles come from having our asses squarely in the saddle . . .' Our job is to sit you down anatomically, socially, and somewhat philosophically."

Worst (Highest) Cost of Living in the World: Predictably, it's Tokyo, Japan, where gasoline goes for as much as two dollars a gallon and, at a coffee-shop counter, a Coke can run you a dollar or more. The Japanese industrial boom has inflated the city's cost-of-living index to 117.

Worst Horatio Alger Story: The worst Horatio Alger story is the story of Horatio Alger himself, the man who made a fortune writing 119 books on the rags-to-riches theme. Alger was a notorious spendthrift and he died totally destitute.

Worst Monetary System: Postwar inflation diminished the value of the Hungarian pengo in 1946 to 1/828 octillionth of what it had been before the inflation spiral began.

Worst Status Symbol: Bracelets worn by high-ranking Suka tribesmen in Ethiopia are purposely made so tight that they almost stop the flow of blood. The hands of the rich often become shrunken, withered, and virtually useless. To the Suka, withered hands are a status symbol, and the more atrophied their hands become the prouder the aristocrats are of them.

Most Unusual Advertisement: One memorable evening in 1952, Parisians craned their necks and saw the most spectacular display advertisement ever conceived. On the low, overhanging clouds the name of a commercial airline appeared in gigantic illuminated letters. The innovation, which promised to be as momentous in the history of publicity as the appearance of the first sandwich man, was made possible through a complicated system of spotlights and huge color transparencies.

The next day, "skylighting" was the talk of the town. The newspapers predicted that soon the names of wines, cheeses, soaps, underclothing, and movie stars would be flashing on the firmament. But the city council had other ideas. They insisted that the skies of "the City of Light" should remain forever dark, and the projection of brand names on clouds was outlawed.

Most Unusual Auction: In 1970, a London collector auctioned off several Napoleonic relics including the emperor's death mask and a generous portion of his body hair, all for an estimated total of $72,000. *Punch* reported on what was "undoubtedly the saddest news item in a long time: The fact that Napoleon's penis was withdrawn (sorry, that's the auctioneer's word, not ours) from a sale at Christie's because no one was willing to pay more than $40,000 for it." The item, described in the auction catalog as a "small, dried-up object," was placed back in its box and then taken back by its American owner.

In March of 1890, Leventon and Company of Liverpool, England, auctioned off 180,000 mummified cat bodies from an Egyptian burial ground near Beni Hassan. While Leventon felt they might command a higher price as a novelty gift item, the cats went for a little less than ten dollars per ton.

According to Herodotus (Book I, 196), the Babylonians ran an unusual marriage auction. All the young women of marriageable age were brought to the central market place. The attractive girls naturally commanded high prices, and the money raised from their sale was put toward dowries for the homely ones (with the ugliest receiving the largest endowment). There was only one concession to romance: If either party was dissatisfied with the transaction, the monies were refunded to the general pool and the marriage annulled.

On March 28, 193 A.D. the Roman Empire was put up for auction by the Praetorian Guards. In *The Decline and Fall of the Roman Empire* Gibbon tells how a wealthy senator named Didius Julianus bought most of Europe and the Mediterranean for a donation of 6,250 drachmas to each guard. Didius ruled for only two months before he was assassinated.

Most Unusual Billion: In the United States as well as in France, a billion is a thousand millions. But in Great Britain a billion is defined as a *million* millions. To check this, just ask yourself how many British billionaires you have met.

Most Unusual Business Enterprise: A group of Venezuelan businessmen announced in 1972 their intention to breed cats and market the bodies. The paws would be sold as good-luck keychains, the fur would be sold for brush bristles, and the insides would be sold as surgical gut—and, presumably, violin strings.

Most Unusual Checks: Artist Marc Chagall pays for even his smallest purchases—toothpaste and cigarettes—with personal checks. Years ago he discovered that most merchants would not cash them, figuring that Chagall's signature makes the checks valuable collector's items. As a result, Chagall easily maintains a healthy balance in his account.

Most Unusual Convention: "Pretzels in a Changing World" was the theme of the 1974 annual convention of the United States Pretzel Manufacturers' Association. Equally unusual was a convention of Pakistani eunuchs who gathered in Sukkur in 1970 to discuss common problems.

Most Unusual Counterfeiter: As a youth, Diogenes the Cynic, who spent his life searching for an honest man, was forced to leave the town of Sinope when he and his father were convicted of counterfeiting. Much later an adversary attacked the philosopher for his unsavory past, and Diogenes replied "Such as I was, so you are now; such as I am, you will never be," which was more sophisticated than saying "Sticks and stones may break my bones."

A nonsequitur: Before his death Diogenes requested to be buried with his head pointed straight down because he believed that the world would soon be topsy-turvy.

For the *most unusual case of counterfeiting:* Six men were arrested by police in Florence, Italy, in 1974. The charge: trafficking in counterfeit blue jeans. Eight thousand pairs of the contraband slacks were seized in the bust.

Most Unusual Millionaire: At the time of her death, Hetty Green (1834–1916), known as "the Witch of Wall Street," was reckoned the richest woman in the world with a fortune totaling nearly $100 million. She inherited $6 million from her father and accumulated the rest through a long series of spectacular investments in the stock market. But despite her uncanny talent for making money, she was utterly mad.

For years she wore the same dress which was originally black but turned green and then brown with age. For undergarments she used old newspapers collected from trash baskets in Central Park. Her home was an unheated tenement in the Chelsea section of Manhattan and her diet consisted almost entirely of onions, eggs, and dry oatmeal, since preparing hot food would have added precious pennies to her fuel bill.

Perhaps the saddest instance of Hetty Green's stinginess involved her son Edward who at age nine was run over by a wagon drawn by a St. Bernard dog. Although his leg was seriously injured, his mother refused to call a doctor, taking him instead to a number of free clinics. Eventually Edward's leg had to be amputated, an operation that might not have been necessary if he had received the medical attention that his mother could certainly afford.

Most Unusual Miser: Sheik Shakhbut, the former leader of Abu Dhabi, was one of many Arab potentates who made a killing in oil revenues. But while Shakhbut was crafty at making money, he was no great shakes at spending it. Eventually, a lot of people in Abu Dhabi began wondering why, with all the oil being pumped out of their land, they weren't seeing any income, and Shakhbut was deposed. An inspection of the royal bedroom provided at least a partial solution to the mystery of the disappearing treasury. It seems the sheik had been hoarding a tremendous fortune right in his chambers,

Hetty Green

stuffing currency in his mattress and dresser and hiding it under his bed and in his closet. It was impossible to determine precisely how much Shakhbut had socked away because at least $2 million in paper money had been devoured by rats.

Most Unusual Money: Yap Islanders in the South Pacific used to measure their wealth in giant stone wheels that measure six to twelve feet in diameter and weigh over a ton. Such stones do not occur naturally on the island; they were brought there over a century ago by an Irish trader.

On the island of Santa Cruz in the West Indies, the original Indian tribes used chains of beautiful feathers for currency. At the opposite extreme are the Amazon rainforest tribes who use curare poison (in which they dip the tips of blowgun darts) as a medium of exchange.

Traders from Connecticut used strings of onions for currency on voyages to the West Indies and South America; they were strung in standard lengths with a standard trade value.

Finally, the Incas never used money and had no word for

it in their language. Yet their treasures of gold, jewelry and art, stolen by the Spaniards, enabled Spain to put the world on the gold standard.

Most Unusual Philanthropy: For years a national glass firm has had a standing offer to fix windows broken by sandlot baseball players for free; on the average they replace 3,000 per year.

Most Unusual Receipt: The French philosopher Voltaire once composed a biting epigram about his patron Frederick the Great of Prussia. Frederick was a tolerant man, but he could not permit such impertinence from a mere author living off the royal bounty. To teach the wit a lesson he ordered him flogged and instructed the flogger to demand a receipt for his services. Voltaire complied with the following voucher:

"Received from the right hand of Conrad Bochhoffer thirty lashes on my bare back, being *in full* for an epigram on Frederick II, King of Prussia, *Vive le Roi.* [Signed] Arouet de Voltaire."

Most Unusual Salary: Of course, it is chicken feed by today's standards, but in 1930 Babe Ruth's salary of $80,000 a year looked pretty good. When someone asked whether it was fair that he was receiving more than President Hoover, the Babe remarked, "Well, I had a better year."

Most Unusual Speculative Boom: In 1906 someone started a rumor that the mint accidentally mixed gold with the copper in 1902 pennies. Soon throughout Virginia and North and South Carolina speculators were buying up 1902 pennies at incredible prices; in some places pennies were going for as much as twelve cents apiece. Within a week, however, the government discredited the rumor, and the penny market crashed.

At the risk of starting a new speculative boom in pennies, as of this writing, the copper in pennies is valued at slightly more than one cent.

Most Unusual Status Symbol: According to Hall's law, there is a statistical correlation between the number of initials in an Englishman's name and his social class. Members of the upper class have significantly more than three names and/or initials, while members of the lower class average 2.6.

Most Unusual Tax: Rhode Island State Representative Bernard C. Gladstone decided his constituents would not stand for a state income tax. As an alternative source of revenue, he introduced a bill calling for a two-dollar tax on each act of sexual intercourse.

Most Unusual Tax Deductions: W. C. Fields once claimed deductions for charitable contributions to churches in the Solomon Islands and depreciation on his lawnmower.

Most Unusual Union: In 1968 a convention of beggars in Dacca, India, passed a resolution demanding that "the minimum amount of alms be fixed at 15 paisa [three cents]." The convention also demanded that the interval between when a person hears a knock at his front door and when he offers alms should not exceed 45 seconds.

Consumer Products

Best Airline: Once *Newsweek* could say, Freelandia is "America's newest and freakiest airline." Now Freelandia is no more, but it was great while it lasted. On board, the stewardesses served organic peanut butter and honey sandwiches, while the carrot juice flowed like wine, and the rock bands blared. It was an airborne party. And best of all, Freelandia was technically operated as an air-travel club, which kept the fares incredibly low: New York to Geneva for $100 as an example.

Painted bright banana yellow, with a hand waving by-by on the tail assembly, the Freelandia jet was unmistakable. It will be missed.

Best Airship: To detractors the early dirigibles were known as "sick whales," and their miserable safety record proved that they were worthy of such abuse. All three candidates for the best airship lived in fame and went down in flame. The queen of the airships was the *Hindenburg*, which exploded so spectacularly in Lakehurst, New Jersey, on May 6, 1937; she featured staterooms for seventy-two passengers, showers, a grand piano, and a cargo capacity of over fifty tons. The airship *Akron*, built for the United States Navy, was outfitted with a retractable runway in her underbelly capable of launching and landing five sparrow hawk fighter planes. After the *Akron* met disaster in 1933, her sister ship *Macon* inherited the sparrow hawks. In addition to being the world's only flying aircraft carrier, the *Macon* was the fastest dirigible ever built, with a top speed of eighty-five knots, as well as the first flying machine with a dial telephone system. One especially popular device on the *Macon* was a "sub-cloud car," which allowed an observer to be lowered down through the clouds, like a bucket down a well.

Out of hometown chauvinism we mention that the *Macon* and the *Akron* were both constructed at the Goodyear Air-

Airship *Akron* in hangar at Akron, Ohio

ship hangar in Akron, Ohio, the largest building in the world without internal supports, enclosing over 55 million cubic feet of Akron air. Sudden temperature changes often cause clouds to form in the top of that mammoth structure, resulting in brief indoor showers.

The word blimp, by the way, has a curious etymology; it was inadvertently coined in December 1915 by Lieutenant A. D. Cunningham during an inspection tour of the British air station at Capel. While Cunningham was examining His Majesty's airship *SS-12,* he could not resist tweaking the gasbag with his thumb and forefinger. The inflated fabric responded with a deep rubbery echo. Amused by the odd noise, Cunningham tried to imitate it: "Blimp!" he said experimentally, then straightened his face and continued with the formal inspection. Officers accompanying him spread the story, and since that date nonrigid airships have been called blimps.

Best Automaton: Archytas, a craftsman of Tarentum, Greece, is said to have assembled a mechanical pigeon that could

217

actually fly in 400 B.C. This intriguing but unlikely claim aside, a Monsieur Vaucanson exhibited what was probably the most unusual automaton ever constructed. His windup flute player, displayed in Paris in 1738, would put a miniature flute to its lips, finger the valves, and blow a real tune.

Best Bottle: A bottle blown in Leith, Scotland, in 1751, is believed to be the largest ever produced by human lungs. It reportedly measured forty by forty-two inches and held nearly two hogsheads (126 gallons).

According to *Gourmet* magazine, the largest standard bottle for champagne is the Nebuchadnezzar, containing five gallons of bubbly.

Best Light Bulb: Clarence Whited screwed a 150-watt light bulb into a ceiling socket in his home in Raven, West Virginia, over thirty years ago and has been using it ever since.

Best Mirror: Looking into mirrors can be fun again, thanks to Milton Doolittle, inventor, industrial engineer, and "friend of the overweight." Doolittle has invented a mirror, which he calls "Select-a-Size," that reflects favorably on overweight persons by making them look thinner. How much thinner? That depends on the user: A special control knob alters the curvature of the glass, so that the mirror-gazer's girth will wax or wane before his or her very eyes. In fact, thin people can fatten up without stuffing themselves with chocolate malteds and Drake's Ring-Dings simply by adjusting the control knob appropriately.

Aside from flattery addicts, who will buy the Select-a-Size? In the two years since it was put on the market, its buyers have included health spas, fashion designers and, most significantly, doctors and therapists who have used it as an aid in helping obese patients slim down.

Best Pen: For $400, Randy Meyer, of Lexington, Kentucky, purchased a set of steel-belted tires touted to be impervious to bullets, bombs and spikes. Perhaps. Shortly after they were installed, Meyer ran over a sharp object and had a blow-out. The sharp object was a ballpoint pen. "It still wrote," he said.

Best Protection Against Obscene Phone Calls: An electronics company called Telident, Inc., has come up with a device that strips the obscene phone caller of his anonymity and makes it a snap to trace calls. It consists, essentially, of a box that attaches to the receiving telephone and provides a digital read-out of the caller's phone number and area code, even if he is calling from a pay phone or from a private phone with an unlisted number. Telident says that the device also provides protection against telephoned bomb threats and ransom demands as well as salesmen offering real estate deals in the Poconos. Makes a wonderful gift for the insecure.

Best Toilet: Imagine a flush toilet that uses no water, no energy to speak of, produces no odor, and turns all wastes deposited therein, along with kitchen scraps, into rich, usable compost. Such a device does, in fact, exist, and the Swedes have a name for it—which is only natural, since they invented it. It's called a Multrum.

The Multrum is hardly a new invention—it's actually been around since the mid-1940s—but its price—$1,500—still keeps it beyond the means of all but the very rich or the very fastidious. There are about 1,000 Multrums in use today throughout Scandinavia and Germany as well as in the New Hampshire and Massachusetts homes of Abby Aldrich Rockefeller, daughter of Chase Manhattan Bank President David Rockefeller. Miss Rockefeller read about the Multrum in a gardening magazine not long ago and was so impressed that she purchased American rights to it, founding a company called Clivus Multrum USA Inc., and named herself president.

Best Toilet Paper: Top honors go neither to Scott, Charmin, or an old Sears-Roebuck catalog, but rather to the neck of a well-downed goose, according to Gargantua, the gargantuan protagonist of Rabelais's *Gargantua and Pantagruel*. At the age of five, Gargantua experiments with all manner of materials—feathered bonnets, a lady's neckerchief, an adult cat, gourd leaves, cabbages, beets, a pillow, a slipper, a hat, a lawyer's briefcase, and then several varieties of fauna, including a hen, a chicken, a rabbit, a pigeon, an otter, and a cormorant, before settling on a goose's neck. "Do not imagine that the felicity of the heroes and demigods in the Elysian Fields arises from their asphodel, their ambrosia, or their nectar, as those ancients say," he tells his doting father. "It comes, in my opinion, from their wiping their arses with the neck of a goose, and that is the opinion of Master Duns Scotus too."

Worst Ashtray: Our mind is aswim with early memories of ghastly ashtrays shaped like grotesque faces with the laughing mouth serving as the bowl, ashtrays shaped like half-shut eyes, and one model in the shape of an unshod foot, embossed with the legend, "I get a kick out of Rhode Island." The worst, however, is most likely a toilet-shaped number imprinted with an image of the Basilica of St. Anthony and sold at a gift shop across the street from the Basilica in Padua, Italy.

Worst Picture Postcard: A Dallas picture postcard magnate turned out a souvenir postcard of the assassination of President Kennedy early in 1964. The card shows an aerial view of the scene of the shooting, pinpointing the Texas Schoolbook Depository, the grassy knoll, and the motorcade route. A smiling inset of the late president looks down at the scene from the upper righthand corner.

A series of twelve postcards depicting the high points of the life of Napoleon I also represent some sort of peak in conceptual stupidity and historical inaccuracy.

Worst Toilet Paper: An unnamed Swabian shoemaker published a pamphlet two centuries ago in which he attributed the moral decay of mankind to the use of indoor plumbing and toilet paper. The solution to man's woes, he said, lay in man's tending to his needs in the "great outdoors," using leaves and moss instead of paper. In so doing, the poisons that defiled his body and soul would be released into the surrounding air and he would undergo a complete physical and spiritual purification. Love among men would be enhanced, people would be humbler and more diligent, and the Kingdom of God on Earth would be brought much closer to realization.

Worst Toy: In 1968 a Japanese firm introduced a toy atomic bomb that flashes, bangs, and emits a cloud of real smoke.

Worst Vehicle: "So get your girl and take her tandem down the street/Don't you know you're an asphalt athlete. . . . Grab your board and go sidewalk surfing with me." Jan and Dean sang about it, the *Quarterly Skateboarder* wrote about it, and millions of kids all over the world did it.

The skateboard was an outlet for all those would-be surfers

stranded in Des Moines or Cincinnati, hundreds of miles from the nearest salt water wave. It was a unique vehicle that offered the combined thrills of surfing, skiing, and soap-box derby racing, along with the economy of roller-skating. The skateboard required the balance of gymnastics and the grace of the dance. Also, the skateboard was a menace.

As one California company was turning out 100,000 boards a day, hospitals were admitting countless young people with broken arms, broken legs, and severe concussions. A number of deaths were reported as reckless hoedaddies rode that imaginary perfect wave down their driveways into oncoming traffic. But what caused the greatest concern were those scabs. "Wiping out" in the warm Pacific is undoubtably preferable to wiping out on macadam, asphalt, or cement. And it was probably the sight of all those grisly scabs, and not the more serious injuries, that caused many communities to outlaw skateboards.

Most Unusual Bed: Khumarawayh, the Mohammedan caliph of Egypt from 884–895, was a man who enjoyed the good things in life. For example, he believed that a man's castle is his home, so he covered the palace walls with his favorite metal—gold. But in the twentieth century Khumarawayh should be remembered fondly as the man who invented an early prototype of the waterbed. In *The Age of Faith* Will Durant informs us that Khumarawayh "taxed his people to provide himself with a pool of quicksilver on which his bed of inflated leather cushions might gently float to win him sleep."

During the last six weeks of his life, Cardinal Armand Jean du Plessis de Richelieu, Louis XIII's powerful and devious minister, occupied another extraordinary bed. Sorely afflicted with headaches, hemorrhoids, boils, and a disease of the bladder, Richelieu slept and worked in a vast litter transported by twenty-four bodyguards, in this way managing to continue with his diplomatic duties. In addition to his bed, the Cardinal's magnificent litter contained a chair, a table, and his private secretary who penned Richelieu's letters and made notes of his conversations. When the traveling bed proved too large to enter through the doors of any building Richelieu proposed to occupy, he commanded his bodyguards to batter down the walls.

Most Unusual Bell: Cast in 1733, the gigantic Moscow Bell, also known as the Czar Kolokol Bell, weighs 440,000 pounds and measures twenty-two feet eight inches in diameter. It fell when workmen attempted to hang it, and a twelve-ton "chip" broke off the lip. For a while it was used as a small chapel; now it rests atop a platform in front of the Kremlin.

Most Unusual Cigar: Cigars shaped like matzohs, the flat, unleavened breads eaten by Jews during Passover, are manufactured and sold by the Nat Sherman Company, a New York tobacconeer. The Sherman company also markets a corkscrew-shaped cigar known to the public as the Sherman Twist.

Most Unusual Clocks: Nicholas Grollier de Serviere invented a clock in 1679 that consisted of a small lizard climbing a post on which the hours and minutes were marked. The lizard's snout, Grollier claimed, always pointed directly at the correct time. He also devised a similar clock which featured a mouse crawling along a calibrated horizontal block.

In A.D. 807, the emperor Charlemagne was presented with a more elaborate timepiece by Caliph Haroun-al Raschid. It was round, as were most clocks of the day, and powered by water. In place of twelve numbers on the dial there were twelve doors. At six o'clock, for example, the sixth hour door would open and six brass balls would be dropped out in succession and strike a bell. All the doors would remain open until twelve o'clock, when figurines of mounted horsemen appeared from each of the holes and paraded around the dial.

A bicycle clock was constructed by Frenchman Alphonse Duhamel. Twelve feet high, the works, the dial, the ornament, and every other detail are all made out of bicycle parts. It strikes the hours and quarters on a bicycle bell and reputedly keeps very good time.

A clock in Worsley Hall, Lancashire, England, always struck 13 o'clock instead of one. The Duke of Bridgewater, who was once master of Worsley, was constantly complaining that his workmen returned late from their lunch hour. The workers explained that they did not notice when the clock struck only a single time—the signal for them to go back to work. Consequently, the Duke had the mechanism adjusted so that it struck a loud, insistent thirteen times.

Most Unusual Cup: It was a classical custom to take impressions of beautiful bosoms to serve as molds for golden drink-

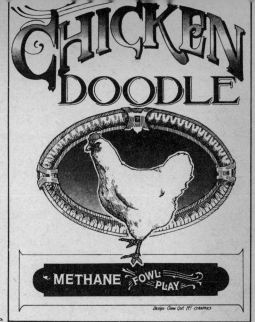

Chicken Doodle

ing vessels. Marc Antony, for instance, used to drink from a goblet shaped around the breast of Cleopatra; a cup in the antique fashion, molded on the breast of Marie Antoinette is still on display in the porcelain factory of Sèvres.

Most Unusual Fuel: In the grip of the Great Fuel Panic of '73, a Belvedere, California, outfit calling itself "Captain Calculus and the Normal Street Mechanics Institute" published a booklet offering detailed instructions on how to run an automobile on chicken excreta. The major step in the Great Conversion is to build a special cauldron in which the wastes are heated to produce methane gas. Entitled "Chicken Doodle," the guide sells for $1.25.

In addition, Harold Bate, an English inventor, has devised the ideal rural vehicle for times of energy crisis—an automobile that runs on pig manure. To the relief of antiodor pollutionists, there is an intermediate step between pig and tank, in which manure is distilled into methane gas.

Most Unusual Lock (and no doubt the best): At the French Crystal Palace in the eighteenth century, a combination lock

223

was exhibited which required 3,674,385 turns of the dial to open and close it. It reportedly took one man 120 nights to lock and another man an additional 120 nights to unlock.

Most Unusual Oil Spill: According to the *Smithsonian* magazine, a storage tank in Allen Park, Michigan, developed a leak and spilled nearly 10,000 gallons of oil into the Rouge River during the winter of 1973. Since the river was frozen, much of the oil collected in a huge, slippery puddle on top of the ice. When ecologists analyzed the puddle they were surprised to find that it was 100 percent pure vegetable oil. The tank, it seems, was the property of the Frito-Lay Company and it contained the oil they used to fry potato chips. In fact, the oil had been oozing its way across Frito-Lay's executive parking lot in a one-inch slick for several weeks. Walking to and from their cars, the oblivious potato chip execs splashed through the oil twice a day without complaint.

Most Unusual Picture Postcard: When the United States took possession of the Philippines after the Spanish-American War, there was a rumor that an army patrol exploring the interior of Luzon had discovered an isolated tribe of headhunters, called the Ingorot, with long, prehensile tails. According to the rumor, the government was trying to hush up the Ingorot story to protect the tailed people from harassment. Still, the evidence was undeniable. Several soldiers returning from the Pacific swore they had seen men with tails. In Manila someone produced a photo of an Ingorot, complete with tail; the photo was reproduced as a picture postcard and thousands were mailed all over the world.

Needless to say, the rumor was totally false. Anthropologists at the Smithsonian Institution discovered the original photo of the Ingorot man, and he had a very ordinary posterior; the postcard was a fake. Apparently the rumor got started because, like many tribes, the Ingorot dressed up in animal costumes, sometimes wearing horns and tails for their religious ceremonies.

This is just the most recent yarn about the existence of tailed men. Such stories, always tinged with racism, have been around since man first noticed that he was lacking what most mammals had. Marco Polo told of a tailed race on the island of Lambri: "In this kingdom are found men with tails, a span in length, like those of a dog, but not covered with hair." For centuries it was the half-believed gossip of the Continent that Englishmen had tails in their britches.

Most Unusual Radio: The world's most unusual radio, when it's perfected, will be worn in the vagina and send out electronic signals to the doctor's office when the wearer ovulates. It is still in the drawingboard stage at the Tyler Clinic in California.

Most Unusual Ropes: According to Bishop Charles Henry Fowler, a Methodist missionary who visited Japan in 1888, all the women of a northern province cut their hair and wove it into three tremendous ropes, the largest measuring ten inches in circumference and 2,600 feet in length. The half-mile-long braids were used in the construction of a magnificent wooden shrine.

Most Unusual Silk: A large Mediterranean clam secretes milky strands up to twelve inches long from its foot. The fibers of this "beard" were gathered by the ancients and woven into a beautiful golden silk. Pulitzer-prizewinning science writer Thomas R. Henry has speculated that this remarkable fabric may have been the Golden Fleece sought by Jason and his Argonauts. Small quantities of golden silk are still being produced in Italy, and a glove made of this rare material is on display in the Smithsonian Institution.

Most Unusual Toilet Paper: During the mid-1960s, when the Indonesian rupiah was valued at 325 to the dollar, travelers throughout the Indonesian archipelago discovered that the cheap, porous paper used in the printing of one-sen notes, worth $1/_{100}$ of a rupiah, made a more-than-satisfactory toilet tissue and was vastly less expensive than commercially marketed tissue since 32,500 one-sen notes could be obtained in most banks for one dollar.

Most Unusual Toothpaste: Doggy-dent is a beef-flavored toothpaste for dogs developed and patented by Ursula Dietrich, a California dentist.

Most Unusual Vehicle: When future archaeologists are digging through the ruins of our civilization, one find they will have difficulty in comprehending is a strange stick with a metal spring at one end to which two pedals are fastened. The pogo stick, which originated somewhere in France, infected England and America in 1921. There was international rivalry over who would perfect the pogo: "American pogo sticks are in every way superior to ours," complained the British magazine *Punch*. And there were pogo stick competitions, like the hula hoop competitions a generation later. A young lad won the first New York *Daily News* pogo contest in 1921 by hopping 1,600 times in fifteen minutes and traversing 600 yards in eight minutes.

Recently a Los Angeles firm introduced a motorized pogo stick, powered by a single-cylinder, two-cycle engine. It gets 30,000 hops per gallon of gas.

Most Unusual Vending Machine: A major breakthrough in the vending machine industry is the Liquormatic, patented by a man named Billy Utz in 1970. The would-be buyer inserts a special plastic ID in a slot to establish that he is of legal age. Then he is required to pass a simple mechanical test to demonstrate his sobriety. (For many drunks, getting the coins in the slot would be test enough.) Only then will the machine sell the customer his bottle of J & B.

Most Unusual Wallpaper: In the Crystal Palace at the Great Exhibition in London, held in 1851, a wallpaper pattern was displayed, which depicted a hunting scene in a lush forest. Twelve thousand separate blocks were used in the printing.

Food

Best Advice Handed Down to Us by the Ancients: "Avoid beans as you would matricide." (Pythagoras in *Golden Verses*)

Best Banquet: *Larousse Gastronomique* describes a banquet that François I hosted for Catherine de Medici (1519–1589) in Paris. It was one of the most sumptuous ever staged: "30 peacocks, 33 pheasants, 21 swans, 9 cranes, 33 ducks, 33 ibises, 33 egrets, 33 young herons, 30 young goats, 99 young pigeons, 99 turtle doves, 13 partridges, 33 goslings, 3 young bustards, 13 young capons, 90 quails, 66 boiling chickens, 66 Indian chickens, 30 capons, 90 spring chickens in vinegar, 66 chickens 'cooked as grouse,' were served at the banquet. There were a great number of other dishes from which butcher's meat was excluded, being considered too ordinary, which, however, did not prevent the organizer of this monster banquet from serving to his guests many young piglets, rabbits, and a vast quantity of vegetables such as asparagus, broad beans, peas, and artichokes."

Best Barbecue: A folksier feast was staged by John Calloway when he became governor of Oklahoma in the 1930s. Nearly 100,000 Sooners were served at a barbecue that sounds like a Texas joke come true. The cooking was done in giant trenches; coffee was brewed in a 10,000-gallon vat; and the victuals included beef, pork, mutton, chicken, goose, duck, buffalo, bear, antelope, squirrel, 'possum, 'coon, rabbit, and reindeer.

Best Beer: If you doubt that beer is a serious subject, just consider how it changed the course of American history. In *The Pilgrim Journal* New England's first colonists tell why they decided to put to shore at Plymouth Rock instead of sailing south toward a warmer site. "We could not now take time for further consideration, our victuals being spent and especially our beer."

The definition of a snob is a person who insists that European beers outclass American brew. Actually, a panel of tasters assembled by the Consumers' Union in 1969 judged two American products, Coors and Miller High Life, to be among the very best. They were ranked well above Löwenbrau, Wurzburger, and other prestigious European brands, although it must be remembered that the imports may deteriorate with the long shipping delays. For our money, the best beer of all is Labatt's, a rich, middle-bodied beer produced in New London, Ontario. Labatt's is widely available in the Midwest at competitive prices.

Best Candy: In Kuala Lumpur, Malaysia, in 1969, police impounded a cache of chocolates containing large doses of sexual stimulants which, they said, had been smuggled into the country from Thailand and Japan. The candy came in six or seven varieties.

Best Chicken: For unsurpassed tenderness, try Chicken a la Toulouse-Lautrec. The great, grotesquely formed painter of Paris lowlife scenes was also a gourmet chef, and a number of his favorite recipes have been collected in a beautifully illustrated book entitled *The Art of Cuisine*. Toulouse-Lautrec reveals that the secret of delectable chicken is in the killing. "In order to make chickens immediately edible," he writes, "take them out of the hen run, pursue them into open country, and when you have made them run, kill them with a gun loaded with very small shot. The meat of the chicken, gripped with fright, will become tender."

But suppose some night you are too tired for the chase, where can you find the best carry-out fried chicken? Several authorities recommend Colonel Sanders' Original Kentucky Fried Chicken. In a recent full-length profile of Harland Sanders, *The New Yorker* said, "His fast frying process produces fried chicken of a quality unknown in New York restaurants and rare even in Southern restaurants." An editor of *The Ladies' Home Journal*, who surveyed 153 fast food restaurants was even more enthusiastic. "Kentucky Fried Chicken is terrific," he said, "and I don't care who knows. I cannot resist the stuff."

But when picking up your chicken, it might be wise to resist the mashed potatoes and gravy. The gravy has been the

Colonel's pet peeve ever since he sold his recipe and franchises to a McDonald's-like supercorporation. After sampling the gravy that the corporation substituted for his own, the colonel sputtered, "How do you serve this goddamned slop? With a straw?" A corporation executive interviewed by *The New Yorker* was apologetic. "Let's face it," he explained, "the Colonel's gravy is fantastic, but you have to be a Rhodes scholar to cook it."

Colonel Sanders now spends most of his time at the hotel and restaurant he operates in Shelbyville, Kentucky. In the Louisville–Lexington area he is an honored citizen, and on slow news days the local papers often send a reporter around to solicit his views on world affairs. Once a reporter asked him what he thought about hippies. The colonel smiled benevolently and said, "They eats chicken, don't they?"

Best Diet: The weight loss regimen offered by Weight Watchers, Inc.—an adaptation, really, of a diet that's been available at the New York City Board of Health's obesity clinic for years—provides dieters with the most filling, varied menus, the most sensible approach to eating, and the best track record of any diet now being popularly touted. The Weight Watchers' program, with its frequent snacks, ingenious recipes (Weight Watchers Moussaka; Weight Watchers Blue Cheese Dressing; Weight Watchers Veal Parmigiana) and filling meals does not merely keep you full and pacified. You will actually feel uneasy about eating as much as you are required to on the diet, and then be amazed when the excess pounds come off so easily.

Best Hamburgers: The best hamburgers in the United States are at Winstead's Drive-In in Kansas City, says food expert Calvin Trillin, and the *best chopped chicken liver* is at the Parkway, a kosher restaurant at 163 Allen Street on New York City's Lower East Side. For the *best fish chowder*, he claims, it's Glady's Canteen, in Lunenberg, Nova Scotia.

Best Ice Cream: Valla's hand-packed ice cream, sold in Chicago, wins out over Breyers' hand-packed, Basset's ice cream, made in Philadelphia, and Häagen-Dazs. All four are marked by a smooth texture and a purity of flavor. Chocolate marshmallow is the flavor to try if you're sampling Valla's for the first time. Breyers' vanilla fudge and the chocolate of both Basset's and Häagen-Dazs are also superb.

Best Pizza: While pizzas of all shapes and varieties are served in restaurants and trattorias throughout Italy, the true birthplace of this delicacy is the United States. Thus, while Italians who visit American shores are often critical of the quality of Italian cuisine in the States—even the food served in the finest Italian restaurants rarely meets their standards—they cannot afford to be so uppity when it comes to pizza. The fact is, the best is found right here.

Most pizzas we've sampled are good, a few are very good (most notably the unconventional offerings of Goldberg's pizzerias in New York City). The best, however, is in Chicago, and is made by Due's. Visitors to the Windy City often pick up a pie or two, or as many as they can stuff into their baggage, and bring them home frozen. It makes sense; even frozen, Due's pizzas are better than anything else we've tasted fresh. The crust is as thick as a bagel; you can literally get lost in the cheese; and there is enough chopped meat in a single pie to keep a McDonald's freak happy for days. There is also something indescribably *different* about Due's pies, a level of quality that transcends the bounds of conventional pizzadom, breaking through into the sphere of the godlike. It's still the best food bargain in Chicago.

Best Restaurant in the United States: As a crusty old restaurateur who ran a charming little Polynesian bistro in Honolulu told us some years ago: "One man's meat is another man's poi, son." The fact is, there is no accounting for taste, and there is even less accounting for taste in matters gastronomical. Nonetheless, we'll side with food expert Calvin Trillin who calls Kansas City "the best eating town in the world," and Arthur Bryant's Barbecue there, "the single best restaurant in the whole world." The specialty of the house is hickory smoked meat baked in a brick oven. The tables are covered with yellow oil cloth.

A more conventional choice for best restaurant in the United States—one that would sit better with connoisseurs—is Lutèce, in New York City. The cuisine is French and the appetizers are superb, particularly the mousseline of pike with lobster sauce. A party of ten can share, as an appetizer, an escallop of salmon served on a three-foot-long wooden platter. If you go for dinner, expect to pay at least sixty dollars for two. The 1974 Mobil Travel Guide gives Lutèce five stars—its top rating—along with only five other restaurants in the country: La Grenouille in New York City, La Maisonette in Cincinnati, La Dome in Fort Lauderdale, Florida, and

Lutèce

the Mandarin in San Francisco. Oddly, Mobil makes no mention at all of New York's Chinatown, which, viewed as one sprawling, multistreet restaurant, might well be the best single place to eat in the whole country.

Best Soft Drink: Vernor's Ginger Ale, produced and marketed in Detroit, Michigan. Even the canned stuff is better than the bottled brew of most other brands. The secret, says *Esquire* magazine, is in the aging process. Vernor's lets its extract mellow for four years.

Worst Alcoholic Beverage: In 1974, police in Pocatello, Idaho, arrested two women on charges of manufacturing and selling an ersatz brandy which was distilled from water, vodka, and urine. Meanwhile, a whisky distillery in Calcutta, India, proudly proclaims on its labels: "Excellent whiskey made from high-quality Scotch grapes."

Insecticide was the secret ingredient in one particular batch of *guajiro lina,* a rumlike brew distilled from sugar cane and sold widely in Nicaragua. A tavern keeper there made the mistake of decanting a supply into some empty insecticide cans and the unfortunate mixture killed eleven customers. His own end came when he defiantly quaffed a pint of the stuff to discredit public accusations that his liquor was poisoned. He died within minutes.

Worst Beer: The advertisements exclaim: "Oh, my gosh, it's Frothingslosh!" Old Frothingslosh beer, bottled only around the Christmas holiday season by Iron City Brewing, is billed as the "pale, stale ale with the foam on the bottom." It is not a breakthrough in brewing, however, which enables them to make this revolutionary claim; they simply paste the label on upside down.

The worst beer according to a Consumers Union tasting panel was Tudor, the A & P store brand. Most tasters concluded that Tudor was excessively sweet, lacking in bitterness, and low in carbonation; several remarked that "Tudor tasted more like apple cider than beer." The CU test was conducted before the introduction of Hop 'n Gator, which was without doubt the saddest event in the history of brewing. Hop 'n Gator, as the name makes insipidly plain, combines the flavors of beer and citrus juice. It is an abomination.

Worst Beverage: The Uape Indians of the upper Amazon cremate their dead. To absorb the admirable qualities of the deceased, his ashes are mixed with *casiri,* the local alcoholic beverage, and drunk by all the members of the family with great reverence and fond memories.

Masai tribesmen from East Africa mix blood drawn from their cattle with sweet milk. Blood is an indispensable part of their diet because it provides salt, which is very scarce in the Masai territories.

Paiwari, another slightly alcoholic drink from the Amazon, is made by scorching meal from the cassava plant. The Indian women chew this preparation, then expectorate it into a vat to ferment. The *paiwari* chewers are a highly professional group who have their lips specially tattooed to ward off evil spirits that might enter their saliva.

Worst Candy: Next time you sink your choppers into a Three Musketeers or a Mary Jane, try not to think about the 200,000 bars and 7,100 boxes of factory-fresh candy that were found by the Federal Food and Drug Administration in 1971 to be riddled with rat pellets and dead bugs. Unfortunately, the FDA released its findings after most of the candy had been sold.

Worst Chicken: *Atlas* magazine reported in 1971 that the Japanese had begun breeding and marketing a new type of chicken, called the *buroira* (a mispronunciation of *broiler*). The chicken is cooped up in a cage so small that it can neither walk, scratch around, or flap its wings, and growth is artificially accelerated by twenty-four-hour lighting and a diet that includes cyclamates, tranquilizers, antibiotics, hormones, a heady dose of miscellaneous nutritional acids, and laxatives. The main objection to the new product was the hormones, which reportedly could produce enlarged breasts in men.

Worst Cookbook: *The Joys of Jell-O*, published in 1964.

Worst Diet: The Doctor's Quick Weight Loss Diet, more commonly known as the Stillman Diet, with its monastic adherence to meat, cottage cheese, and tap water, drains all the charm and pleasure from the eating experience and turns it into a purely biological function. And the quick-loss variation diets that Dr. Stillman has devised—his Baked Potato and Buttermilk Diet, his Yogurt Only Diet, and his Bananas and Milk Diet ("By considering a banana as one meal, and a glass of skim milk as another meal . . . you can eat nine . . . 'meals' a day and still total only 900 calories") are as laughable as they are unsatisfying, and less unsatisfying than they are nutritionally unsound.

The sacrifice-all-for-the-sake-of-your-body type of regimen has proved that when the calories go down, emotional tension goes up. Doctors in Jerusalem's Hebrew University Medical School recently studied the emotional effects of massive weight loss on ten people who had dieted off between 110 and 240 pounds apiece. One of them committed suicide; all the others required in-hospital psychiatric care. However, when they stopped dieting, lifted the ban on Hostess Twinkies, and regained the lost poundage, their depression vanished and all was bright and rosy again.

Worst Diet Book: *Calories Don't Count*, by Dr. Herman Taller. Oh, but they do, *they do!* the Federal Trade Commission countered in an injunction that barred Dr. Taller, in 1963, from continuing to distribute his book. By that time,

233

he had been catapulted to fame and fortune on a wave of Hershey Kisses and Hostess Snowballs, exhorting millions of adipose Americans to consume as much as 5,000 guilt-free calories a day. ("Extra slices of chicken? Ridiculous! I eat extra chickens.") Dr. Taller's prescription for losing unsightly pounds was to eat as much as you wanted so long as you took care to maintain a balance of two-thirds fats, one-third proteins, and practically no carbohydrates. Low carbohydrate diets, of course, are nothing new, and while doctors debate their safety, it is true that some people lose weight on them. What made Dr. Taller's diet unique, however, were the miraculous CDC tablets that one took while following this regimen; the pills, he said, were the key to maintaining your health while shedding weight. Moreover, CDC pills purportedly decreased cholesterol, prevented heartburn, fought colds, and increased sexual potency.

A month's supply of CDC tablets ran as high as $600, a hefty sum by any standards. But when the Food and Drug Administration found that the tablets were not only ineffective but contained nothing but safflower oil, they pressed charges. Investigators discovered that Taller and the pharmaceutical company had a little deal arranged whereby Taller was getting a percentage on all the CDC tablets sold, and together they were getting fat off the overweight. The company and Taller were both convicted of mail fraud and violations of the Food, Drug and Cosmetics Act.

Taller's spiritual ancestor in dietary folly was the French writer Gleizes, who wrote some ten books on vegetarianism, all of which endlessly repeated the same theme: Meat is godless, vegetables are holy. Gleizes is said to have deserted his wife because she refused to stop eating beef.

Worst Food Faddist: Horace Fletcher (1849–1919) is believed to have composed the motto: "Nature will castigate those who don't masticate," and certainly it is the finest statement of his firmly held conviction that we chew too little and, therefore, do not get the full nutritional value out of our food. It is basic Fletcher dogma, still defended by many grandmothers, that one should chew each morsel thirty-two times, once for each tooth. Furthermore, soup and milk should be sloshed around in the mouth for a full fifteen or twenty seconds until the saliva has had ample opportunity to do its work.

Fletcherism was good for Fletcher. On his fiftieth birthday

Horace Fletcher

he bicycled two hundred miles in a single day; and in 1903 he tested the endurance of his legs on Yale's ergometer, raising three hundred pounds 350 times, twice the record of Yale's most formidable athlete. His meals, consisting primarily of milk, maple sugar, and prepared cereals, cost him an average of eleven cents a day, and once as an experiment he lived on potatoes alone for fifty-eight days.

John D. Rockefeller and Upton Sinclair were among the millions of Fletcher faddists in the early 1900s who were determined to chew their way to good health and long life. Novelist Henry James publicly declared, "Horace Fletcher saved my life, and, what is more, he improved my disposition." Gradually, however, the chewing craze faded, in part because it made for incredibly long and boring meals, and in part because it conflicted with another favorite maxim of grandmothers: "Eat your food before it gets cold."

Worst Fruit: The durian. It's about the size of a bowling ball, covered with sharp, stiff, spiny points, and grows on trees throughout southeast Asia, most predominantly in Malaysia, Thailand, and Indonesia. The business end of a durian, which is the inside, is mucuslike in consistency, and the unique flavor is reminiscent of garlic, smoked ham, and rancid cheese. Durians, known throughout the orient as the "king of fruits," are prohibitively expensive when not in season—a medium-sized fruit may go for five or six dollars—and potentially lethal in the hands and stomachs of the unanointed. (One danger is in their weight. Unwitting foreigners have been known to be struck fatally on the head by durians falling from trees. Others have made the mistake of washing down a durian dessert with a quart of beer. The resultant gas has blasted their insides to smithereens.) Walk through the vegetable stalls in Singapore or Bangkok during durian season and you'll swear the city's sewage disposal system is on the blink. English novelist Anthony Burgess, in fact, has said that dining on durian is a lot like eating vanilla custard in a latrine.

Worst Ice Cream: A few new flavors released and mercifully retracted in recent years have been especially offensive to our palates: bubblegum (a Baskin and Robbins' specialty), fig, and licorice. If you're dieting, take special care to avoid Weight Watchers' vanilla or strawberry "frozen dessert" (the chocolate is passable). The taste of the strawberry is virtually indistinguishable from that of the carton in which it is packed (try it if you don't believe us) and the vanilla is the chalkiest, most indigestible substance we've seen short of the barium mixtures they make you swallow in preparation for gastrointestinal X rays.

Worst Meal: In 1971, Hans and Erna W., a Swiss couple vacationing in Hong Kong stopped to eat at a Chinese restaurant there and asked the headwaiter to take their pet poodle, Rosa, into the kitchen and find it something to eat. The waiter misunderstood their request, however, and the couple was aghast when Rosa was brought to their table done to a turn in a round-bottomed frying pan, marinated in sweet-and-sour sauce, and garnished with Chinese vegetables. The meal was left uneaten and the couple were treated for shock.

Worst News for Health Food Addicts: Dr. Alice Chase, who wrote *Nutrition for Health* and other books on the science of proper eating, died recently of malnutrition.

Worst Peanut Butter: Just what are those chunks in Hoody Chunky Style Peanut Butter? A 1972 Oregon health department investigation disclosed that some were peanuts, some were rodent hairs, and some were rat pellets. The investigators also found that some of the peanuts used in Hoody were contaminated with rodent urine.

Hoody executives were sentenced to serve ten days in prison for health code violations. It was not, as you might think, the mere presence of rat hairs that got the Hoody executives in trouble; it was the presence of an unconscionable number. In an effort to crack down on unsanitary conditions at food processing plants, the United States Food and Drug Administration issued strict new guidelines in 1972 on the amount of foreign matter permissible in packaged foods. They make very depressing reading: 1) no more than an average of 50 insect fragments or two rodent hairs per 100 grams of peanut butter will be acceptable; 2) no more than ten fruit fly eggs or two larvae will be allowed in 100 grams of tomato juice; 3) no more than 150 insect fragments are acceptable in an eight-ounce sample of chocolate.

Bon appétit!

Worst Recipe: Here it is, the recipe that *The Joy of Cooking* dared not print, *Homme Rôti avec Patate*. The method of preparation we present was the favorite among cannibals in the Fiji Islands, although the Irish, the Picts, the Congolese, the Aztecs, and the eleventh-century Danes also enjoyed interesting variations of this dish.

Most anthropophagists agree that selecting the right brand and cut is very important, and on the island of New Britain, human meat was sold in butcher shops, greatly simplifying this problem. A number of cultures, notably the Fuegians, distinctly preferred females, ranking their flesh even higher than a good dog (which "tastes of otter"). In the Solomon Islands, women were fattened for roasting like pigs. Some connoisseurs favored white meat, including a Tahitian chief who explained that "The white man, when well roasted, tastes like a ripe banana." But the Fijians generally found other Polynesians more delectable; Europeans were "too salty."

For the details of a Fijian feast, we are indebted to anthropologist A. P. Rice, who published this eye-witness account in a 1910 issue of *The American Antiquarian and Oriental Journal:* The first step is to eviscerate the carcass and wash it thoroughly in salt water. Next, "the carver, with his huge implements of split bamboo, cuts off several members of the body, joint by joint. His assistants then fold them separately in (plantain) leaves and carefully place them in an oven, a simple contrivance of a hole in the ground, lined with hot stones." Roasting time is approximately the same as for pork—forty minutes per pound—and the meat is served with baskets of yams. "The heart, thighs, and arm above the elbow are termed dainties by skilled epicureans," Rice notes.

Worst Sandwich: The Hubert Humphrey Special. "My favorite sandwich," says the senior senator from Minnesota, "is peanut butter, bologna, cheddar cheese, lettuce, and mayonnaise on toasted bread with lots of catsup on the side. Another favorite is toasted peanut butter, cheese and bacon or, if I am in a hurry, just peanut butter and jelly."

Worst Seafood Dinner: In 1974 fishermen from Cebu Province, in the Philippines, landed an eighteen-foot-long hammerhead shark weighing over a ton and brought it to market in Manila where they prepared to cut it up before the very eyes of a throng of eager customers-to-be. The customers lost their appetite for fish, however—and, presumably, for anything else—when the severed head of a woman slid embarrassingly out of the fish's stomach. Those who hung around for more watched the fishermen cut deeper into the shark's innards and exhume several human limbs as well as the remains of a dog.

Worst Soft Drink: Two soft drinks, Squirt (bottled in the United States) and Pshitt (French) vie for dishonors as the worst name for a beverage; no one knows how many customers decide not to buy these products rather than going through the embarrassment of asking, "Do you have Squirt?"

A small Ohio pop company, now defunct, adopted the brand name Norka. In their radio and billboard advertisements they hammered in the slogan, "And remember, Norka spelled backwards is Akron."

But the more significant question is which soft drink *taste* the worst, and in the course of our research a clear choice emerged: Diet Moxie, vintage 1962. Moxie is a New England concoction, first developed in 1884, with a flavor that compares unfavorably with horehound drops. The brand name has entered the American language as a colloquial noun meaning "vigor" or "spunk," perhaps because it takes a good deal of spunk to swallow the stuff.

In the late 1960s Frank Armstrong, the president of Moxie Industries, contemplated introducing Old Moxie to the Old South. He hired a crack research organization to find out whether Southerners liked the taste. "It had the worst ratings they ever recorded," Armstrong confessed to *Forbes* magazine. "Nine out of ten said they wouldn't buy it again."

Moreover, back in 1962, soda manufacturers were still a long way from perfecting the technique of artificial sweetening. Moxie and bitter saccharine combined to form a flavor that defies description, although one who dared try it volunteered the adjective "painful."

Worst Source of Nutrition: If one is really down on his luck and starving, he might consider licking some cancelled or uncancelled postage stamps. The glue is a mixture of cassava (the source of tapioca) and corn—starchy but nutritious.

Worst Vegetable: The rabage. In 1924 a Soviet geneticist named Karpenchenko successfully crossed a cabbage and a radish, producing an entirely new vegetable—the *Rephanobrassica* or rabage. (An unfortunate name, but clearly rabage is preferable to cadish.) Rabages in turn could produce little rabages, and there was great hope for a plant with a plump, edible root and delectable, leafy head. Much to the world's misfortune, despite determined efforts at selective breeding, the rabage yielded only the straggly greens of a radish and the small, useless roots of a cabbage.

This suggests another brief disputed story about selective breeding. Isadora Duncan sat next to George Bernard Shaw at a dinner party one evening in London. Miss Duncan had recently read a book on eugenics, and she was much impressed with the idea that people of ability had an obligation to find each other and produce talented offspring. Confidently, she suggested to the playwright that theirs would be the eugenically ideal marriage—the most graceful and beautiful woman in the world and the wittiest, most talented writer. "Yes, Miss Duncan," Shaw replied politely. "But what if the child should have my body and your brains?"

Worst Wine: Two-hundred seventeen Italian wine merchants were arrested in 1969 for producing and attempting to market nearly three million gallons of a mysterious brew which consisted, in part, of ox blood, ammonia, and banana skins and contained not a single grape.

Most Unusual Appetizer: Muktuk is an Eskimo delicacy consisting of whale skin and a layer of whale blubber, often served as an appetizer before dinner. The best is found in Nome, Alaska, probably at the Nugget Inn No. 3. First-time tasters of the dish find it a bit like cod-liver oil in solid form.

Most Unusual Bread: A Cairo museum displays a loaf of bread found in one of the Pyramids. Archaeologists say it is 4,500 years old and very stale.

Most Unusual Cake: In June of 1730, Frederick William, King of Prussia, invited his entire army—30,000 guests in all—to a picnic dinner. To top off the meal the King ordered a team of eight horses to draw in the most colossal cake of all time: eighteen yards long, eight yards wide, and one-half yard thick. The cake was made from thirty-six bushels of flour, 200 gallons of milk, one ton of butter, one ton of yeast, and over 5,000 eggs. Frederick's army was too full to finish the dessert, so slices were distributed to civilians in nearby villages and towns.

Most Unusual Cheese: It is mind expanding to contemplate that there are more microbes in a two-and-a-half-pound wedge of cheese than there are people on this earth. Imagine then, how many tiny organisms lived in the 34,591-pound cheddar made by the Wisconsin Cheese Foundation in 1964. Well over 10,000 thoroughbred Guernsey and Holstein cows contributed to the project, which was displayed at the New York World's Fair.

Most Unusual Cocktail: Pliny the Elder foisted thirty-seven volumes of hearsay on the world, which it took scholars fourteen centuries to correct, and he is the source of this tidbit. Nevertheless, there is sufficient scientific substance to the following story to make it somewhat credible.

Cleopatra, Pliny says, once made a wager with Mark Antony that she could spend over three million dollars on an evening's entertainment. There were dancers garbed in specially made costumes of gold and rare feathers; there were jugglers and performing elephants; there were a thousand maid servants attending to the couple's every need; and there was a seemingly never-ending banquet of indescribable splendor. At the end of the evening, Cleopatra proposed to toast her lover with a vessel of vinegar. But first she dropped her exquisite pearl earrings into the cup, each worth a small kingdom, and watched them dissolve. Then she raised the sour cocktail of untold value to her lips and drank it down.

Pearls, it is true, are largely carbonate and will dissolve in a mild acid solution such as vinegar. Complete dissolution, however, would probably take several hours in vinegar too potent to quaff with a smile. But if Cleopatra crushed her pearls first, the powder would have melted immediately with a gentle effervescence in a solution that one could drink without severe gastrointestinal distress. So perhaps, just perhaps, Pliny was telling the truth about this grandly romantic and profligate gesture.

This story leads us to a discussion of *aurum potabile* or liquid gold, which was considered the greatest wonder drug of them all during the Middle Ages. Even in the Renaissance a cocktail of gold was occasionally prescribed for patients who could afford it. Court records show that Louis XI took an emulsion containing ninety-six gold coins for treatment of his epilepsy. Usually the gold was mixed with borage, balm, sugar, cinnamon, and other exotic ingredients to make it more healthful and more palatable. Gold therapy was believed to be especially effective for smallpox and warts and was also considered an excellent enema.

Most Unusual Coffee: Frederick the Great of Prussia is said to have preferred his coffee brewed with champagne rather than water.

Most Unusual Cookies: First prize in the 1972 Susquehanna Valley Science Engineering Fair went to high school student Velma Anstadt, of Turbatville, Pennsylvania, who whipped up a batch of cookies made with earthworms. She told the judges that they were "an excellent source of protein."

Most Unusual Dessert: A favorite in Tanzania is white-ant pie made by mixing sweet white ants with banana flour. The taste is a little like honey nougat.

Most Unusual Food: Manna is first mentioned in Exodus when the Lord promises to "rain bread from heaven" for Moses and the children of Israel starving in the desert. This

Sylvester Graham

is the description found in Exodus 16: 14–15: "And when the dew that lay was gone up, behold, upon the face of the wilderness there lay a small round thing, as small as the hoarfrost on the ground. And when the children of Israel saw it, they said one to another, 'It is manna': for they wist not what it was."

Now, however, we do "wit" with some certainty what it was. Manna is a sweet, granular substance secreted by two varieties of scale insects that live on tamarisk shrubs. In the Sinai region through which the Israelites passed in their flight from Pharoah, manna accumulates only during the month of June; sometimes it is plentiful, sometimes it is scarce. As Marston Bates reports in *Gluttons and Libertines: Human Problems of Being Natural,* the Arabs still collect this substance, which they call *man-es-simma* (bread from the sky). And in Iraq nearly sixty thousand pounds of scale secretions are gathered each year and sold in the bazaars of Baghdad. Manna is mixed with eggs and almonds to make candy, which is perfectly in keeping with the Biblical description: ". . . it was like coriander seed, white; and the taste of it was like wafers made with honey."

Moving from the sublime to the ridiculous, we note that cereal magnate C. W. Post introduced a brand of corn flakes in 1904 which he called "Elijah's Manna." Fundamentalists everywhere were incensed by the desecration of the prophet's name and the vulgar reference to the bread of heaven. England refused to register the trademark. Under fire, Post changed the name to Post Toasties.

Most Unusual Food Faddist: Sylvester Graham (1794–1851) was a temperance lecturer who became convinced that a purely vegetable diet would depress the appetite for demon rum. His thought found full flower in the classic work *Bread and Bread Making* in which he developed the idea that whole wheat bread is more healthful than white. In 1847 his advocacy of this position caused a riot of Boston bakers intent on lynching the "mad enthusiast." The police were unable to control the crowd, and the disturbance was quelled only when Graham's followers shoveled slaked lime on the mob from the second-story windows of the lecture hall.

Graham survived to espouse other visionary reforms: taking cold showers, sleeping on hard mattresses with the windows open, eating rough cereals, wearing looser and lighter clothing, and practicing cheerfulness at meals. He had many enthusiastic adherents, among them Horace Greeley, some of whom lived and ate together in Graham boarding houses. Emerson called him "the poet of bran bread and pumpkins." Now, alas, Sylvester Graham is virtually forgotten, but his spirit lives on in the cracker bearing his name.

Most Unusual Ice Cream: Long before Dolly Madison and all that, the emperor Nero had ice imported from distant snow-capped mountains for frozen desserts.

Most Unusual Meat: In 1896 a woolly mammoth was found frozen in a Siberian glacier, his flesh perfectly preserved by the long deep freeze. What meat could be rescued from the wolves was canned and shipped back to Moscow, where Czar Nicholas II and a select group of scientists are said to have dined on the prehistoric fare. Several other mammoths have been found in the Siberian permafrost over the last century; those who claim to have tried it say the flesh is black in color and tastes like a cross between bear and whale.

As far back as the first century, mammoth steaks were reported to have graced royal tables. During a Roman meat shortage, Herod Agrippa I, governor of Judea, served glacier-preserved Pachydermata from the Caucasus at a dinner party for the emperor Caligula.

Archaeologists say the ancient Greeks almost surely must have stumbled on a number of mammoth skulls, which are common throughout the Mediterranean area. The most im-

243

pressive thing about a mammoth skull is its large nasal cavity. Since few Greeks had ever seen a living elephant, they may have mistaken a mammoth skull for the head of a gigantic one-eyed man, giving rise to the story of Polyphemus in the *Odyssey*. As late as the fifteenth century mammoth skulls were occasionally identified as the crania of Cyclops.

Most Unusual Milk: Dehydrated milk is not new; the warriors of Genghis Khan dried mares' milk in the sun until it became a fine powder which could be stored indefinitely. To reconstitute it, they would mix the old-fashioned Samalac with water in a leather pouch and tie it to a horse. A day's galloping homogenized it into a thin, white soup.

Most Unusual Mug: The glass-bottomed tankard enabled a drinker to hoist a few beers and still keep an eye on potential cutthroats. This common drinking vessel (with an uncommon history) is said to have occasioned the friendly admonition: "Here's looking at you."

Most Unusual Pie: Born in 1619 in Oakham, England, Jeffery Hudson was only seven years old and eighteen inches tall when he entered the service of the Duke of Buckingham. One evening, as a merry entertainment, the Duke decided to serve Jeffery in a cold pie to his guests, Charles I and Queen Henrietta Maria. The Queen was so pleased with this little practical joke that she convinced the young dwarf to join her own retinue.

Most Unusual Poison: Tomatoes were widely thought to be poisonous in the American colonies until 1733 when a Virginia physician named Dr. Siccary demonstrated that not only were they not poisonous but they were delicious and healthful. Dr. Siccary was so enamored of the lowly tomato, known in those days as the "love apple," however, that he went to his grave sincerely believing that "a person who should eat a sufficient abundance of these apples would never die."

Most Unusual Restaurant: In this vast and wondrous land of ours there is, happily, only one restaurant catering exclusively to dogs and cats, and it is the Animal Gourmet, on Manhattan's Upper East Side. For the "pet owner who cares," there is a menu that compares favorably to the bills-of-fare offered at New York's finest biped restaurants, and it includes

Richard Nixon eggplant

shrimp cocktail, liver paté, beef bourguignon, steak and kidney ragout, braised chicken livers, poached fish filet, and beef Wellington.

"We sell about three hundred meals a week," says Bill Poulin who, with Joe Mitseifer, owns and operates the restaurant. "The food we serve our customers is bought in the same places you and I buy our own food."

Poulin's and Mitseifer's love for animals—and good food—has turned an aversion to feeding animals canned pet foods into a profitable enterprise. As the sign above the entrance proclaims, "We do not prepare dog and cat food. We prepare food for dogs and cats." Meals are served at small tables with white table cloths; the beverage of the day, every day, is water. Animal Gourmet also caters birthday parties for animals and with advance notice they'll provide flowers, favors, and a birthday cake made of dog meal, liver, whipped powdered milk and cream.

"I'm a Pennsylvania hick and Bill once worked as a lumberjack," says co-owner Mitseifer, "and we have had the Duchess of Windsor here to feed her two pugs. And we have the lady from the Bronx who takes a bus and subway and lugs a forty-pound metal crate with her alley cat in it. She feeds it here with a little silver spoon. Just think how lonely she'd be without her cat."

Most Unusual Steak: A ten-pound steak arriving in Circle City, Alaska, during the gold rush was sold for a price that seemed unbelievably inflationary until recently. At first there was open bidding for the meat, with offers soaring as high as thirty-five dollars per pound. When fist fights broke out among the bidders, it was decided to raffle off the steak instead. Over $480 worth of tickets were sold with each of the winners receiving one slice.

One of the most highly honored pieces of meat in history was served to Charles II of England who exclaimed, "For its merit it should be knighted, and henceforth called Sir-Loin." Some authorities have claimed that this was the origin of the butcher's term, but the Oxford English Dictionary cites earlier mentions of sirloin. Rather than coining a new word, they credit Charles with making a bad pun.

Most Unusual Vegetable: *New York* magazine reported in 1973 that an eggplant bearing a startling resemblance to the beleaguered President Nixon had been purchased by a Manhattan housewife in a midtown supermarket.

Life-Styles

Best Life-Style: The Kalapalo Indians who live on the savannas of central Brazil have the world's most relaxed society, spending well over half their lives in their hammocks. Adults average twelve hours of sleep a night and catch two or three naps during daylight hours as well. At most the men work two or three short days a week fishing for picuda in the tributaries of the Amazon. And though wild game abounds, they are too peaceable to hunt.

Simplicity characterizes all aspects of their lives. In addition to fish, they dine mainly on manioc, lice, and butterflies. The men wear only a belt of beads around their waists; married women wear a string of shiny wedding bells. Although women often have several lovers and a fish occasionally disappears from its owner's pot, the Kalapalo are not troubled with problems such as infidelity or theft. To accuse a neighbor of theft or a mate of infidelity is considered far more dishonorable than the acts themselves. But the most distinctive aspect of Kalapalo life is leisure, and in their abundant spare time they enjoy gathering together and improvising melodies on wooden flutes.

Best Proof That Californians Are Not Like the Rest of Us: California is currently the scene of a mushrooming "gluers" movement spearheaded by people who like to glue things—small things, preferably, like costume jewelry, rubber mice, teeth, baby beads, tennis balls, bottle caps, plastic salt shakers—to bigger things, like cars and buildings. Dickens Bascom, a noted northern California gluer, looks forward to the day when he can join other gluers and purchase a large office building and decorate it in their fashion. "I'm determined to do it," he says. "I think it's something people need."

Best Streakers: Most college administrators were very tolerant of the mercifully short-lived fad of streaking; few suspensions or expulsions were recorded, and it is apparent that deans and policemen would rather see students running around in nothing but their tennis shoes than engaging in sit-ins or occupying buildings. In short, most streakers had nothing to lose. In this permissive climate, two dozen West Point cadets emerged as the best streakers and the only heroes. With their clothes off and their military careers on the line, they raced across the campus of the United States Military Academy, pursued, Keystone-cops style, by a platoon of apoplectic officers—and they got away with it.

Worst Gift: Victor Emmanuel II (1820–1878) was the first king to rule over a united Italy, and he might therefore be a prominent figure in history even if he hadn't won immortality as the giver of one of the most vulgar gifts imaginable. For some unfathomable reason of his own, the monarch allowed the nail of his big toe to go untrimmed for one whole year at a time. Each New Year's Day was the occasion for the annual paring ceremony, and by that time the nail had grown to be a full half-inch long, or even longer in good years.

The royal clipping was then passed on to the king's jeweler, who took the unpromising "gem," polished it, shaped and edged it with gold, and encrusted it in diamonds. In the hands of the skilled craftsman, the nail was transformed into a presentable and quite valuable bauble. Victor Emmanuel made it a custom of turning over this little piece of himself to his favorite mistress of the moment. The most stunning collection of *ongles de roi* was accumulated by the Countess Mirafiori, whom the king ultimately married.

Worst Life-Style: The Yanomamo tribesmen who inhabit the dense rainforests near the Brazil-Venezuela frontier are male chauvinists unexcelled in viciousness. They beat their wives savagely at the least provocation, real or imagined, and nearly all Yanomamo women are covered with scars and ugly welts—tokens of their husbands' affection. A common punishment for a misbehaving wife is to rip the bamboo earring right out of her pierced lobes.

But the women also contribute to the incomparable cruelty of Yanomamo society, most notably by murdering their own male infants (strangulation with vines is the preferred method) until they deliver a son. And once they have born a male heir, the women are permitted to kill all unwanted children, regardless of sex.

248

The two principal pastimes of Yanomamo males are drug-taking and war. A man and his brother-in-law tend to be the closest companions in Yanomamo society, and they spend much of their days lying together in a hammock blowing the hallucinogenic powder *ebene* into each other's nostrils. Under the influence of this powerful substance, as anthropologist Marvin Harris has recounted, they experience incredible illusions, walk around on all fours growling, and chat with demons. At war, the Yanomamo are notoriously dirty fighters. Whenever possible, they sneak into enemy villages at night and club in the skulls of unsuspecting sleepers.

Nor is it safe to be a Yanomamo's friend. When one village invites another over for a friendly feast, it is understood that there will also be "competitions." The favorite sport is a chest-pounding duel in which one man takes a rock into his hand and slams it against the chest of the other competitor as hard as he can. The opponent, if he is able, then returns the blow, and they exchange wallops until one or the other sinks to his knees. Those who prefer more aggressive play take turns smashing each other over the head with bamboo poles. The Yanomamo are proud of the gashes they receive in these games and they shave their heads and paint the wounds bright red to exaggerate them.

A dinner guest is fortunate if he comes away with just a few scars on his head and chest. Not infrequently one village invites another to dinner only to massacre all the men and gang-rape the women. Well aware of this tradition, the guests are always on their guard and may come with the intention of striking first and slaughtering their hosts.

Worst Singles Party: For weeks in advance newspaper advertisements in Chicago and Toronto inquired naughtily, "Can singles parties lead the way to a better understanding of international affairs?" Those answering yes were invited to what the promoters billed as "the largest, highest, and longest singles party in the history of Western civilization." The original, grandiose plan called for 2,000 Canadians to fly to Chicago where they would join 8,000 Americans at the Regency Hyatt O'Hare Hotel for an amorous November (1973) weekend. There, among North America's most eligible unmarrieds, they would enjoy an ultrahip fashion show, seven big-name rock bands, "the biggest, most sumptuous buffet ever presented," and of course the pleasures of companionship.

To their credit, only 200 Canadians invested $130 to join

the gathering, but swarms of local young people more than made up for the poor Canadian turnout. The festivities began well enough: The sexes were about evenly represented; the rock bands were loud, if not well known; the dancing was spirited; there was the usual amount of disrobing and tossing of the fully dressed into the heated swimming pool. The first sign of trouble came when the buffet was opened. The ravenous socializers were disappointed to see only cold cuts, pickles, and rye bread, and even that was soon devoured. Then as the crowd continued to swell and incidents of gate-crashing began to occur, the hotel management grew nervous and they decided to close the bars. Starved, thirsty, and suspecting a rip-off, the crowd turned nasty. There was a lot of littering, some property destruction, and a false alarm that brought a hook and ladder and a lot of firemen to the party.

George Russell, writing in *The New York Times* described the event as "an ugly form of social Darwinism," which promoted the "survival of the swingingest, of the least sensitive." Well, that may have been the reason for the party's failure, but more likely it was the shortage of booze.

Worst Streakers: The worst streak, as far as consequences for the participants, occurred when two naked students parachuted from a rented Cessna 182 over the University of Georgia campus. Blown off target, one landed in the playground of a married students housing complex and the other touched down in a cesspool. This was followed the next day by the most disingenuous streak when the two parachutists performed the whole scene over again for photographers.

Most Unusual Aphrodisiac: In 1929 an incomplete skull of Peking Man was discovered—one of the most important archaeological finds of all time. Also that year, the Japanese were readying for their invasion of China. Hurriedly, Peking Man's remains were packaged for transport out of China to safety, but when the trunk containing the priceless skull arrived in Shanghai, it was empty. No one is certain what became of Peking Man, but one report maintains that the bones were stolen by local blackmarketeers, ground into a fine powder, and sold as an aphrodisiac.

Most Unusual Aryans: In 1938 a rising Nazi journalist faced a stumbling block in his career. Although three of his grandparents were of indisputable Teutonic blood, his maternal grandmother was a full-blooded Sioux Indian. The Chamber of the Press consulted with National anthropologists, who huddled, referred to their books, and concluded that the young man had no problem: The Sioux, it turns out, are Aryans. Some of the same anthropologists probably worked on the tremendous scholarly effort of 1941-1942, assembling evidence that the Japanese allies were also of solid Aryan stock.

Most Unusual Bastard: Perhaps the most talented illegitimate of all time was Leonardo da Vinci, although those other bastards, Richard Wagner, Napoleon, and Boccaccio, might argue the claim.

Grover Cleveland (see also *Most Unusual Draft Dodger*) fathered an illegitimate son; he publicly admitted the fact and made a generous provision for the boy's welfare. Much to the credit of the electorate, they forgave him his indiscretion and twice elected him president—the only chief executive to serve two nonconsecutive terms.

Most Unusual Beauty Contest: Ivan the Terrible was among several Russian czars who chose their brides in a nationwide beauty contest. As many as 2,000 eligible young ladies and their parents, the pick of the provinces, were brought to Moscow for the long and rigorous selection process. After weeks of interviews and fancy balls, the czar and his advisors would single out the woman with the most pleasing figure, manners, and wit to become the czarina.

Not surprisingly, this relatively democratic procedure was popular with the proletarian parents of pretty daughters, who aspired to become in-laws to the most powerful man in all of Russia. By the time of Alexis Romanov, the beauty contest was such a well established tradition, that it posed an obstacle to his extraordinary plan to marry a woman he loved. To avoid disappointing hundreds of families, Alexis staged a contest, as usual, but rigged it so that beautiful Nathalie Narychkine, his beloved, would emerge the winner. Nathalie and Alexis were the parents of Peter the Great.

Most Unusual College: In Morogoro, a suburb of Dar es Salaam, Tanzania, a "sex college" was established—next door to the town's busiest bar, according to a news item in *Baraza*, a local paper. The school's *raison d'etre*, according to a promotional brochure, "is to teach girls new and modern ways of welcoming rich men." Only the cream of the area's secondary school dropouts are eligible for admission and classes are held for four hours a day. The degree offered is the mysterious D.W.D.

Most Unusual Courtesy: A number of practices that are now codified as "good manners" are the outcome of the old practice of emptying chamber pots in the streets. A common expression in Elizabethan London was *Gardez, l'eau*—or look out below—the polite scream before you dumped your chamber pot out of an upper story window. The streets had open sewers, which presented a constant hazard to pedestrians as coaches sloshed by near the curb. To protect a lady and her garments from an unexpected splash of sewage, gentlemanly escorts took to walking between the lady and the dangers of the street.

The hero in this brief history is Sir John Harrington, who was one of the men who invented the flush toilet—a device that has been invented and reinvented several times in history. According to one disputed derivation, it is in his honor that the privy is known as the john or jakes. (See also *Best Invention*.)

Most Unusual Curse Words: The ancient Arabs used to invoke the awesome laxative powers of the fig when swearing. Similarly, the Greeks often uttered a phrase that loosely translated means, "Rhodesian cabbage!" (Rhodesian cabbage was highly valued as a hangover cure, but that hardly explains why it became a swear word.)

Louis IX of France had a very low tolerance for swearing, which is one of the reasons why he became known as Saint Louis. He became very upset when he heard people say *pardieu* (by God) or *cordieu* (God's heart) and finally he decreed that cussers should have their tongues branded with a hot iron. To protect their tongues, the courtiers began to swear by the king's dog Bleu, hence the curses *parbleu* and the ever popular *sacrebleu*, which have come down to the Frenchman of today.

Most Unusual Duel: Two gentlemen of equally high merit, one German and one Spanish, sought the hand of Helene Acharfequinn, the daughter of Maximilian II. In their ardor, the suitors proposed to fight a duel over who should have the privilege of marrying the beautiful Helene. But their prospective father-in-law would not allow them to risk their noble blood, and instead he proposed an unusual contest: Whichever gentleman could put his rival in a gunnysack would become his son-in-law.

The rivals wrestled with skill and vigor for more than an hour until the German, Baron von Talbert, succeeded in bagging his opponent. Talbert hoisted the bag, carried it across the room, and placed it at the feet of Helene, proposing then and there.

Most Unusual Euphemism: During World War II, overly demure members of the French Resistance announced their need to use the toilet by saying, *"Je vais telephoner à Hitler."*

Most Unusual Greeting: It is the custom among some tribes in New Guinea to greet a woman with a kiss on her bare left breast. A fine how-do-you-do.

Most Unusual Life-Style: A very subjective judgment: In 1971 a Philippine government official made contact with the Tasaday people of Minanao Island. The most isolated and primitive tribe yet known to anthropologists, they are true stone-age men who have never seen metal tools. The concept of war is unknown to them, and in fact they have no word for it in their language. Most of their goods are held in common, and the lush rainforest provides them with all the food they can eat. Most of the families live together in one central cave. When asked if they had any wants or needs, one bachelor asked for a wife. But except for the shortage of women in the tribe, they appear to be perfectly content with life as it was lived 10,000 years ago.

Sadly, we must report, all that is changing. A recent article asserts that since establishing contact with the outside world, the Tasaday have taken to smoking commercial menthol cigarettes.

Most Unusual Manifestation of the Victorian Ethic: *Lady Gough's Book of Etiquette* notes that arranging books on shelves must be done with the utmost discretion so that a book written by a male author is not placed adjacent to one by a female author to whom he is not married.

Most Unusual Marriage Proposal: In January 1964 a Masai chieftain offered to buy the blonde actress Carroll Baker for 150 cows, 200 goats, and $750 cash. As a measure of how highly he thought of Ms. Baker, a Masai warrior usually spends about $200 and 12 cows for a wife.

It is of economic and sociological interest to note that in the *Odyssey* the slave girl Euryclea was purchased by Laertes for twenty oxen. So the price has remained relatively constant.

Most Unusual Masher: Enrico Caruso was once arrested for making a pass at an attractive young woman in the monkey house of the Central Park Zoo.

Most Unusual Sexologist: In 1776 the Temple of Hymen, established by the eccentric Dr. James Graham, opened its doors and began teaching "the art of preventing barrenness, and propagating a much more strong, beautiful, active, healthy, wise, and virtuous race of human beings than the present puny, insignificant, foolish, peevish, and nonsensical race of Christians, who quarrel, fight, bite, devour, and cut each other's throats about they know not what." Graham furnished his pleasure dome with erotic paintings and statuary, as well as providing the most tasteful vocal and instrumental music. The overhead was tremendous, and from the first it was a losing proposition, but Graham continued to support the operation for several years with money out of his own pocket.

Dr. Graham was a strict vegetarian and drank nothing but cold water. From his point of view, the prime attraction of the Temple of Hymen was his "Eccentric Lecture on Generation," which was a mishmash of puerile eugenics and sexual "how-to" all presented in the chastest of words. From his audience's point of view, the prime attractions were the handsome females—among them Lady Hamilton and other daring ladies of the upper crust—who appeared naked, in the interest of science.

Most Unusual Sexual Ethics: Not surprisingly the Toda language has no word for adultery. The Todas of Southern India expect a woman to have at least one lover in addition to as many as six husbands. Todas are of the opinion that if a girl is still a virgin at her wedding, her maternal uncle will be taken ill and die. Fortunately, if the doomed uncle discovers the bride's shameful innocence in time, he can save himself by shaving off her hair.

If a Toda woman dies without having acquired a lover, the

elders of the village are forced to appoint one because the grieving lover plays an important role in the funeral service.

Most Unusual Streakers: The most unusual streaks were the so-called "reverse-streaks." At a number of nudist camps, residents raced across the grounds fully clothed in defiance of camp regulations.

Most Unusual Waiters: In 1973 Jack Cione's night club in Honolulu introduced the bottomless waiter. Business has been booming ever since with a predominantly female clientele.

Most Unusual Wedding: In the Marquesas Islands a bridegroom walks to his father-in-law's house on a human street formed by the prone wedding guests. He steps from back to back at a stately pace. (If there are too few people to pave the entire route, the people at the back race up to the front of the line to be stepped on again.) At the altar the groom eats a raw fish that has been fileted and diced on a human body. Presents are distributed and there is a great feast, and finally at the end of the festivities, the street of bodies is formed again for the groom's return home.

People

Best Anti-intellectual: History's most effective anti-intellectual was Shih Huang Ti (259–210 B.C.). Shih was the complete man of action who rose to the throne of the small state of Ch'in at the age of twelve and waged constant warfare for twenty years until he had unified the countless squabbling states of China into a single nation; the effort cost some 1,500,000 lives. Having "pacified in turn the four ends of the earth," he became China's first emperor and turned his attention to the problems of administration. He standardized the written language, devised a harsh penal code, built long straight roads, and began construction of the Great Wall of China.

Scholars were an irritation to Shih; they constantly compared his actions to the standards for a good ruler set down in the Confucian texts—and found him wanting. When a few dared to criticize his cruelties outrightly, the emperor decided to remove them. He summoned the 460 most prominent wise men to his palace and put them on trial. But when it became clear that distinguishing the innocent from the guilty would be a long and difficult process, Shih simply ordered that all 460 be buried alive.

The books were next to go. One copy of each book (actually huge bamboo scrolls) was brought to the Imperial Library and every other manuscript in the country was ordered destroyed. Those caught concealing books were gruesomely tortured and executed, but many book-lovers learned the Confucian works by heart in order to preserve them. Poetry, philosophy, and history fed the huge bonfires that lit up the night sky in China.

Shih's motives for the conflagration were threefold. First, he did not wish to be bound to the code of conduct and ancient rites set down in the Confucian texts. He also felt that literary freedom was divisive and hindered the cultural unification of his country. And finally he reasoned that if all the old history books were destroyed, recorded history would begin with the reign of Shih.

Best Gambler: A consistent winner at the tables is highly unusual. Therefore, it is indeed noteworthy that Charles Wells broke the bank at the Monte Carlo roulette table fifteen times in 1890. Understandably encouraged by his success, he returned in 1891 and broke the bank five more times.

Best Linguist: Cardinal Mezzofanti of Bologna, Italy, taught Cockney slang to Lord Byron. It was merely one of over 100 languages and dialects the cardinal could speak and understand. Reliable sources insist that he was fluent in at least fifty tongues, including Walachian, Guzarati, Algonquin, and Pegu. He could chat a little in Frissian, Chippewa, Lettish, Quechua, Tonquinese, and many others. He found Chinese to be the most difficult language to master, requiring approximately four months of study. Perhaps the most cosmopolitan speaker of all time, Cardinal Mezzofanti never traveled outside of Italy.

Worst Alchemist: Heinrich Kurschildgen was no less successful than the alchemists of old, but he merits the title "the worst" because he was the most recent flop in this great tradition of failure. Kurschildgen was a dye worker who managed to convince a gullible university professor that he had discovered mysterious rays that made all matter radioactive. With a little tinkering, he promised, a device could be developed which would split the atom and make gold.

The professor described the plan to some of his right-wing friends, among them Herr Hugenberg, an important industrialist and newspaper publisher. Patriotic businessmen were interested not only because it was a chance to make huge personal fortunes but also because they saw alchemy as a way to pay off the Weimar Republic's debts under the Treaty of Versailles. As Kurschildgen embellished his claims, asserting that the rays might also cure cancer and purify steel, eager investors sunk tens of thousands of marks into the scheme. Soon, word got around of this promising enterprise and before Kurschildgen was exposed as a fraud, inquiries about the process were coming in from America, Britain, and Switzerland.

There is a persistent rumor that Hitler employed a number

of alchemists who worked full-time throughout the war trying to turn lead into gold. While we could find no evidence of this, perhaps the Kurschildgen story is the source of the Hitler rumor.

Worst Job in the Court: During the reign of François I, 1515 to 1547, the exalted position of chair-bearer was introduced to the French court for the first time. It was surely the worst job any courtier ever brown-nosed to earn, and yet because it provided a rare opportunity to be with the king in the most intimate of circumstances, the office was much coveted. The chair-bearer, you see, was charged with carrying around His Majesty's portable toilet and attending to his royal needs thereon.

Following François's initiative, Catherine de Medici also acquired a "chair," appointed chair-bearers, and dressed them in elaborate uniforms. Ordinarily Catherine's chair was outfitted with seat cushions of red and blue velvet, but for one year following her husband's death, Catherine, in her grief, substituted a black velvet seat as a symbol of mourning.

The toilet, portable and stationary, continued to play an important role in French politics for years to come. Louis XIV, for example, announced his marriage to Madame de Maintenon while astride his *chaise d'affaires* (business seat) as he delicately called it. Hopefully for such momentous public occasions he observed the custom of earlier monarchs, who sweetened the fragrance of their chairs with tansy and other mild herbs.

Louis XV boasted of a remarkable toilet decorated with Japanese landscapes and birds worked in gold and brightly colored relief, inlaid mother-of-pearl borders, bronze fittings made in China, a merry red lacquer interior, and a padded seat of green velour. An inventory conducted at the Versailles Palace shortly before the French Revolution noted the presence of nearly three hundred toilets. From that you may draw your own conclusions.

Worst Reformer: Carrie Nation (1846-1911), America's most extraordinary temperance agitator, stood six feet tall and had the arms and shoulders of a professional wrestler. When she stormed into a saloon, swinging her legendary hatchet, few dared to oppose her. She was jailed more than thirty times in her crusading career and there is little doubt that in her time she was, in the words of writer Ishbel Ross, "by all odds the most meddlesome woman in the country."

Cartoon of Carrie Nation

Carrie had fanaticism in her blood. Her mother was absolutely convinced that she was Queen Victoria and always wore the long purple velvet gowns and crystal crown that befitted a monarch. Early in life Carrie began to develop fixed ideas of her own and her first marriage to Dr. Charles Gloyd gave direction to her eccentricity. It is not unfair to say that the meek doctor was driven to drink by his overbearing wife. Eventually he fled his spouse, took refuge in the Masonic Lodge (where women were not admitted), and drank himself to death. From then on Carrie was a confirmed foe of drink and the Masons.

Her second husband was a preacher, the Reverend David Nation, who also found Carrie more than a little intimidating. During his sermons she used to sit in the front pew and embarrass him by loudly correcting his grammatical mistakes; when he announced a hymn, she would overrule him and insist on singing one of her own favorites. Probably the reverend was relieved when his wife deserted him to take up her "divinely appointed" career of "hatchetation," as she put it.

Mrs. Nation's first triumphs were in Topeka, Kansas, where she organized ministers, college students, and the teetotalers of the Women's Christian Temperance Union into a holy mob bent on destroying every saloon in town. They marched through the streets arm-in-arm singing "Onward Christian Soldiers" or chanting "Smash, smash, for Jesus' sake, smash!" When they came to a gin mill, all hell broke loose. Following Carrie's lead, the marchers threw rocks through the mirrors, destroyed all the glassware, and chopped up the bar, furniture, walls, and floors with their inevitable hatchets. Carrie's favorite feat was to rake an entire counter of good booze onto the floor with a single sweep of her hatchet. The place in ruins, she would shout with the fury of a prophet, "Praise God, another joint gone."

Soon she developed a nationwide reputation and formed the National Hatchet Brigade, which published a periodical called *The Smasher's Mail*. She took on national figures, such as Teddy Roosevelt, whom she characterized as "that bloodthirsty, reckless, and cigarette smoking rummy." No saloon in the country was safe. Once she stormed into John L. Sullivan's drinking establishment in New York City, and tradition has it that the bare knuckles champ fled in terror. Toward the end of her career her zeal extended to other reforms besides temperance. She took to knocking cigarettes out of men's mouths as they walked down the street, hatcheting paintings of nudes, and covering nude statuary with her own cape.

Could one expect less of Victoria's daughter?

Most Unusual Explorer: In 1823 Captain John Cleves Symmes, a hero of the War of 1812, brought his case to Congress. For several years he had been researching and documenting his marvelous and sincerely held beliefs about the interior of the world: "I declare the earth is hollow and habitable within, containing a number of solid concentric spheres, and that it is open at the poles twelve or sixteen degrees," he wrote in a circular addressed "To All the World." All he desired was a ship and a few brave scientists to accompany him in the descent through the "Symmes Hole" at the North Pole into the "warm rich land, stocked with thrifty vegetables and animals, if not men" that they would surely find within.

Captain Symmes was a popular figure on the lecture circuit and thousands of Americans, moved by his arguments, petitioned Congress to support an expedition to "Symmezonia,"

John Cleves Symmes

as they called it. Representative Richard M. Johnson of Kentucky (who later became vice-president) championed Symmes's cause on the House floor and finally forced the question to a vote. Symmes's proposal was defeated, but twenty-five congressmen did vote in favor of a "journey to the center of the earth." Circumventing the unimaginative Congress, John J. Reynolds, a Symmes disciple, persuaded the secretaries of the Navy and the Treasury under President John Quincy Adams to outfit three ships for a voyage to the interior; before the adventurers could set sail, however, Andrew Jackson came into office and quashed the plan.

Captain Symmes died in 1829, but his vacuous theory survived him, inspiring a short story by Edgar Allen Poe ("Ms. Found in a Bottle") and Jules Verne's novel about the subterranean world. In 1878 the captain's son, Americus Vespucius Symmes, edited his father's collected works, which continued to interest unconventional thinkers until Robert Peary reached 90°N in 1909 and found no hole.

Most Unusual Hero: We shy away from calling Paul Revere the worst hero, because he made many unheralded contributions to the Revolution. But the "Midnight Ride," so highly touted by Longfellow, was not all it was cracked up to be.

First of all, according to an article in the *Smithsonian* magazine, Revere was not alone on that April night in 1775. Two other colonials, William Dawes and Dr. Samuel Prescott, rode with him, and they had not gotten to many Middlesex villages and farms before they were approached by a British patrol. Both Dawes and Prescott escaped, but Paul Revere was captured. The British put a loaded pistol to his temple and ordered him to talk. Showing discretionary valor, the famous Boston silversmith told them everything they wanted to know about where he had been and why. And another thing Longfellow forgot to tell us: Revere was riding as a mercenary that night; the Boston patriots paid him five shillings for his efforts.

Most Unusual Hypnotist: Franz Mesmer (1734-1815) believed that there is an invisible magnetic fluid coursing through the body that controls a person's physical and mental health. To heal, he reasoned, it was necessary to control the flow of this fluid. Mesmer began conducting experiments in which he waved magnets slowly back and forth in front of his patients; on other occasions he immersed them in tubs filled with warm water and iron filings. All this soaking and waving sent some of his clients into a deep trance. Mesmer was jubilant: They were magnetized!

Later, Mesmer found that he could induce a trance without the tubs and magnets, simply by waving his hands in front of the subject. But instead of discarding the magnetism theory, he concluded that there was a strange "animal magnetism" in his hands. Moreover, iron and people were not the only things he was convinced he could magnetize. "I have rendered paper, bread, wool, silk, stones, leather, glass, wood, men, and dogs—in short, everything I touched—magnetic to a degree," he wrote.

Mesmer's penetrating eyes, entrancing gestures, and long purple robes, set in the soothing environment of his office with a pianoforte playing softly in the background, combined to make Mesmer a competent, though theoretically naive, hypnotist. In fact, "mesmerism" appears to have had a genuinely therapeutic effect on some people, particularly those suffering from hysteria. A few exceptional cures and the public's eternal enthusiasm for miracle healers made Mesmer immensely popular in Paris. But establishment physicians and the French government were less enthusiastic about his methods. A board of inquiry (of which Benjamin Franklin was a member) was set up to investigate whether Mesmer was a quack, fake, or medical hero. The verdict was quack, with a measure of fake, and Mesmer was forced to retire to Switzerland, where his popularity declined.

Most Unusual Mathematician: There are numerous accounts of people who have performed incredible feats of calculation instantaneously. Karl Gauss, a pioneer in non-Euclidean geometry, had this ability. Another well-documented case of a man with a mind swifter than a pocket calculator is the story of George Bidder, who won the mathematics prize at Edinburgh University in 1822. Bidder was once asked to figure how far a pendulum that swings 9¾ inches in one second would travel in 7 years, 14 days, 2 hours, 1 minute, and 56 seconds—taking the year to be 365 days, 5 hours, 40 minutes, and 50 seconds long. After meditating for a little less than a minute Bidder replied, "2,165,625,744¾ inches!" (Check it yourself.) George Bidder went on to become an accomplished civil engineer.

Most Unusual Name: Boxing buff Brian Brown, of Wolverhampton, Great Britain, named his daughter, born in 1974, after all twenty-five world heavyweight champions. Brown told newspaper reporters that he planned to take the child—Maria Sullivan Corbett Fitzsimmons Jeffries Hart Burns Johnson Willard Dempsey Tunney Schmeling Sharkey Carnera Baer Braddock Louis Charles Walcott Marciano Patterson Johanssen Liston Clay Frazier Foreman Brown—to see her first professional boxing match "when she is three or four months old, so that she can soak up the atmosphere." That would prepare her, he said, for a career in "promotion or management or something similar." Brown explained that he had been hoping for a boy.

At her christening in 1883, Arthur Pepper named his daughter Anna Bertha Cecilia Diana Emily Fanny Gertrude Hypatia Inez Jane Kate Louisa Maud Nora Ophelia Quince Rebecca Sarah Teresa Ulysses Venus Winifred Xenophon Yetty Zeus Pepper—one name for every letter in the alphabet with P for Pepper displaced to the end.

Most Unusual Occupational Hazard: For schoolteachers, sportscasters, even telephone operators, sore throats and laryngitis are all in a day's work. Rock 'n' roll singers, however, frequently are prey to a much more serious and longer-lasting deterioration of the vocal cords. In fact, many rock stars, in the pursuit of their careers, literally scream their lungs out.

Recently, Dr. Eugene M. Batza of Cleveland Clinic's Department of Otolaryngology, examined a five-member rock combo and found that all of them suffered from chronic, aggravated laryngitis, as well as nodules and inflammation of the vocal cords. The symptoms were so serious, in fact, that the group was forced to call off a long string of engagements and undergo medical treatment. "The risk of permanent degenerative change is always present," says Dr. Batza, who has since taken a closer look into the hazards of singing rock 'n' roll for a living.

What makes the rock singer's plight so much worse than the operatic soprano's or the folk singer's is, more often than not, a hectic schedule that has him singing three or four hours perhaps four or five nights a week for several months at a stretch in addition to rehearsals and recording sessions. Moreover, rock singing puts an intolerable strain on the voice. Nonetheless, rock singers are generally unwilling to take the care needed to avoid permanent damage to the larynx.

"They fear that a radical change in their vocal style will lead to oblivion as artists," the doctor says. "They rely on their youthful resiliency to carry them through, but they would do well to remember that singing is a physical activity. Abuse of the pitching arm, particularly after fatigue has noticeably set in, can be catastrophic to the serious athlete."

Contemporary orchestral music is as hard on the nerves of its performers as rock music is on their vocal cords. After studying 208 orchestral musicians, two West German psychiatrists concluded that musicians who frequently play present-day compositions are often beset by a broad range of symptoms, including chronic nervousness and irritability, insomnia, earaches, and impotency.

Most Unusual Old Man: R. S. Kirby, author of *Kirby's Curious and Eccentric Museum,* recounts the story of Old John Weeks of New London, Connecticut, who married his tenth wife when he was 106. (The blushing bride was sixteen.) Kirby also insists that after Weeks lost all his gray hair, he began growing a new head of brunette locks. In 1798, he died—at the age of 114. A few hours before his passing, Weeks dined on three pounds of pork, two pounds of bread, and nearly a pint of wine.

Most Unusual Part-time Job: Serving working-class families who could not afford an alarm clock, Mrs. Mary Ann Smith of London ran a thriving business. For a few pennies a month, she would shoot a volley of peas against their windows to awaken them at the specified hour.

Most Unusual Philosopher: Historians would have us remember Jeremy Bentham as the founding father of utilitarian philosophy, passing over his other, more remarkable accomplishments. For example, Bentham invented scores of neologisms, including the words "maximize" and "minimize." He also devised a round prison called the "panopticon," which permitted a single jailer to sit in the center and watch over a full house of convicts. All in all, he lived a full, happy, eccentric life, organizing all of Western thought into a single system, and doting on his beloved teapot (named Dickey) and his cat (named Reverend Dr. John Langborne).

In his last will and testament, Jeremy Bentham left a large fortune to University College in London on the condition that his preserved body be displayed annually at the board of directors' meeting. Dr. Southward Smith, Bentham's physician and the executor of his will, has described the exhaustive effort invested in carrying out the philosopher's wishes. "I endeavored to preserve the head, untouched," the doctor wrote, "merely drawing away the fluids by placing under it . . . sulphuric acid, but 'twas without expression. Seeing this would not do for exhibition, I had a model made in wax by a distinguished French artist. I then had the skeleton stuffed out to fit Bentham's own clothes and this wax likeness fitted to the trunk. The whole was then enclosed in a mahogany case with folding glass doors, seated in his armchair and holding in his hand his favorite walking stick."

The body was dutifully displayed at every board meeting until 1924, when it was relegated to an exhibit area. During the London blitz in World War II, University College was heavily bombed, and the wing that housed Jeremy Bentham's body was almost completely destroyed. Miraculously his remains came through unscathed.

Most Unusual Shepherds: Much of the rich pasturage of the Landes district of France is partially covered with water. If they had to slosh through the bogs and shallow pools on foot, the Landesmen would never be able to keep up with their roaming flocks. To solve this problem, the Landes shepherds wear tall stilts. Each man also carries a long walking stick, which he uses to keep his balance on rough terrain. When he wants to rest, the shepherd uses this third pole as a seat, forming a high and steady tripod. If a Landesman has some spare time, he knits while seated atop his tripod—a rare sight indeed.

Most Unusual Wet Nurses: In many primitive societies, an unweaned baby whose mother has died is fed directly from the teats of cows or milk goats. And among some reindeer herding tribes, even adults commonly take nourishment directly from their does. Conversely, anthropologists have reported that in some African and South Seas cultures women think nothing at all of nursing orphaned baby animals right along with their own children.

Yet, in industrial societies, most people find something strange and unsettling about drinking anything but pasteurized cows' milk poured from bottles or cartons. For example, men and women lunching along the Bois de Boulogne in Paris used to marvel at and cheer the daily ritual of Monsieur Le Comte, the father of Toulouse-Lautrec. Each morning Le Comte rode a brood mare to his favorite cafe. There, he would invariably order a sherry, return to the hitching post, and milk his steed right into the glass.

This leads us to a delightfully Oedipal story about John D. Rockefeller: As he passed his ninetieth birthday, the withered millionaire was troubled by the absence of teeth and a shattered digestion. The only food that he could keep down was pure mother's milk. Reportedly, several wet nurses on his domestic staff were kept busy lactating his meals. (We searched in vain for a written version of this anecdote, but we offer it here on the authority of writer Gore Vidal, who recounted it on David Susskind's television show.)

Fashion and Grooming

Best Bath: The Baths of Caracalla, in Rome, Italy, constructed during the reign of the Roman emperor Marcus Aurelius, were a mile in circumference. They offered hot and cold running water and a lot more: theaters, temples, a festival hall, and complete facilities for nearly 30,000 bathers.

While he could not compete with Marcus Aurelius, George Blumenthal of New York City owned the top of the line in the personal tub. He floated his rubber duck in a $50,000 bath carved from a single block of Italian marble.

Worst Color: It caused a sensation in the French court when the young Dauphin, son of Marie Antoinette, publicly displayed his ignorance of toilet training. The delightfully uninhibited boy inspired the fashion designers to create a whole line of clothes in a new color, *Caca Dauphin*.

Worst Cufflinks: In 1969 Dino Drops, Inc. introduced a matching cufflink and tie-pin set made out of petrified dinosaur dung.

Worst Fashion: English nankeen was quite the fashion in France during the abbreviated reign of Louis XVI. Because this fad was undercutting the market for French fabrics and unfavorably affecting the balance of trade, the monarch decided to take drastic action. He decreed that executioners wear only nankeen. Given this macabre endorsement, the nankeen fashion soon died.

In 1793, of course, Louis XVI went to the guillotine himself. Louis's death considerably unnerved Czar Paul I of Russia and every other king and queen. Paul believed that the clothes make the man, and thus he attributed the French Revolution, in part, to recent radical innovations in men's

Lenin in vest

clothing, particularly the popularity of the vest. To prevent any revolutionary nonsense in Russia, he ordered that any man caught wearing a vest should be executed. If you think Paul was a fool, take a look at this picture of Lenin.

Worst Oppression of Females: Until quite recently, a Bulgarian woman was permitted only one bath in her lifetime—on the day prior to her wedding. And in South Sclavonia, females could bathe only rarely during childhood and not at all as adults.

Most Unusual Bald Pates: Samuel Johnson mentions a theory current in the eighteenth century, "That the cause of baldness in men is dryness of the brain, and its shrinking from the skull." Whatever the cause, baldness has been throughout the ages the bane of men, both great and small.

Suetonius records that Julius Caesar was extremely self-conscious about his receding hairline. When the most exotic massages and hair tonics failed to produce new follicles, like so many others, he resorted to combing his hair forward to cover the bare spots. Suetonius notes wryly that of all the honors conferred upon him by the Senate, Caesar most treasured the laurel wreath because wearing it helped to disguise his baldness.

The chronicler Claudius Aelianus asserts that the death of the Greek playwright Aeschylus was indirectly attributable to hair loss. Forewarned by a soothsayer that he might die from the impact of a falling object, Aeschylus left the cities, with all their hazards, and retired to the countryside with its safe, wide-open fields. Alas, his precautions were in vain. One afternoon as Aeschylus was walking through a meadow, an eagle, carrying a tortoise in its talons, spied the dramatist's bald pate and mistook it for a rock. Intending to crack open its dinner, the bird released the tortoise from a height of one hundred feet; it struck Aeschylus squarely on the skull, killing him instantly.

Most Unusual Bathtub: The *National Geographic* recently described a solid gold bathtub weighing 313½ pounds that is a popular feature in a Japanese hotel. The management charges two dollars a minute for a dip and hints that bathing in the tub ensures long life.

Less regal but more imaginative was the "bag bath," which was first invented by a Doctor Sanctorius of Padua (d. 1636), only to be forgotten and reinvented several other times in lavatory history. The bather crawled into a large leather (later, rubber) sack, took off his clothes within, and had the top of the bag sealed around his neck like a collar. Hot water was then poured in through a funnel at the bather's shoulder; it washed over his body and down towards his feet where it drained out of a long spout. If the bather preferred a leisurely soak, the spout could be plugged. And certain models had watertight arms and gloves, like oversized spacesuits, enabling one to read or write while enjoying the continuous cleansing flow. But Dr. Sanctorius believed that the principal advantage of his bag bath was that it allowed the bather to receive visitors in all modesty and decency.

Water is definitely the preferred fluid for bathing, but milk has also enjoyed some popularity. In the Roman era, bathing in milk was a rather common luxury, and Nero's wife, Poppeia, insisted on something a little better, she-asses' milk. More recently, Beau Brummell (1778–1840), the wealthy English fop, made a habit of bathing in ordinary cow's milk.

Most Unusual Beads: In some coastal areas of Italy, squid eyes are strung and used for necklaces and bracelets.

Most Unusual Beard: Banary Bhat, a farmer in South India, was dismayed over the commonly held belief that bee-keeping is dangerous, and ventured to prove otherwise. He found that by placing a queen bee on his cheek, he would soon attract a huge swarm of her followers and that they would cling beardlike to his face. According to an item in the *Asia Magazine,* a Sunday newspaper supplement that cir-culates throughout the Far East, Bhat's wife ran screaming from the house the first time she saw her husband in his beard. However, he eventually reassured her by showing that he could eat dinner, smoke, play cards, and do just about anything else, without bodily risk.

During Abraham Lincoln's campaign for the presidency, a dyed-in-the-wool Democrat named Valentine Tapley from Pike County, Missouri, swore that he would never shave again if Abe were elected. Tapley kept his word and his chin whiskers went unshorn from November 1860 until he died in 1910, attaining a length of twelve feet six inches. In his de-clining years Tapley developed an obsessive fear that someone might rob his grave to get at his remarkable beard, and in his will he was careful to set aside a large sum of money for a double-strength tomb.

For a while Frederic Chopin, the composer and pianist, wore a beard on only one side of his face. "It does not matter," he explained. "My audience sees only my right side."

Presumably Chopin would have been required to pay only one-half of the standard beard tax had he lived in eighteenth-century Russia. Czar Peter the Great aspired to Europeanize his nation in every conceivable way, and since beards were the exception in Europe, Peter wanted his own subjects to be clean-shaven. An ill-conceived attempt to outlaw chin whiskers nearly touched off an armed rebellion, so in 1705 the czar resorted to a more moderate strategy—taxation. Bearded men were required to pay the tax collector fifty rubles a year. Excepted were poor peasants who were per-mitted to wear their beards tax free in their own villages; but on entering or leaving a town, unshaven peasants had to remit one kopek.

Most Unusual Cosmetic: In the court of King Louis XV, many of the women took to wearing false eyebrows made of

270

moleskin. And in Greenland a few centuries ago, wealthy women dyed their faces blue and yellow.

In 1969 Mr. Kenneth, one of America's foremost cosmetologists, brought out a line of creams, rouges, and special applicator brushes for bosom makeup.

Most Unusual Earmuffs: Work elephants near the Bangkok, Thailand, airport were constantly disturbed from their labors by sonic booms and other loud noises, so the considerate Thai government is supplying them with elephant ear protectors.

Most Unusual Eye Makeup: To continue in this scientific vein, researchers have found that men are more attracted to women with dilated pupils. This comes as a justification of the practice of women in Renaissance Italy who enlarged their pupils by applying drops of belladonna. (Note that belladonna means beautiful woman.)

Most Unusual Fashion: Marie Antoinette was the Jacqueline Kennedy of the eighteenth century. If the queen styled her wig in a particular fashion, all the ladies of the court were soon wearing their hair the same way. And when the First Lady of Louis XVI became pregnant, the best-dressed of Paris and Versailles wore cushions under their gowns in imitation. For nine months they inserted larger and larger cushions, to keep pace with Marie's expansion. Then suddenly, with the birth of the Dauphin, cushions became passé.

Most Unusual Hair: Because of the overdevelopment of his scalp muscles, a nineteenth-century Frenchman, Pierre Messie, was able to make his hair stand on end at will. For variety, Messie could even make one patch of his hair stand up while the rest lay flat.

Most Unusual Haircut: The Athenian orator Demosthenes had difficulty disciplining himself to tend to his studies instead of going out on the town. His solution was to shave one side of his head, leaving the hair long on the other; he looked so ridiculous that he was ashamed to be seen in public.

Most Unusual Hair Dressing: The Warraus of the Orinoco Delta in Venezuela pomade their hair with honey and shiny colorful fish scales.

Most Unusual Hair Restorer: Balding Peter Biggs of England reported in 1973 that he had gotten good results from horse manure rubbed into his head.

Most Unusual Hat: The three qualities one looks for in a hat are style, comfort, and durability. For generations New Guineans have been wearing a headdress that embodies all three virtues: a close-fitting turban made from spider webs.

Most Unusual Jump Suit: Rock singer-guitarist Dan Hartman does his performing these days garbed in a $5,000 silverized jump suit that is music's answer to pantyhose. It's called the Guitar Suit, simply enough, and it's made of Laurex, a stretchy synthetic. The guitar fits into a pelvic pouch fitted with electrodes that transmit the signal through wires sewn into the lining of the suit into a small but powerful transmitter in the thigh. To adjust tone and volume, the singer presses a button on his left sleeve.

"It's a dynamite way to perform," says Hartman of the suit, which he designed in collaboration with Los Angeles fashion stylist Bill Witten. "I can feel the vibrations in my body. I know what an expectant mother must feel like. I am the music."

Most Unusual Mustache: Elizabethan gentlemen perfumed and tinted their mustaches; the favored colors were bright red, orange and purple. Shakespeare pokes fun at this practice in several of his comedies: In *A Midsummer Night's Dream,* for instance, a character speaks derisively of "your straw colour beard," which presumably did not match the rest of the hair in view.

Most Unusual Ornament: Certain tribesmen of New Guinea deserve mention. They wear the tusks of wild boars inserted through gradually enlarged slits in their nostrils.

Most Unusual Pearl: The Pearl of Allah is neither round nor especially beautiful, but it has the virtue of weighing over fourteen pounds. Currently owned by Wilburn Cobb of California, its value is estimated at about $4 million. As any spectacular ornament should, the Pearl of Allah has a deadly curse connected with it: The first diver who tried to harvest it had his hand trapped in the giant Tridacna clam which produced the gem and was held underwater until he drowned.

The Tridacna clam of the East Indian Ocean is itself a wonder. When mature, it measures up to four feet in diameter and weighs nearly six hundred pounds, shell included. The slippery animal living inside can grow as large as twenty pounds—enough to make 150 gallons of clam chowder.

Most Unusual Perfume: Scientists have established that certain perfumes have a real physiological effect on males. It is amazing, however, what people think smells good. For instance, Plutarch noted that Spartan ladies perfumed themselves with butter. The emperor Augustus, on the other hand, believed in mixing scents, applying mint to his arms, palm oil to his royal chest, and essence of ivy to his knees.

Most Unusual Purse: Who says you can't make a silk purse out of a sow's ear? Arthur D. Little, a pioneer in synthetics, took the old Shakespearean adage as a personal challenge. He boiled down hundreds of sows' ears into a milky fluid, and then, through an elaborate spinning and drying process, reduced the juice to a long, continuous strand of synthetic silk. A purse woven from this silk is on display in the Smithsonian Institution.

Most Unusual Shaving Cream: A Barry Goldwater nostrum: "If you don't mind smelling like a peanut for two or three days," says the Arizona Republican, "peanut butter is a darn good shaving cream."

Most Unusual Tattoo: Even though it is almost surely legend, the story of lightning prints is worth repeating simply because it is so bizarre. Various venerable and unreliable sources claim that when people are struck by lightning or are very near a place where lightning hits, through some process that is a cross between tattooing and photography they may be imprinted with images of nearby objects. The most believable story took place in 1830 at the Chateau Benatonière in Levandee, France. A young woman was seated in a chair with an ornately carved back when lightning struck the castle. She felt a painful burning and when she stood up, her host noticed that her dress and back had been imprinted with the design of the chair.

Most of the stories, however, are more like this: A man was hanging up a horseshoe in the middle of a storm, when lightning hit the good luck charm. Through the mysterious process of lightning printing he received a horseshoe-shaped scar on his neck.

Most Unusual Zipper: In 1964 an intrepid inventor patented the "Forget-Me-Not." The device attaches to a little boy's zipper and causes an alarm bell to ring if his fly comes open.

Places

Best (Safest) City in the United States: Lakewood, Ohio. And Lakewood is not only safe from crime but from fire as well, with an all but obsessively enforced municipal program for inspecting homes and businesses for fire-code violations.

David Franke, author of *America's 50 Safest Cities,* combed through the crime statistics of the 396 cities in the United States with populations over 50,000, fed them into a computer, and found this bedroom suburb of Cleveland to have the lowest crime rate of all. Lakewood is an old city, with a top-grade police force, excellent radium-arc street lighting, and a predominantly middle- to upper-middle-class population that evidently is comfortable living cheek-to-jowl with Cleveland, one of the nation's less endearing cities and hardly a paragon of urban tranquility itself.

On a smaller scale, Coal Township, Pennsylvania, (population 12,000) is even more halcyon. In 1973, according to statistics released by the F.B.I., Coal Township reported no murders, no rapes, and no cases of grand larceny. It was, in fact, the largest of only nine towns in the country with populations in excess of 10,000 to have no incidence of major crime.

Best City in the United States if for No Other Reason Than: The Chicago city council outlawed pay toilets in the Windy City by a 37–8 vote in 1974, a direct response, evidently, to the efforts of the Committee to End Pay Toilets in America. "You can have a fifty-dollar bill," the committee's nineteen-year-old president, Michael Gessel, told newsmen as he kicked off a national crusade against coin-operated commodes, "but if you don't have a dime, that small metal box is between you and relief."

Best Country to Visit: New Zealand. Our authority is J. Hart Rosdail, of Elmhurst, Illinois, who is enshrined ungrammatically in *The Guinness Book of World Records* as "the man who has probably visited more countries than anybody." More precisely, Rosdail has set foot in all but five of the world's 225 countries, and New Zealand, he says, offers the finest combination of scenic wonders—including breathtaking mountain-and-fjord coastal country—native hospitality, and general ambience. The cost of living is still reasonable there and the quality of living in major cities like Wellington and Christchurch far outshines urban life throughout the United States and most of Europe. One discouraging note, however: according to a study conducted by the New Zealand Cancer Society, two out of three New Zealand children smoke cigarettes before they are seven years old.

Best Museum in the World: If you have even the remotest interest in ancient civilizations, then it's London's British Museum where you can spend a rainy afternoon or two trying to decipher the Rosetta Stone.

The Stone, they say, is to the British Museum what the Spirit of Saint Louis is to Washington, D.C.'s Smithsonian Institution—unquestionably the greatest non-art museum in the world. (Clarifying it more specifically than that would be impossible. Millions know it as "America's attic.") Running a close second in the non-art category is Chicago's Museum of Science and Industry.

The world's best art museum—if we can exclude the British Museum—is the Louvre, in Paris, which is not only the world's largest museum but architecturally its most beautiful. The best art museum in the United States is New York City's Metropolitan Museum of Art, which has the best temporary exhibits anywhere in the nation.

Best Place to Hitchhike: It is probably easier—and more fun—to hitchhike in Australia than it is anywhere else in the world, according to free-lance writer Jourdan Houston, writing in *Saturday Review World*. Hitchhiking-related crimes are rare there, he says. Cars with willing drivers are available, and hitchhiking is not only commonplace but supported by the government. Tourist bureaus, in fact, are only too happy to provide you, on request, with inside tips for hitching in the outback, where you'll need all the help you can get. (Towns in the outback are tiny for the most part and spaced hundreds of miles apart, with nothing but sagebrush and billabongs in between.)

Native hospitality also makes for easy, pleasant hitchhiking in Japan. Thumb a ride there and you may also find yourself invited to dinner and an overnight stay. In Poland, tourists and natives alike pay a registration fee to enroll in a government-administered hitchhiking plan. Thumb-riders are given a block of coupons which are used as "carfare" to be paid to drivers who pick them up. Drivers with the most coupons are eligible for prizes.

Best Rest Spot in the World: If it's absolute peace and quiet you're after, visit the territory staked out by the Mabaan tribe in the Sudan. Religious dogma among the Mabaans forbids noise of any kind, and the only sounds ever heard in Boing, their main town, are the patter of raindrops and the occasional lowing of a cow. Background noise, in fact, has been judged to be about one-tenth as loud as a refrigerator's hum. Incidentally, don't try whispering secrets in the area. The Mabaans, nurtured on years of silence, can pick up conversational tones at 100 yards, and your average seventy-five-year-old Mabaan hears as well as twenty-five-year-olds.

Best Zoo in the United States: For millions of wilderness-loving urbanites, New York, with its magnificent zoological gardens in the Bronx and Central Park, used to be known as Zoo City. (There are plenty of people who still call it that, but for different reasons.) Today, however, the best zoos in the United States are in San Diego, Chicago and St. Louis, Mo. The Saint Louis Zoo, the best of them all, has been redesigned in recent years to allow its animals to roam about with a greater degree of freedom in the closest duplication possible of their natural environment. (The Bronx Zoo, which does run a close second, has also done this.) The result is a unique and nontraditional experience for the zoo-going public.

Worst Air of any United States City: New York City and Chicago are probably the worst places in the United States to breathe, according to statistics issued by the Environmental Protection Agency. Automobile emissions, as well as fumes from fuel burning, incineration, manufacturing, and other sources give the air in both cities their characteristic bouquet.

As for water, Cleveland's Cuyahoga River is probably the *nation's foulest waterway.* At its dirtiest points the river is more than 50 percent acid and industrial wastes. It has even caught fire on several occasions.

Worst City (United States): Edward A. Hanna thinks that Utica, New York (population 91,000) is "A lousy place to live," and that its young people would do well to leave the place as soon as they can. Hanna should know: He's the mayor of Utica.

The spectacle of a mayor publicly holding his own town up to ridicule is a rare one, indeed, but then Utica's sorry economic state, its skyrocketing unemployment figures, its all-around urban decrepitude are singular. As Hanna sees it, it's the business interests, the banks, and what he calls "the chamber of no commerce" that have sucked the life-blood from the scraggly neck of this wheezing, underfed chicken of a metropolis. Because of the business establishment's efforts at keeping new business out of the city, Hanna said in a city hall press conference, "Progress is our least important product."

In July 1974, the banks, by turning down his repeated requests for a mortgage, throttled a builder's plans to put up a hotel on a lot that had been vacant and unused for fourteen years. For Hanna, it was the last straw. He responded by withdrawing all of the public funds—several million dollars—from the banks and storing it out of the city.

Worst City (World): Calcutta. Sir George Otto Trevelyan wrote in 1863: " . . find, if you can, a more uninviting spot than Calcutta. . . . The place is so bad by nature that human efforts could do little to make it worse; but that little has been done faithfully and assiduously." That judgment is still accurate today.

A creation of the British colonists, Calcutta is by nature plagued by sultry summers and stifling humidity. Mark Twain complained that the weather is "enough to make a brass doorknob mushy." Today, perhaps as many as 10,000,000 people are crowded into the metropolitan area; the population density is appalling—102,000 per square mile, as compared with 27,900 per square mile in New York City. Visitors are invariably shaken by the awful and inescapable beggary, and they find it difficult to reconcile it with the fact that Calcutta is the richest and most heavily industrialized city in India. Thousands sleep in the streets at night; 35,000–40,000 lepers live as outcasts within the general misery. Calcuttans live a nightmare spawned by colonialism and the Industrial Revolution. Yet Winston Churchill said he was glad to have seen it once, "so I will never have to see it again."

278

Worst College Campus: Imagine 1,400 well-scrubbed youngsters carrying biology textbooks and hymnals, scurrying in and out of the abandoned hulls of an old "World of Tomorrow" exhibit at Disneyland or the '64 New York World's Fair, and you'll have a fair picture of the plastic-and-aluminum wonderland that is Oral Roberts University, in Tulsa, Oklahoma. Tulsans like to tell tourists that "unless you've seen ORU, you haven't seen Tulsa," unaware, evidently, that not seeing Tulsa does have its benefits. Just the same, the $50-million campus is worth looking at if you are in the area, especially for the 200-foot-high "Prayer Tower," which looks like nothing so much as an upended vibrating dildo girdled with an inner tube. It may well be America's ugliest religious structure.

Worst Country to Visit: The Union of Soviet Socialist Republics, says Rosdail. It isn't that the country lacks for scenic wonders, cultural diversity, or native hospitality. It's just that "the Russian secret police, combined with the stifling governmental bureaucracy make it all but impossible for the traveler to move freely from place to place. Traveling in the Soviet Union," says Rosdail, "is more frustrating than it is anything else."

Worst Crime Rate in the United States: Compton, California, a suburb of Los Angeles. Its proximity to Los Angeles means, of course, that if the muggers don't get you, the smog will. Compton heads Franke's "most dangerous" list, followed by Newark, New Jersey, and then Detroit. Interestingly, neither New York, Saint Louis, Los Angeles itself, Chicago, nor Philadelphia appear among the top ten.

Worst Family Entertainment: Hong Kong's Tiger Balm Gardens. Tiger Balm itself is a godsend—a eucalyptus salve sold commercially throughout the Far East and used to treat everything from chigger bites to hangover. It's the closest thing we know of to an all-purpose drugcounter nostrum that works. But the Gardens are another story! Designed by Tiger Balm industrialist Aw Boon Haw, the Gardens are a concrete-and-plaster Disneyland of the Vulgar, consisting largely of loudly colored murals and friezes that depict graphically the sadistic torture and mutilation of the prisoners and enemies of mythical Chinese kings. One memorable series of relief-painted panels shows the poor wretches being disemboweled,

Wilbur Glenn Voliva

dismembered, crushed by steamrollers, having their eyes plucked out by hot irons and their organs gnawed by beasts.

There's fun for the family to be had in your nearest nuclear bomb test area as well. Former Atomic Energy Commissioner James Schlesinger took his family to view the controversial Amchitka Island atomic bomb test in 1972 and told reporters, "My wife is delighted to get away and it's fun for the kids."

Worst Geographer: During the Apollo moon flight of Christmas 1968, Astronaut Frank Borman looked back on the old globular earth and wondered aloud whether their historic flight would influence the thinking of Samuel Shenton—the organizer of the International Flat Earth Society. It didn't. Nor would it have shaken Wilbur Glenn Voliva, the Christopher Columbus of flat earthology and the worst geographer of the twentieth century.

Voliva was a millionaire fundamentalist who for many years had complete ecclesiastical and secular control over the small theocratic community of Zion City, Illinois. Taking the Bible as his sole authority on all questions, Voliva was absolutely convinced that the earth is as flat as the proverbial pancake—circular, yes, but certainly not spherical. At the center of the pancake is the North Pole and the edges are surrounded by a vast wall of ice, which we mistakenly call the South Pole. We can praise God that this ice wall exists, Voliva said, because it prevented Antarctic explorers like Sir James Ross from sailing right off the edge of the world. As for Magellan and others who claimed to have circumnavigated the globe, they merely sailed all the way around the outside edge of the disc; it was an extraordinary achievement, but it did not prove the earth was round.

Voliva also had fixed ideas about the firmament. The sun, he said, is only three thousand miles away and it moves in a continuous circle above the disc. The sky is exactly what it appears to be, a great blue-black vault to which the stars are fastened. And the moon, like the sun, spirals freely above us at a constant height.

Wilbur Glenn Voliva had confidence in the validity of his beliefs: "I can whip to smithereens any man in the world in a mental battle," he said. "I have never met any professor or student who knew as much on any subject as I do." Every year he ran an advertisement in the Chicago and Milwaukee papers offering $5,000 to anyone who could convince him that the world was not flat. No one ever could.

Worst Museum: The Syphilis Museum in Liverpool, England. The museum has long since gone the way of the dodo, but when it was in business, fathers took their progeny there to gaze in horror at an endless display of the withered organs, diseased tissue, and shriveled corpses of men and women who had flirted with Sin and thus met the grisliest of ends. Douglas Day describes the museum in his 1973 biography of English novelist Malcolm Lowry who was taken on several rather traumatic visits there during his boyhood.

Worst Park: To Western visitors one of the most peculiar aspects of Hinduism has always been cow worship. But orthodox Hindus hold *all* animal life in high esteem and there are sects devoted to the worship of snakes, monkeys—and rats. In the city of Bilaner, in Rajasthan, there is a temple consecrated to rat worship; thousands of the ravenous rodents gather there to be fed and pampered. On the main street in Calcutta, Hindus of similar persuasion maintain what is surely the most repellent public recreation facility in the world, rat park. As William Drummond, a reporter for the Los Angeles *Times,* describes it, "dozens of the fat brown creatures play and cavort in broad daylight while human pedestrians pass nonchalantly by." As a footnote: Rats and mice in India consume an estimated 2.4 million tons of grain a year.

Worst Place to Hitchhike: Hitching is illegal in Mexico and generally to be avoided. Violators are often summarily deported unless they can show that they've got sufficient funds to support themselves. In Afghanistan hitching is an exceptionally dangerous activity, as it is in Uganda, where several hitchers in recent years have reported being shot at.

In the United States thumb your rides with discretion, or not at all, in Maine and Nevada, where the talmudic proscriptions against hitchhiking are strictly enforced. This does not necessarily mean that violators are thrown in the slammer for a day or two. We know of a few people who, while trying to flag down a ride on a state highway in Nevada, were picked up by troopers, driven some distance (in air-conditioned comfort, of course) and dropped off in the middle of nowhere.

Worst Taxi Drivers: As a group, the rudest, most opinionated taxi drivers in the world are in New York City. Naturally exceptions exist, hundreds of them no doubt, but the major impression one forms after trafficking in New York's taxi system for any length of time is the greed and thickheadedness of its drivers. In 1974, one unknown driver charged an unsuspecting French tourist fifty-two dollars for the ride from Kennedy International Airport to midtown Manhattan, about five times over the going rate; another took a $168 fare from a Guatemalan family of three for a similar half-hour drive. Anomalies? Perhaps. Just as likely to happen outside New York? Hardly.

Similarly, taxi drivers in Bangkok, Thailand, can make getting there considerably less than half the fun. Most cabs in the Thai capital are equipped with meters that no doubt work, but it's a rare driver there who won't tell you that his meter is broken and then set a fixed price for the ride in advance. Go along with his offer and you'll most probably pay a higher fare than what you'd have to pay on the meter. As for reckless drivers, the world's worst are in Paris, France, and Taipei, Taiwan.

Worst Tourist Attractions: Visit the Indianapolis Speedway on an off-day, and for twenty-five cents you can ride around the two and one-half-mile track in a small touring bus operated by a driver who doubles as a tour guide with a penchant for the grotesque. "We're coming around the first half-mile bend," he says. "This is where Bill Vukovich slammed into the retaining wall in the 1973 Memorial Day race and died instantly. . . . There's the third turn. Eddie Sachs's car blew up here in 1966 and he died on the way to the hospital. . . . In 1972, a car crashed through the fence crippling the driver and incinerating several spectators in the first few rows." The tour takes about twelve minutes. Refreshments are available at a small souvenir stand near the departure point.

The Reversing Rapids in Saint John, New Brunswick, is another attraction that the tourist can pass up. We began seeing signs for the rapids as soon as we crossed over the Maine border into Canada. On arriving in Saint John (which prides itself as the Loyalist City—a haven for British sympathizers during the Revolutionary War), we made directly for the tourist office in the new city hall. There we received a complicated set of schedules and the advice that "to fully appreciate the Reversing Rapids, they must be seen at high, high slack, and low slack tides." Most spectacular of all, according to our advisor, was low slack, when the mighty Saint John River, the largest on the Eastern seaboard, suddenly ceases its swift white water plummet from the interior highlands to the Bay of Fundy. The reason: The treacherous tides of Fundy, ranging up to fifty feet in height, overpower the Saint John at that moment and send it rushing and spilling over itself back up toward the mountains. The Mic Mac Indians believed it was a miracle.

We were in luck. Low slack was only fifty minutes away. So we hurried to Reversing Rapids Park, where we joined about fifty other people from all over Canada and the United States. The Saint John itself wasn't as we'd pictured it. It was wide, and muddy brown, and rather tired looking. Across from the park, there was a large factory that was churning out great quantities of white, and rather polluted-looking foam, which drifted casually downstream. "Well," we thought, "isn't it a crime how they've ruined this great natural wonder! It's like the American side of Niagara Falls." Still, we had visions of the wild, clean tides of Fundy surging in—a tremendous wall of sea water driving the Saint John back toward its source—so we positioned ourselves as close as we dared to the river, fearful that the powerful waters might engulf us there.

Everyone checked his watch. It was 5:35. The foam wasn't sliding downstream quite so rapidly now. Then it was the appointed moment: 5:37 ADT. The foam and current came to an exceedingly gradual halt. Everyone looked seaward, expecting the deluge. Nothing. Then, imperceptibly at first, the white foam began moving again, regurgitating dully back toward the factory. After another few minutes someone in the crowd asked, "Is that it?" That was it.

If the recent war has not thrown the schedule off, a new hotel called Lot opened in the town of Sodom late in 1973. Israeli officials say the Lot is just one of several new hotels that have gone up in recent years due to the extraordinary tourist boom in Sodom. Incidently, the discovery of gas wells in the area has led some geologists to speculate that a natural gas explosion might have caused the destruction of the sinning cities. The effect of such massive combustion, they argue, would resemble the description in Genesis 19: "The Lord rained upon Sodom and upon Gomorrah brimstone and fire from the Lord out of heaven."

Another place that is attracting a lot of tourists these days is Alcatraz Island. The government recently opened the abandoned maximum security prison to visitors. There is now a regular ferry, and a number of ex-convicts have landed jobs as tour guides.

Worst-zoned Neighborhood: For years the Carioto family of Pittsburgh has lived next door to a tombstone workshop, across the street from a cemetery, and just a few houses away from yet another tombstone workshop. But when an entrepreneur applied to the local zoning board for permission to put up a crematorium within smelling distance of the Cariotos' kitchen, the family begged the zoners for mercy.

"We've managed to adjust to living with graveyards and tombstone factories in our midst, but the prospect of a crematorium twenty-five feet from the kitchen window is too much to bear," Mr. Carioto told the zoning board. "It's already changed our lives."

Said Mrs. Carioto, "If someone says something like 'You burned the chicken,' I fall apart. The children's friends will say something like 'What did you do with this meal, cremate it?' and we push our plates away. I just can't take the jokes."

Most Unusual City: With a population of 500,000, Brasilia is the largest "new" city in the world and certainly the strangest. Laid out in the shape of a swept-wing jet, Brazil's new

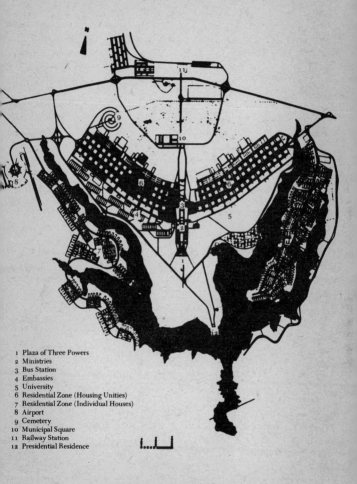

1 Plaza of Three Powers
2 Ministries
3 Bus Station
4 Embassies
5 University
6 Residential Zone (Housing Unities)
7 Residential Zone (Individual Houses)
8 Airport
9 Cemetery
10 Municipal Square
11 Railway Station
12 Presidential Residence

Plan for Brasilia, the federal capital of Brazil

285

capital rises above a stark and treeless plain. Chief architect Oscar Niemeyer pledged at the beginning of the staggeringly expensive project "Never to fall into the hitherto customary banal style of building." True to his promise, Niemeyer's concrete, glass, marble, and steel designs are unique and disturbingly surreal. The streets are the widest in the world; the central avenue, for instance, is 370 yards wide—five times the width of the Champs Elysées.

Poet Elizabeth Bishop, who has lived in Brazil for many years, believes the new capital is a stunning experiment and yet a failure: "Individual buildings are very beautiful . . . but there is little feeling of scale; the buildings are lost in the surrounding vastness, and even within the city limits the sensation of being on another planet—as everyone puts it—is overwhelming." John Dos Passos has called it "an inverted Pompeii," rising from the bleak landscape in an eerie way that is reminiscent of the Roman resort excavated from the lava flats.

Pakistan is also building a new capital from scratch. It remains to be seen whether Islamabad will be what Brasilia was meant to be, the world's best-designed, most comfortable, and most human environment.

Most Unusual Island: Santorini, also known as Thera, is a small island in the Aegean Sea not far from the coast of Greece. Actually what was once a single island is now three small islands due to the cataclysmic volcanic eruptions that periodically rearrange the geography. The hills of Santorini were last shaken in 1866 when an underwater volcano shot flames and brimstone up through the ocean and thirty feet into the air.

But this rare and spectacular display must have been insignificant compared to the tremendous explosion that shattered the volcanic cone of Santorini in the fifteenth century B.C. The mammoth tidal wave which resulted wiped out the flourishing coastal cities of Crete, hundreds of miles away. Moreover, several archaeologists have speculated that the Minoan colony on Santorini, which was heaved into the sea and covered with a thick layer of black ash, may have inspired the myths about the lost city of Atlantis.

Architecture

Best Building in the United States: The Chicago Civic Center. Not just another pretty place, the Chicago Civic Center made it with ease to *Fortune* magazine's 1966 list of the ten best buildings in the United States. Here is what architect Douglas Haskell has written about the 465,000-square-foot skyscraper, completed in the mid-1960s with public financing from an $87 million bond issue: "In Chicago the random viewer slowly begins to understand that the big new Civic Center . . . has a reason for looking so wonderfully light on its feet. There are just four full-height columns across that entire wide front, and the eight seven-foot spans of the horizontal trusses between them are Bunyanesque. But all is carried with casual grace and charm. Nobody standing outside would guess that there are several theatre-sized courtrooms on some upper floors inside . . ." Visually, the most striking feature of the building is the steel itself, which has begun to turn a "fiery red" as it rusts, and, says Haskell, will eventually turn to "a dark whiskey tone, flattered by adjoining windows of amber-colored glass."

Best Hotel in the United States: The Plaza, in New York City. When the Plaza opened its doors on a crisp fall day in 1907, hundreds of New Yorkers lined the streets to watch the hoopla and to see the Alfred Gwynne Vanderbilts arrive by limousine to check in as the hotel's first guests. It was billed then as "the world's greatest hotel" and its magnificence has never waned. The Plaza is best known for the efficiency of its staff, and *Esquire* Travel Editor Richard Joseph who, by his own count, has checked into well over 1,300 hotel rooms over the years, numbers the Plaza, along with the Mauna Kea Beach Hotel on Hawaii's Kona Coast, among the three greatest hotels in the world.

The Mauna Kea, incidentally, is Joseph's choice for best resort hotel in the world. Built in 1966 at a cost of $15 million, the hotel sits in the shadow of the 13,800-foot volcano after which it is named, comfortably isolated from the plasticized commercialism of Waikiki on what may well be the most beautiful stretch of beach in the entire island chain. Every one of the 154 guest rooms has its own *lanai* (porch), and is decorated with bedspreads and upholstery material handwoven under the direction of a Siamese princess. Says Joseph, "Walking through it is like strolling through an open-air museum and art gallery—past Hawaiian quilts hung as tapestries, bronze ceremonial drums and red-and-gold scroll boxes from Thailand . . . Japanese and Chinese scrolls and paintings, New Guinea carvings and masks, brass candelabra from Hindu temples, an antique wood and brass chest from Zanzibar . . . Buddhist figures from all over the Orient."

Best Hotel in the World: The Gritti, in Venice, Again, the considered opinion of Richard Joseph—and of Ernest Hemingway, journalist John Gunther, French mystery writer Georges Simenon, Somerset Maugham, and Elizabeth Taylor, all of whom have been regular guests at the Gritti. Built as a Doge's palace in the sixteenth century, it was converted into a hotel only recently—1948, in fact—but, as Joseph writes, "You'd be willing to swear that you read about Keats staying at the Gritti, or about something happening there to Henry James." With almost no staff turnover at all from year to year, even the one-time guest is remembered when he returns to the Gritti, and his preferences—for idiosyncratic drinks, for flowers in his room, for overdone steak smothered in tomato ketchup—are accommodated without his asking.

Best (Most Beautiful) Structure in the World: The Taj Mahal. When Arjumand Banu Begum, the wife of the seventeenth-century Mogul emperor Shah Johan, died in childbirth, the Shah knew that your standard garden variety funeral and burial plot simply wouldn't do. For twelve years, beginning in 1632, 20,000 laborers toiled at his behest to complete the Taj Mahal, and when the Shah himself died some sixteen years later, he was interred there as well in a separate casket next to his matchless wife. Located in Agra, India, about 110 miles south of New Delhi, this paragon of architectural symmetry is best viewed on a clear night with a full moon, although its magnificence remains undimmed even if you view it with a bad hangover in a heavy drizzle. Architect H. R. Nevill wrote that the Taj Mahal "is within more measurable distance of perfection than any other work of man." Even if you've never seen it—never been to India, in fact, or even east of Philadelphia—call it "the Taj." Your friends will be impressed.

There is a nameless but awesome beauty to Stonehenge, located on Salisbury Plain in England, that is as sobering as it is thrilling, and Chicago architect Laurence Ogden Booth calls this ancient monolith the world's most beautiful structure. It was built, most likely, by the Druids, probably around 3,600 years ago, and appears to have been a temple of sky worship, although no one knows for sure. The symmetry and perfection of the Taj are absent, of course, and so is the comforting feeling that you know what you're looking at. Stonehenge is at its best at sunset.

Worst (Ugliest) Hotel: An affront to any tourist's eye is the Marlborough-Blenheim Hotel, on the boardwalk at Atlantic City, New Jersey. Occupying five acres of choice real estate, its architecture borrows from the Spanish, Moorish, and Queen Anne styles. Or so they say. All the same, for the benefit of its guests the Marlborough-Blenheim makes up in creature comforts what it lacks in outward beauty, and is probably the only hotel in the world to offer hot and cold running salt water in each room.

Worst House: Mrs. Sarah Winchester was the superstitious heiress to the Winchester rifle fortune. In 1880 she consulted a medium who confirmed what she already suspected; her house was haunted. It's the restless souls of those murdered with Winchester rifles, the medium told her. The only way to ward them off was to build a house with endless rooms. If the house were ever completed, the medium warned, the angry ghosts would carry Mrs. Winchester off with them into the other world.

Mrs. Winchester took this advice quite seriously. For thirty-eight years she kept nearly fifty carpenters working full-time until her Victorian mansion in San Jose, California, sprawled to an incredible 160 rooms. Only a fear of the supernatural could explain the totally absurd construction. There are stairs leading nowhere; hallways come to a dead end; a window opens to a wall; a door leads to another blank wall; towers have been completely closed off so there is no entrance. To further confuse any intruding spirits, Mrs. Winchester planted a mammoth hedge that completely conceals

Marlborough-Blenheim hotel, Atlantic City, New Jersey

the house from the road. But few of the carpenters or gardeners ever met the lady of the house. She walked quietly around the grotesque structure in a long black veil, and only the butler, who served her meals on the $30,000 gold dinner set, ever saw her face.

You can now visit Winchester House. But we wouldn't advise it if you suffer from the willies.

Worst Monument in the United States: Squat and sinister, and designed with a mysterious dearth of windows, the Lyndon Baines Johnson Library, on the campus of the University of Texas in Austin, reminds one of a malevolent flat-headed fish resting on the ocean floor. The storage bin for some 31 million documents that Johnson collected during his thirty-two-year political career, it is not simply a memorial to a president, but a monument to anal retentiveness. As *Time* magazine architecture critic Robert Hughes says, "It may be that no politician has ever been so gripped by the indiscriminate urge to retain everything he produced, initialed, touched, or was sent." Stored in the library are still-classified documents on the Vietnam War. There is also a 1951 covering

Victor Emmanuel monument

letter which Richard Nixon sent Johnson along with a three-pound box of jumbo deluxe dried California figs, courtesy of the California Fig Institute.

Worst Monument in the World: The Victor Emmanuel Monument, in Rome. A competition was held throughout Italy in 1884 to determine who would have the honor of designing a monument to Victor Emmanuel II. The winner was the architect Count Giuseppe Sarconi, and construction began under his direction in 1885. Sarconi died, however, long before the monument could be completed, and so it bears the thumbprints of a half-dozen mediocre architects. The monument is huge and grotesque, suggestive of a retarded giant dressed up in Sunday finery. Architectural historian Henry-Russell Hitchcock calls it "the most pretentious of all nineteenth century monuments."

Worst Office Building: The world's worst office building was also, until recently, the tallest—the twin towers of New York City's World Trade Center, 110 stories of steel-and-concrete mediocrity on Manhattan's nether tip. Besides blighting the skyline and affronting the eye, the World Trade Center is also a wretched place to work. "When I approach the building, I just don't want to go in there," says one employee. Says another, "Sometimes I just walk out, intending to get out for an hour for lunch, and can't make myself come back."

The Center's horrors are many—inexplicably sealed mail chutes, hopelessly snarled telephone lines, centrally controlled office lighting that can be controlled after hours only by means of a written request submitted at least a day in advance—but the building's denizens reserve a special place in their spleens for the elevators. Plummeting downward so fast that their walls shake audibly, they break down frequently, spilling over with humanity during rush hours. "Sometimes I feel like a lemming—or a salmon swimming upstream," says a New York State employee who works in the building. "If I can't leave at 4:45 I wait until a quarter past five or I walk down stairs rather than be squeezed into the elevator." A woman whose office is on the eighty-second floor describes the noontime trip to the cafeteria: "I have to take a local elevator to the seventy-eighth floor, than an express to the first floor, then an express to the forty-fourth, then an escalator to the forty-third, where I get a lousy meal."

Many workers have complained of psychosomatic ailments that are directly traceable to the Center—one Manhattan physician has treated five such patients. Leonard Levin, a staff member of the New York Racing Board, whose office is in the Center, says, "There *is* one wonderful thing about the World Trade Center. It feels sooooooooo good when you get home at night!"

Most Unusual Apartment Building: The Spanish architect Antonin Gaudi designed Casa Milá in Barcelona, one of the most singular living spaces in the world. Albert B. Brown of S.U.N.Y. at Buffalo has paid tribute to it as one of Gaudi's "highly imaginative and dramatic experiments" that gain their effects through "bizarre form and ornament." There are very few straight lines in the entire building, and even the rooms themselves take on organic shapes rather than the traditional Western cube. The front of the building, far from being flat, is a series of gentle swells, suggesting waves. Overall the effect is one of curves and swirls, like a natural object formed by the wind or the sea. Casa Milá is universally recognized as one of the very finest examples of "art nouveau" architecture.

Most Unusual Bridge: Ever since it was erected in 1831, London Bridge had been sinking into the muddy bottom of the Thames at a rate of one-eighth-inch per year. Thus in 1967 Queen Elizabeth sadly announced that the venerable span designed by John Rennie would have to be torn down and replaced before it fell down once and for all, as promised in the children's song. The old bridge was put up for sale and the highest bidder was Robert McCulloch, an oil and chain-saw tycoon, who offered a cool $2,460,000 for the ten thousand tons of granite slabs.

Piece by piece, the famous structure was dismantled, numbered, and shipped by boat and truck to Lake Havasu City, Arizona. The total moving bill amounted to $5,600,000. McCulloch built an artificial island in Lake Havasu, and London Bridge was reassembled across the narrow channel between island and mainland. Appropriately McCulloch has named the channel the Little Thames.

The Lord Mayor of London joined 40,000 celebrants for the rededication in October 1971. To mark the event, sky-divers dove, skywriters wrote, and balloons and doves were released while a recording of Big Ben tolled sonorously over the loudspeakers. In its first year among the palm trees, pubs, and fish-and-chips joints of Lake Havasu's three-acre English Village, London Bridge attracted over a million tourists.

Most Unusual Campsite: Wesley Hurley, President of Hi-Rise Campsites, Inc., believes that most weekend backpackers don't want to sacrifice the comforts of city living in order to go camping. Acting on that belief, Hurley's firm plans to build the world's first hi-rise campground, in downtown New Orleans.

The twenty-story building, to be constructed at a cost of $4 million, "will be unique," Hurley claims. "It is designed for today's different brand of camping. People don't want the woodsy bit now; they want to camp in comfort near the city." Campers will park their cars on the eight lower floors of the building and then take the elevator up to one of 240 individual campsites on the upper twelve stories, all of which will be equipped with electrical connections and carpeted with Astroturf.

"Le Manneken-Pis"

Most Unusual Drawbridge: One of the smallest achievements in civil engineering is Somerset Bridge at Ely's Harbor, Bermuda. It opens just wide enough to let a sailboat mast slip through.

Most Unusual Fountain: Brussels is the home of one of the world's most beloved fountains: Le Manneken-Pis. The innocent brass boy with the protruding belly has been passing water from his inexhaustible bladder into the pool below since 1619; the people of Brussels refer to him now as "our oldest citizen." Designed by sculptor François Duquesnoy, the little boy has received medals, swords, honors, and offers of clothing from three and a half centuries of distinguished visitors including Louis XV and Napoleon Bonaparte.

Most Unusual Hotel in the World: La Parra, located 49 feet below water off the coast of Spain near Malaga. Getting there is half the fun, since there are no boats or other craft that serve the hotel. Thus, guests must swim there, with their gear sealed in a watertight rucksack.

The Parra, which can accommodate twelve guests at a

time, is the brainchild of underwater explorer Dr. Hans Hass and Austrian businessman Theodor Soucek. Its "rooms" are a complex of glass bubbles (a social area bubble, a kitchen bubble, a dormitory bubble, etc.) and accommodations are quite comfortable. At present the major attraction at La Parra is its nightly underwater concerts in which the audience lolls about on the floor of the sea while music is piped through speakers in the surrounding gardens. Says Hass, "The music comes from all sides and you can feel it all over your body. It's as if you're right in the middle of the orchestra."

For the mountain-climbing public, a hotel was opened for business in December 1970, 12,800 feet up the side of Mt. Everest in Nepal. You can fly to your room directly from Katmandu Airport, or go it on foot, a twelve-day trek. The rooms all have views of the world's fifteen highest mountains and the beds are equipped with optional oxygen tents.

The most unusual hotel, architecturally, is shaped like an elephant drinking from a trough and called, reasonably enough, The Elephant House, located in Margate City, New Jersey. The building is 75 feet long and 85 feet tall and topped by a howdah which serves as an observation deck offering a splendid view of the Atlantic. It was designed by architect James V. Lafferty in 1883, who built another elephantine edifice that same year in Coney Island, New York. One hundred twenty-two feet tall, it was bigger than its New Jersey cousin, housing a cigar store in one foreleg, an elevator shaft in the other, and staircases in both hindlegs. Patrons could rent rooms in whatever part of the animal's anatomy they desired. The Coney Island hotel burned down in 1896.

Most Unusual House: In tropical Africa, several tribes hollow out the baobab tree and set up housekeeping inside. The trunk can reach a thickness of 30 feet, for tree house living that is both spacious and gracious.

The baobab has such a peculiar shape that an Arabian legend maintains that the devil must have pulled it up and replanted the tree with its branches underground and its roots in the air.

Most Unusual Igloo: A Toronto architect is manufacturing pre-fab igloos. Already he has sold a number of the structures, made of fiberboard and covered with frosty-looking polyurethane foam, to Eskimos in the vicinity of Hudson Bay.

Baobab tree

Most Unusual Mortar: How often mortar is taken for granted! Truly memorable mortar was used in the construction of the Alexander Column in Leningrad. Erected in 1834 during the bitter Russian winter, workmen mixed the lime and sand with vodka instead of water to prevent the goo from freezing.

The Koutoubia, a holy tower in Marrakech, Morocco, is nearly 800 years old, and a sweet scent still lingers around it. The sultan who built the Koutoubia ordered 960 bags of musk mixed with the mortar.

Most Unusual Motel Chain: There's free parking for guests and all major credit cards are accepted (including Heed-thy-Master Charge and BankAmericat) at American Pet Motels, Inc., a one-million-dollar nationwide motel chain enterprise based in Chicago. Dogs and cats sleep in brass beds in private rooms that are carpeted with wall-to-wall Astroturf.

St. John's Animal Inn, in Cockeysville, Maryland, provides essentially the same accommodations to dogs and cats, but on a smaller scale. All rooms have piped-in music and hotel staff members are available around the clock to console homesick guests.

Going one step further, at Margaretsville, New York, dog-lover Ron de Strulle directs Campo Lindo, America's only summer camp for dogs. De Strulle offers his charges a well-balanced diet and a full program of summer-fun activities including counselor-supervised treasure hunts for hidden dog biscuits and after-dark campfires, where the dogs sit around a fire all toasty-warm and the counselors strum their guitars and sing. Sometimes, the dogs join in.

One of the nicest things about Campo Lindo is that the dogs are allowed to do their own thing to a refreshingly large extent, at least where eating is concerned. One animal, for instance, has a passion for Fruit Loops and skimmed milk, another for barbecued chicken; both are catered to without question. There is also a legally blind Bedlington terrier who is accompanied everywhere by her own seeing-eye dog.

In deference to the inevitable anxiety that the dogs' owners will experience during the separation from their pets, de Strulle sees to it that "progress reports" on the animals, signed in ink with the animal's pawprint, are sent regularly. "It's like getting a postcard from your dog," he explains.

Most Unusual Pyramid: "Coin" Harvey was a self-taught economist and journalist who wrote a fuzzy-minded yet influential book entitled *Coin's Financial School*. Harvey was an advisor to William Jennings Bryan during each of his three campaigns for the presidency, and many of the theories set down in *Coin's Financial School* became part and parcel of the populist ideology. Yet it is not so much Harvey's economics as his ambitious plan to attain immortality that interests us here. For Coin Harvey dreamed of becoming the American Tutankhamen.

Egypt has magnificent pyramids, as does Mexico, but there are no noteworthy pyramids in the Ozarks, and Coin Harvey set out to remedy that oversight. The Harvey Pyramid was to be less ostentatious than Cheops; the blueprints called for a 60-foot square base, with the apex rising 130 feet into the air. The architects decided to use concrete rather than limestone blocks in the construction and the tip was to be crowned with stainless steel. Harvey selected an isolated valley near Monte Ne, Arkansas, as the site. He anticipated that over the centuries the valley would fill with soil eroded down from the surrounding mountainsides, covering and preserving the pyramid. Thousands of years hence, archaeologists would rediscover the Harvey Pyramid and open it to find the treasures and memorabilia of our age—including, of course, a copy of *Coin's Financial School*.

At first the fund-raising went very well, and soon there was enough money to sink a shaft into the bedrock and begin a foundation. Then, tragically, the depression hit and the flow of contributions dried up. As a last hope, a crowd of supporters gathered at the Monte Ne excavation site in 1931 to nominate "Old Coin," the people's economist, for the presidency. If Harvey had been elected could he have gotten the economy back on its feet? That remains one of history's big "ifs." In his last hurrah, Coin Harvey received 800 votes to Franklin Delano Roosevelt's 22,829,501.

The Unexpected

Best News for Bartenders: The California Board of Equalization once ruled that bartenders cannot be held culpable for misjudging the age of midgets.

A boon to bartenders of an earlier age was the ancient Greek law which made it a crime *not* to get drunk during the annual festival of Dionysus. Sobriety was considered an affront to the god.

Worst Kiss: In Pontoise, France, recently, a girl was attacked on the street by a masher who tried to kiss her. In self-defense she bit off his tongue.

Worst Luck: Caesar Beltram of Lyons, France, was struck by lightning five times. He died of pneumonia.

Worst Noise: When the volcano on Krakatoa Island erupted, the sound of the tremendous explosion was heard on Rodriguez Island in the Pacific 3,000 miles away.

Most Unusual Augury: When Julia, the daughter of Caesar Augustus, was curious about the sex of her unborn child she consulted a trustworthy oracle. The wise man advised her to carry a fertile chicken egg between her breasts. After twenty-one days she hatched a healthy rooster. And sure enough, Julia presented Augustus with a grandson.

Most Unusual Disappearance: Out of many candidates, probably the most romantic of all unsolved disappearances is the story of the Roanoke Island Colony off the coast of North Carolina. Roanoke was the birthplace of the first child of English parentage in the New World, Virginia Dare (born August 18, 1587).

After the initial exploration of the island, most of the settlers returned to England for the winter, leaving only fifteen men to maintain the settlement. When a subsequent party arrived, the fifteen had disappeared.

A new colony of 100 settlers was established before the ship again returned to England. The next visitors to Roanoke found that all the members of the colony had vanished. There were no signs of violence and no graves or bodies to suggest illness. In fact, all they found was the word "Croatoan" carved on one tree and "Cro" carved on another. An extensive search turned up nothing.

While there have been many legends—the existence of a blue-eyed tribe of Indians in the vicinity, and so on—no satisfactory explanation has ever been brought forward.

Most Unusual Escape: A modern Jonah: In February of 1891 James Bartley, a British harpooner for the whaling ship *The Star of the East*, fell overboard near the Falkland Islands and was swallowed by a wounded sperm whale. Several hours later the whale was captured. While it was being rendered, Bartley was discovered in the gigantic stomach, still alive. After a three-week bout with insanity, Bartley recovered and told about his incredible adventure. (It was easy to breathe, he said, but the heat and the humidity were terrible.) Bartley suffered no lasting injury, although his hair and skin were permanently bleached white.

	S	C	H	W	A		S	E	L	I	M		Q	U	I	T	E
	C	H	I	R	R	S		A	D	A	L	E		U	L	R	I	C	A
C	H	A	M	O	I	S		B	U	T	Y	L		A	L	O	N	G	O	F
C	H	I		A	L	T	A	I		C	H	A	T	O	Y	A	N	T		R	E	F
H	I	L	L		F	O	G	A	R	T	Y		N	A	G	Y		K	A	N	E
I	T	I	O	N		F	A	I	T		B	E	I	G	E		B	A	N	N	S
L	O	A	V	E	S		I	N	E	S	S	E	N	C	E		P	A	R	G	E	T
I	N	D	E	N	T	S		T	S	Q	U	A	R	E		C	H	A	L	I	C	E
		M	E	A	T	H		U	P	T	O		C	H	O	L	I
D	R	A	Y		F	E	A	R		A	R	A	B		H	E	R	I		F	F	F
H	U	N	D		F	A	Z	E	N	D	A		I	R	I	S		S	H	O	J	I
O	N	T	O	P		M	I	S	O	C	A	P	N	I	S	T		M	E	L	O	N
T	I	O	G	A		B	E	H	N		E	L	G	R	E	C	O		B	I	R	D
I	N	N		I	C	O	S		E	Y	R	A		E	L	O	N		R	O	D	S
		U	N	H	A	T		S	E	I	S		S	L	A	V	I
K	I	N	G	T	U	T		R	U	N	A	M	O	K		D	I	E	D	O	W	N
A	M	O	R	E	T		M	U	C	I	L	A	G	E	S		R	E	E	C	H	O
K	A	F	I	R		H	I	G	H	S		G	L	U	T		P	A	T	I	N
A	B	A	C		D	O	N	G		M	A	I	S	N	O	N		N	O	R	N
S	U	I		S	A	M	O	Y	E	D	E	S		O	S	T	E	O		B	R	Y
M	T	E	I	G	E	R		W	I	L	C	O		P	H	I	L	T	R	A
	H	E	R	O	I	C		I	N	F	O	R		O	E	N	O	N	E
	S	E	N	N	A		G	O	I	N	G		T	E	S	T	S

If you have candidates of your own to suggest, we'd like to hear about them. Drop us a line care of *Best, Worst, and Most Unusual,* Thomas Y. Crowell Company, 666 Fifth Avenue, New York, N.Y. 10019.

*A BOOK OF SCANDALS ABOUT HOLLYWOOD'S
GREATEST STARS*

Hollywood Tragedy

by William H. A. Carr

Sex is in this book. Crime fills many of its pages. All of
the subject matter is sensational. From the sexually bizarre
orgies and trial of Fatty Arbuckle to the macabre Manson
murder of Sharon Tate, this brutally candid book unveils
much of the fascinating truth about Hollywood.

Profusely illustrated with dozens of photos, this is dramatic,
stunningly detailed reading. A book you will want to look at
many times over.

2-2889-4 $1.95

Send to: FAWCETT PUBLICATIONS, INC.
         Mail Order Dept., P.O. Box 1014, Greenwich, Conn. 06830

NAME _____

ADDRESS _____

CITY _____

STATE _____ ZIP _____

I enclose $_____, which includes total price of all books
ordered plus 50¢ for book postage and handling for the first
book and 25¢ for each additional. If my order is for five books or
more, I understand that Fawcett will pay all postage and handling.

How to Choose and Use Your Doctor

BY MARVIN S. BELSKY, M.D.
AND LEONARD GROSS

2-2966-1 $1.95

Next to choosing a mate, choosing a doctor is the most important decision you'll ever make. And as a patient you must be assertive, questioning, and capable of knowing what is vital to your health and well-being. With the wisdom and information revealed in this book, you will learn:

- How to choose a doctor
- How to get more out of your relationship with your present doctor
- Questions the doctor should ask you
- How to ask the doctor questions
- How to identify your health problems
- Games not to play
- And other essential information to get the most for your health care dollars.

Send to: FAWCETT PUBLICATIONS, INC.
Mail Order Dept., P.O. Box 1014, Greenwich, Conn. 06830

NAME _____

ADDRESS _____

CITY _____

STATE _____   ZIP _____

I enclose $_____, which includes total price of all books ordered plus 50¢ for book postage and handling for the first book and 25¢ for each additional. If my order is for five books or more, I understand that Fawcett will pay all postage and handling.